Waiki
987-345-1

Famous
Jewish Lives

Famous
Jewish Lives
John R. Gilbert

Odhams Books

First published: 1970

Published for Odhams Books by
The Hamlyn Publishing Group Ltd.,
Hamlyn House, 42 The Centre,
Feltham, Middlesex

© *Copyright*
The Hamlyn Publishing Group Ltd, 1970

SBN 6007 2599 5

Printed by Cox & Wyman Ltd,
London, Fakenham and Reading

Contents

Illustrations

Illustrations

Preface

A book on Jewish lives is in one way a simpler proposition than one on Scottish or Irish or Australian lives. One has over three thousand years of history and most of the civilized world to choose from. But it has its pitfalls too. In introducing such a book and trying to justify one's selection there is the risk of being dragged into tedious and insoluble discussions about 'What is a Jew?' and 'Religion or race?' – fine for whiling away those midnight hours in somebody's room at college. There, among the litter of half-filled glasses and cigarette-ends, it all seemed earnest, exciting and significant. In middle age, a war later, it strikes one as a superficial and irrelevant debate.

After all, the Nazis didn't sit down and talk about it. They reduced the problem to its simplest terms. One Jewish great-grandparent was enough. No matter if you had never learned to lisp the traditional morning prayer, never seen the Sabbath candles lit in your parents' house, never been to synagogue. You could be Jewish without even knowing it. As far as the 'Final Solution' was concerned, it was no problem at all.

So the reader will be spared any profound talk about the nature or quality of 'Jewishness', though quite at liberty to ponder the matter as he thumbs through the pages of this book. Perhaps he will be able to decide whether Maimonides was a better Jew, a greater man than Albert Einstein, and whether Moshe Dayan has anything in common – apart from the name – with his Biblical ancestor. I believe he has, but it was no part of my intention to underline the fact.

The choice of subjects was not an arbitrary one. I think a dozen or so of my famous characters would be included in any anthology of this kind. The rest are personal choices. Taken all together they are intended to reflect the many different facets of Jewish genius and achievement. Thus we

9

have outstanding figures – not necessarily the greatest – in theology, philosophy, politics, business, science, the arts, even sport; as well as those who refuse to be fitted into any category – such as Sabbatai Zevi, the pseudo-Messiah of Izmir; Mendel Beilis, the scapegoat accused of ritual murder; and Anne Frank, the child-martyr of the Second World War.

Although I did not consciously attempt to tell the story of the Jews through the ages it so happened that many of these lives were played out against a background of significant events in Jewish history. Some of these lives helped to shape those events. The Biblical period is perhaps the most sketchily covered, but most readers are sufficiently familiar with the Bible story. Nor, except through the innocent eyes of Anne Frank, have I dwelt on the recent, too-familiar horrors of the war years. Other periods and themes may not be so well known – the Golden Age of Jewish learning, in which the early life of Maimonides unfolds; the return of the exiled Jews to Cromwell's England after 400 years, thanks to the efforts of men such as Manasseh ben Israel; or the struggle for parliamentary privileges during the lives of Benjamin Disraeli and Lionel de Rothschild.

I make no apology for describing in such detail the fifty years leading up to the establishment, in 1948, of the State of Israel, as seen through the eyes of Theodor Herzl, Chaim Weizmann, David Ben-Gurion and General Moshe Dayan. Before the war the world of Jewry was sharply divided into Zionists and non-Zionists. Today that division no longer exists. Israel is a fact. For the vast majority of Jews it has been the most positive and hopeful event in modern times. The Jews of Israel have had to fight for their very survival three times in twenty years. We, in the affluent West, have played a safe and secondary role; some have sent sons and daughters, others money and prayers, almost all sympathy and encouragement.

This brings us back – like it or not – to the evasive, inescapable fact of being Jewish. For there is, however tenuous, an invisible bond between the wealthy Jewish businessman in New York or Manchester, the forcibly assimilated lawyer or doctor in Moscow or Warsaw, the *kibbutznik* in the Negev and the most recent immigrant from Rumania, Algeria or Iraq. The language spoken by Moses in the wilderness, by David in Jerusalem, by Jesus on the Mount of Beatitudes, is still spoken – though much modernized and streamlined – by lecturers at the Hebrew University, by actors playing *Hamlet* and *My Fair Lady* in Tel-Aviv theatres, by telephone operators, taxi drivers, tank commanders, members of parliament, sports commentators, housewives and family grocers.

But the language is not the real bond. As like as not, your new immigrant and your American businessman don't talk Hebrew with any degree of fluency – though the former will quickly learn. Nor is religion the answer. Throughout the Jewish world there is a complete range of religious observance, from the ultra-orthodox in their self-imposed modern ghettos to the defiantly atheistic. We Jews in the West have our communal problems, what with Orthodox, Conservative, Liberal and Reform movements. The Israelis have even greater ones affecting every aspect of their lives – politics, transport, food, marriage, divorce, education – and they will probably be arguing about them a generation hence. No, it's not religion, in the narrow sense, which links Jews.

There is simply – and I don't wish it to sound arrogant or presumptuous – a feeling, a response, an intuition, which only a Jew can share fully with another Jew. It cannot be explained. A Jew who has not been to synagogue since childhood wanders into a service, by accident or design, on the evening of the Day of Atonement and feels at home, accepted. It may be in San Francisco, Stockholm, Budapest, Cape Town, Haifa or Hong Kong – it makes no difference. One Jew introduced to another can discover a range of common problems, interests, friends, in a matter of minutes. And when a Jew opens a newspaper there is an immediate spark of interest, or pride, or concern, or shame whenever he comes across a story in which another Jew features. For all I know exactly the same thing happens in a gathering of Irishmen, Yorkshiremen or Australians – we all tend to huddle together in protective, parochial warmth. Probably with us it stems naturally and inevitably from those thousands of years of persecution and its consequences. It is our weakness and our strength and we find it hard to evade it.

Glancing down the list of contents, therefore, it proves impossible to find an obvious common denominator. Barely six of them were pious Jews; three or four, whilst acknowledging their Jewish origin, rejected the idea of being described as such; two of them were formally baptized when young. Yet here they all are within the covers of a single book. And although it cannot be proved, I think their Jewishness, consciously or unconsciously, impinged on the thoughts and actions of every one of them. Disraeli was reminded of it frequently during his lifetime. Mendelssohn who hardly spared it a thought while he lived was shown little mercy after his death.

This may help to explain why I have interpreted the term 'Jewish' fairly freely. I only drew the line with somebody like Karl Marx who not only renounced Judaism but attacked it vehemently. Marx has his rightful place in other anthologies. I don't think he belongs in this one.

Of course I would have liked to include so many more famous men and women. Only shortage of space kept out Judah the Maccabee, Spinoza, Heine, Montefiore, Shalom Aleichem, Nathan Straus, Henrietta Szold, Leo Baeck, Martin Buber, Paul Ehrlich, the Marx Brothers, Yehudi Menuhin, Yigal Yadin and a host of others. To readers who protest at the exclusion of their favourites I can only say, 'I know they exist, I know they all ought to be there. But it's not an encyclopedia, and perhaps a sequel may one day right the balance.'

There is a story, doubtless apocryphal, of a conversation between President Eisenhower and Prime Minister Ben-Gurion. B.G. claimed Eisenhower's job was far easier than his own. 'How so?' inquired Ike. 'You are the President of a nation of 175 million people,' replied B.G. 'I am Prime Minister of a country with 2 million Prime Ministers.'

So perhaps all they really have in common is that they were all individualists, non-conformists, reacting against the normal, the conventional, the expected. Had they not been rebels in their different fields they would not have achieved so much. We might never have had the Ten Commandments, the Theory of Relativity or the Jewish State. It is surely this freedom of thought, this flexibility of mind, this independence of spirit which has proved a source of strength to Jews during their centuries of trials and triumphs.

John R. Gilbert
December, 1968

Acknowledgements

The author would like to thank the following individuals and publishers for permission to reproduce passages from books consulted in the course of research:

Mrs. Katharine Jones and the Hogarth Press Ltd., for an extract from *The Life and Work of Sigmund Freud*, Vol. 3, by Ernest Jones.

Sigmund Freud Copyrights Ltd., The Institute of Psycho-analysis and the Hogarth Press Ltd., for extracts from *An Autobiographical Study*, Vol. 20 of the Standard Edition of *The Complete Psychological Works of Sigmund Freud*.

Macmillan & Co. Ltd., for an extract from *Philosophical and Literary Pieces*, by Samuel Alexander, ed. John Laird.

The Dial Press Inc., New York, for extracts from *The Diaries of Theodor Herzl*, ed. Marvin Lowenthal.

Angus & Robertson Ltd., for extracts from *War Letters of General Monash*.

Hamish Hamilton Ltd. and Harper & Row, Inc., New York, for extracts from *Trial and Error*, by Chaim Weizmann.

Lady Epstein, for extracts from *Epstein: An Autobiography*, by Sir Jacob Epstein.

Weidenfeld & Nicolson Ltd., for extracts from *Diary of the Sinai Campaign*, by Moshe Dayan.

Vallentine, Mitchell & Co. Ltd., and Dr. Otto Frank, for extracts from *Diary of a Young Girl*, by Anne Frank.

Moses
Thirteenth Century BC

Pride of place in this book of famous Jewish personalities through the ages goes to Moses – the leader, law-giver and prophet. Towering above all other characters in the Old Testament, he is the great father figure, the instrument of the divine will, the personification of Jewish values and traditions. More simply, he is the founder of the Jewish nation.

It matters not at all that there is no positive proof that he ever lived. He was a legend in Biblical times and the legends round his name have multiplied with the passing centuries. Faced with this great weight of biographical material one may easily be persuaded that somewhere in the background there lies a framework of valid historical fact, but it can be no more than conjecture.

From the pages of the Bible and the labyrinth of surrounding legends Moses emerges vividly as a man unusually endowed with gifts both of the intellect and spirit. Yet this is no classical-type hero with superhuman attributes or unnatural powers. This is a flesh-and-blood individual with recognizably human weaknesses as well as uncommon virtues. Here is a man capable of inspiring affection, admiration, loyalty, awe and respect; he is not, however, a paragon of virtue, he lays himself open to criticism, his judgement is sometimes faulty, he is racked by doubts and conscience, he has a quick temper, is stubborn and argumentative.

The portrait fashioned by all these colourful stories is of a man of great ability, saddled with a task of appalling responsibility which calls for the exercise of all his powers of faith, courage and judgement. It shows a leader who discharges his mission successfully, though not without cost, and who is denied the personal, material reward of enjoying the fruits of his efforts.

It is worth while trying to isolate the key events of this saga, and – without implying that any one version is more credible than another – to select those versions, whether from the Old Testament or from later legends, which throw interesting light on his character.

The story starts in Egypt at a time when the ancient Israelites were still slaves of the Pharaoh. Exactly when this was we cannot tell. Perhaps they had originally drifted southwards from Canaan to escape from repeated famines, just as in the Biblical account the sons of Jacob travelled down to purchase food. Possibly the influx was linked with the invasion of the Hyksos which brought to an end the Middle Kingdom in the eighteenth century B.C. We do not know the identity of the Pharaoh 'who knew not Joseph' and who set a formerly favoured and prosperous farming community to making bricks and building cities for his own glorification. Rameses II is frequently mentioned, which would help to date the Exodus during the thirteenth century B.C. Other authorities favour a date some two hundred years earlier. All we know for certain is that the Hebrew tribes who had been allowed to settle in the land of Goshen, east of the Nile delta, and who were now treated as little better than serfs, had lived there for several centuries. They had no memories of Canaan, the land of their forefathers, and had no expectation or hope of ever seeing it.

Moses is the son of Jochebed, wife of Amram, a counsellor of the tribe of Levi. He is born at the time when Pharaoh, terrified by prophesies of a Jewish child who would destroy Egypt and save his people, has ordered all male Hebrew children to be drowned in the Nile. He is the third child of his parents, having a brother, Aaron, and a sister, Miriam. His mother, aware of the child's destiny, unable to conceal him any longer, floats him down the river in a basket of bulrushes while Miriam keeps watch over his progress from the bank. He is discovered by Pharaoh's daughter and lifted from the water. Miriam persuades the princess to have the child nursed by his own mother. Later he is adopted by the princess and brought up at court. She gives him the name of Moses – meaning 'drawn out' of the water.

This account of the birth and rescue of Moses has parallels in other mythologies. Especially similar is the tale of Sargon I, king of Babylon, who is born secretly to humble parents, placed in a basket of rushes and rescued by one Akki, drawer of water. The exposure and discovery of Romulus and Remus is another familiar variation of this tradition.

Moses, as a young man, is tall, handsome, unusually intelligent but slow of speech, probably a stutterer. This defect is said to have resulted from an early episode at court when the child reached out and placed Pharaoh's crown on his head. One of the king's counsellors, possibly the angel Gabriel in disguise, suggested testing the child to determine whether the act had been intentional. Given the choice of selecting a precious onyx or a glowing coal, the child's hand was guided to the coal which he placed in his mouth, burning his lips and tongue.

Fully conscious of his Hebrew origins, Moses is angry and distressed at the sufferings and humiliations of his people. He intervenes with Pharaoh to grant them the Sabbath as a day of rest. When, on one occasion, he sees an Egyptian brutally beating a Hebrew labourer, he impulsively strikes him dead. He is betrayed by the brothers Dathan and Abiram, and forced to flee the country. One legend describes how he is sentenced to death, but saved on the scaffold by Gabriel who turns his neck into a pillar of marble and blunts the executioner's sword; and while the Bible account takes him directly to the land of Midian, other versions tell how he becomes king of Ethiopia, marrying an Ethiopian princess (Miriam later accuses him of this in the Biblical text) and reigning over them for forty years. He is finally deposed in the friendliest manner and loaded with riches.

Arrived in Midian, he is recognized by the priest Jethro, formerly in Pharaoh's entourage, as the man destined to bring disaster on the Egyptians. He is therefore imprisoned in a dungeon for seven years, during which time he is kept alive by Jethro's daughter, Zipporah. At the end of this period, convinced that Moses' preservation is miraculous, Jethro frees him, marries him to Zipporah and makes him keeper of his flocks.

Moses works patiently and faultlessly as Jethro's shepherd for another forty years. One day, near Mount Horeb, he sees a thorn bush burning but miraculously not consumed by flames. From the centre of the bush the voice of God tells him that he is the man chosen to lead the people of Israel out of Egypt back to a land flowing with milk and honey. Far from accepting this honour gratefully Moses hesitates, protests, argues: He is unfit, the Jewish people are unworthy, the four hundred years of bondage are not yet up, he himself is slow of speech, the people will not listen to him, let alone believe that the Lord has appeared to him. He is punished for his reluctance and doubts with leprosy, and because of his stubbornness his speech-defect remains uncured. But eventually he is convinced and sets off for Egypt, armed with the rod which will turn into a serpent and draw water from a rock, and assured that God will save his people once Moses has proclaimed it, and that Aaron will act as his spokesman before Pharaoh. He is joyfully reunited with his brother and together they confront the king.

At Pharaoh's court, their faces aglow with a strange radiance, they soothe the lions guarding the gate and make their demand. Aaron demonstrates the powers of his God and throws the king's magicians and soothsayers into confusion by turning his rod into a serpent, curing his own hand of leprosy and turning water into blood.

Pharaoh, however, refuses to acknowledge the Hebrew

God and threatens even harsher oppression. The Egyptians are then punished with ten plagues – blood, frogs, lice, wild beasts, murrain, boils, hail, locusts, darkness – and, as a climax, after Pharaoh has once again refused to liberate the Hebrews – the killing of all the Egyptian first-born. This occurs at midnight as the Jews celebrate their first Passover feast, having sprinkled the blood of the paschal lamb sacrifice on the door posts so that their houses are 'passed over' and the lives of their children spared.

Pharaoh, genuinely alarmed and contrite, asks Moses to intercede with his God and to leave immediately with his people. They gather – 600,000 of them, by traditional accounts, not including the women and children – with sufficient time to pack all their possessions and take away vast quantities of Egyptian money and jewels. Moses brings with him the coffin containing the remains of Joseph, and they set off across the desert, not by the direct coast road with its fortresses and guard-posts, but by a devious, twisting route which brings them to Sinai after three months. Though guided by God's pillar of fire by night and of cloud by day, they suffer terribly from hunger and thirst, they are nagged by doubts and fears, and terrified to learn that Pharaoh is pursuing them with a huge army, including 600 chariots. At this time of crisis Moses needs to muster all his own faith and self-confidence and to exercise all his powers of persuasion. The decision to take this dreary, tortuous route was his; now he must justify this decision and convince them that the Lord is on their side and that their agony and misery will soon be over.

They reach the Sea of Reeds (not the Red Sea, as is commonly believed, but probably one of the Bitter Lakes to the north, or even a narrow isthmus on the Mediterranean coast itself). Here the waters are miraculously divided, either by Moses' rod or by a powerful east wind, and the tribes of Israel pass to the other shore unharmed. As the waves close over the heads of Pharaoh's pursuing army, Moses and Miriam lead their people in a song of triumph and thanksgiving.

Then begins the long journey to Sinai, another frightful

ordeal. But they are sustained by a series of miracles. Bitter water is turned sweet at Marah and at Elim they find twelve wells and a grove of palm trees. But Moses' leadership is challenged again as, hungry and tired, they long for a return to the fleshpots of Egypt. Then comes the fall of manna to satisfy their hunger – white, like coriander seed, tasting of wafers of honey; and later, flocks of quail in such profusion that the people are busy catching them for two days and a night. Legend also tells of Miriam's Well, a rock from which water pours freely, and which follows them until the day of her death. While in camp they are protected by a cloud of glory; and with God's aid, and led by Joshua, they ward off an attack by the Amalekites.

Moses is now joined by his father-in-law, Jethro, who is concerned that he is taking too much responsibility in acting as sole judge and adviser in all internal disputes. It is Jethro who persuades Moses to appoint rulers and judges to assist him. He remains the final arbiter in important cases but leaves minor decisions to others.

Finally they arrive at Mount Sinai. This is the climax of their wanderings, culminating in the gift of the tables containing the Ten Commandments and the sealing of the Covenant between the people and their God.

At this point the legends are exceptionally rich and varied, telling how the people during their journey have gradually renounced idol worship, how they have been enjoined to study the Law in all its ramifications, how they have been purified, circumcised their male children, been cured of their ailments and made fit to receive the Law and enter into their Covenant. But the Biblical version is simple, vivid and impressive in its own right. After three days of purification, amid thunder, lightning and the blast of the trumpet, with the mountain peak shrouded in flames and smoke, Moses ascends to the top and God proclaims his Ten Commandments. The Covenant is sealed and Moses is given the two tables of stone.

Moses has promised to return within forty days. When he is delayed the people become restless and once more prone to doubts. Aaron leads them in fashioning the golden calf which they worship. Joshua waits loyally on the mountainside and when the two men return to the camp Moses breaks the tables rather than hand them over to an idolatrous nation. He pleads with God not to destroy them and when the divine wrath is appeased, and the people repent, a second set of tables is made. To house the holy tables an Ark is built of acacia-wood, then a portable Tabernacle. The people bring their offerings, Aaron is appointed high priest, and the Tabernacle is consecrated as God pledges his love for his people.

In addition to the Ten Commandments, Moses also reveals to the people the entire body of oral and written law, by which they will be expected to live. It covers their relationship both with their God and with their fellow men. Here Moses appears in the role of teacher and interpreter. He appoints seventy elders to help him in his work of counsel and guidance, though he remains senior in rank to all of them.

The children of Israel repeatedly fail to live up to the high standards demanded of them by the Law during the years of hardship that ensue. Moses' powers of leadership are put to the test again and again. His brother and sister rebuke him for having married an Ethiopian woman, and, according to the legends, condemn him for his self-imposed chastity since the Exodus. Moses claims this is in accordance with God's commandment and both are punished with leprosy. Although Moses intercedes for her, Miriam is banned from the camp for seven days. The pillar of cloud disappears until she is cleansed and the people ready to depart.

More serious is the conspiracy of the spies sent out by Moses to inspect the land of Canaan. Twelve of them spend forty days travelling through the Promised Land and find that it is, as prophesied, rich and fertile. But, apart from Joshua and Caleb, they bring back a contrary report to the effect that it is infested by giants and hostile tribes. Joshua and Caleb try to protest but are shouted down. The people threaten to lapse into idolatry. A full-scale civil revolt is imminent. Even in this period of extreme danger, Moses pleads God to be merciful. He and Aaron are protected by the cloud of glory as God decrees the nation's punishment. The generation which left Egypt, everyone of twenty years upward, will die in the wilderness, at intervals, during the forty years which still remain before they come to the Promised Land. Even Moses is not exempted from this decree. Neither he, nor Miriam, nor Aaron, will survive. The disloyal spies are summarily executed, but both Joshua and Caleb are spared to enter the Promised Land.

Shortly afterwards there is another challenge in the form of a religious revolt, instigated by Korah and abetted by Moses' old adversaries Dathan and Abiram. Korah questions the tributes payable to the priests and casts in doubt Moses' spiritual authority. For their presumption, they and their families, two hundred and fifty of them, are horribly destroyed.

The tribes stay encamped at Kadesh Barnea for nineteen years, spend a further nineteen wandering in the wilderness of Zin and return to the same spot. During this time Miriam dies, and with the disappearance of her well the people are again assailed by thirst. At Meribah comes the episode of the striking of the rock, where, according to all the legends, Moses makes a fatal mistake. He has been instructed merely to call water from the rock. Instead, spurred by the taunts and gibes of a disbelieving people, he loses his temper and strikes the rock with his rod. Only on the second stroke does the water gush out. Because of his lack of faith and his failure to sanctify God in the eyes of the people, his fate is reconfirmed. He too will die in the wilderness.

Shortly after his sister Miriam, Aaron also dies, quietly and painlessly, on Mount Hor. His son Eleazar inherits the high priesthood. His place of burial remains hidden. The Israelites now travel by way of the Red Sea to the land of Edom and then northwards, where they are attacked successively by Sihon, king of the Amorites, and Og, king of Bashan. Both are defeated and Moses himself is credited with killing the giant Og with an axe twelve cubits in length. The next enemy, Balak, king of Moab, enlists the aid of the heathen prophet, Balaam. The angel of the Lord appears to Balaam on his ass and his intended curse on Israel is turned into a blessing. The last battle is with the Midianites, in which Balaam is killed.

Now, in sight of the border of Canaan, the time comes for Moses himself to die. The faithful Joshua is installed as his successor. Moses takes leave of his people. The Book of Deuteronomy is traditionally accepted as Moses' address of farewell, with its exhortation to them to love God and obey his laws. Whether or not Moses is the author, the nobility and humanity of its expression accords well with his character and brings his career to a fitting conclusion.

As to the manner of Moses' death, the legends once more vary considerably. Deuteronomy recounts that he ascended Mount Nebo where God showed him the Promised Land, and that he died peacefully in the land of Moab, aged one hundred and twenty years, his eye undimmed and his natural force not abated. The children of Israel mourned for him thirty days and he too was buried in an unrevealed grave. The legends concentrate on the human aspects of the doomed man and abound in fantasy. Moses begs for remission of his sentence, dons sackcloth and ashes, asks the sun, moon and planets, the mountains, rivers and deserts to intercede for him, and performs menial tasks for Joshua in the hope that if he relinquishes his leadership, his life may yet be spared. It is unavailing. He is rebuked for his fears, and there is the interesting suggestion that Israel will only be saved by his own death. He blesses his people for the last time, and after fending off the Angel of Death, yields his soul to God who descends with three angels.

The Jewish people, led by Joshua, come into their inheritance without his physical guidance. But the memory and the inspiration linger on. His name is ever after mentioned in their prayers and psalms. We have no reason to doubt that he exceeded all other men in piety, wisdom and humility, and the more human attributes which appear in the legends and fables in no way minimize his great gifts as leader, teacher and counsellor.

We should not be too hasty in dismissing the story of Moses and the Exodus as merely mythical. There is much pictorial, as well as written, evidence for the years of slavery in Egypt and the departure for the Promised Land – not to mention the Ten Plagues. These may be seen either as extreme examples of normally recurring natural disasters, or as physical effects of an overwhelming cosmic catastrophe. There are innumerable parallel accounts of such disasters in the folklores of other nations.

Although there is a lack of supporting archaeological evidence, all the places mentioned in the Scriptures can be identified, even if the authorities differ as to the exact route of the Exodus, the point of the crossing and the precise location of Mount Sinai. Certainly there is plenty of archaeological evidence of contemporary Canaanite settlement and of Joshua's campaigns in the next generation.

Detailed examination both of the archaeological discoveries of recent years and of comparative accounts in other national mythologies must, if we are fair, lead us to admit that there is a strong backbone of historical truth in the Bible. Moses, the founder of the Jewish people and the man who introduced them to monotheism and the laws by which they have lived for three thousand years, may or may not have existed. But Jews of every place and generation still repeat the Biblical words enshrining his memory: 'And there has not arisen a prophet since in Israel like unto Moses, whom the Lord knew face to face.'

Moses Maimonides
1135–1204

In the year 1170 the Jews of the Yemen in Southern Arabia were faced with a grim decision. Their brutal Moslem rulers demanded exile or conversion. The community was deeply divided. One prominent convert was preaching that Mohammed was the true Messiah; another young Jew was proclaiming that he himself was the forerunner of the Messiah. In his torment and confusion the Yemenite elder, Jacob al Fayumi, turned to the one person who could give advice and sympathy – Moses ben Maimon, otherwise known as Maimonides, the Sage of Fostat.

The great scholar-philosopher was quick to answer the call. Writing from his home in the old city of Cairo, he called on them to stand firm in their dark hour and predicted an end to their sufferings. 'My brethren,' he urged, 'hold fast to the covenant, be immovable in your convictions, fulfil the statutes of your religion.' Ridiculing the claims of Mohammed to be the Messiah, and dismissing the pretensions of the pseudo-Messiah as the ravings of a demented man, he pointed out that Jewish suffering was universal throughout history but that it would not last for ever. 'I beg,' he concluded, 'that you will send a copy of this letter to every congregation, to those who are possessed of knowledge in Israel and to others, so that they may be strengthened in their faith, and may remain unwaveringly steadfast.' Several years later a change of régime brought deliverance, and the Jews who had taken Maimonides' advice honoured him by including his name in their daily prayers.

The fame of Moses ben Maimon had spread far beyond the boundaries of the country where he and his family had themselves taken refuge from persecution ten years previously. The range of his learning, the impact of his personality, his wise and humane approach to religious problems and the conduct of everyday life, had made him the recognized leader of Egyptian Jewry. He was a distinguished author, a prolific letter-writer, an authority on Jewish law, medicine and philosophy, and a practising physician. It was not only his fellow Jews who considered him the greatest religious philosopher of his time.

Cordova, where he was born on 30 March, 1135, the eve of the Passover, had once been a great and glorious city, the pride of Moorish civilization in Spain, a centre of statecraft, learning and culture. During this 'golden age' art, science and scholarship joined hands to create a society which, at its peak, during the ninth and tenth centuries, compared with the finest years of Greece.

In almost every other part of the world Jewish communities were oppressed or submerged. Here, in Moslem Spain, Jews were prosperous and free – free to worship and free to develop their intellectual and artistic gifts to the full. Hebrew language and literature were revived by the poets Solomon ibn Gabirol, Judah Halevi and Moses ibn Ezra, and the scholars Hasdai ibn Shaprut and Samuel ibn Nagrela. Rabbis, philosophers, historians, politicians, merchants, bankers, physicians, scientists and writers – there was no area of communal activity in which Jews did not play a positive and respected role.

This then was the background to the early years of Moses, son of Maimon the theologian, mathematician and astronomer, himself descended from a long line of rabbis and scholars. Yet very little is known of his family environment. One legend refers to his mother as the daughter of a butcher, and his father often referred to him as the 'butcher's boy'. All we really know is that he was an unusually intelligent child, eager to learn, guided by his father and his teachers from an early age into the paths of piety, duty and service. Not necessarily a life devoid of childhood pleasures and diversions, but certainly one in which the quest for knowledge outweighed all else.

Unfortunately, Cordova had seen her best days. The city was as beautiful and imposing as ever, but a corroding, destructive spirit was at work. Internal feuds, political and religious conflicts, the message of the Crusaders – all were beginning to sap the energy of Moorish Spain.

In 1148 disaster overtook Cordova. The Almohades, a fanatical Mohammedan sect from North Africa, swept through Morocco, crossed the narrow straits and captured the proud city. These bloodthirsty barbarians slaughtered and ransacked without discrimination. To the Jews they offered the traditional alternatives – apostasy or exile.

Maimon and his family chose to leave. Surprisingly he did not turn north to Christian Spain or France but wandered, nomad-fashion, through southern Spain. All records of the family's eight or nine years of restless exile are lost, but it was during that dreadful period of adolescence and approach to manhood that Moses learned what persecution meant. There was never any question of abandoning their faith. Under his father's tutelage the young scholar continued his studies and at some stage in his travels embarked on his career as an author, with an *Introduction to Logic*, an *Essay on the Jewish Calendar* and some commentaries on the Talmud.* He also began the first of his three major works on the subject which absorbed him for the rest of his life – the validity of traditional Jewish laws in a foreign environment and a changing world.

Finding no respite from Almohade persecution, Maimon finally embarked, with his two sons and a daughter, for

* The compilation of Jewish civil and ceremonial law.

Morocco. He settled in the town of Fez. Although Fez was still part of the Almohade empire, it was renowned for its stimulating cultural and intellectual atmosphere. Nevertheless, the Jews of Fez and of Morocco were in dire danger. Many of them were leading double lives, outwardly Moslems, at heart Jews. The Maimon family themselves probably paid similar lip-service to Islam. They could hardly have survived otherwise. But in private they spoke out boldly in defence of their faith. The elder Maimon wrote a stirring letter to a friend, which was widely circulated, offering consolation for suffering but urging courage and loyalty. Let Jews pray in Arabic if they did not know Hebrew, but let them remain Jews at heart.

In reply to this *Letter of Consolation* an anonymous writer retorted that any Jew who as much as paid lip-service to Islam was a heretic. Thousands of Jews who found themselves in this predicament took panic, and it was to resolve their dilemma that Maimon's son now took up the cudgels with his famous *Letter on Apostasy*, the first of many such public pronouncements designed to mould opinion and strengthen morale.

It was a brilliant document, forceful, impassioned and tolerant. Assuring the Moroccan Jews that provided they prayed and obeyed the divine commandments – even if in secret – they were still essentially Jewish, Maimonides showed characteristic understanding of human frailties. After all, he too had been forced into just such a compromise. But the ideal course of action, he urged, would be to flee the country: 'The advice I give to myself, to those I love, and to those who ask my opinion, is that we should go forth from these places, and go to a place where we can fulfil the Law without compulsion and without fear, and that we should even forsake our homes and our children, and all possessions.'

A message to inspire his compatriots but not to endear him to his hosts. He was a marked man. In 1165 the eminent Rabbi of Fez was attacked and killed by a frenzied mob. Maimonides decided that the time had come to leave. On a dark Saturday night the family slipped on to a ship bound for Palestine. The month's journey was punctuated by a terrible storm which almost shipwrecked them. In their tiny cabin the family huddled and prayed. When the danger was over Maimonides vowed to observe every anniversary of the storm as a solitary day of fasting.

Finally they landed at Acre. This day too was set aside in future years as a day of thanksgiving. Then he travelled to Jerusalem, spending three days visiting the holy places and the Wailing Wall, and continuing on to Hebron, burial place of the Patriarchs. These days were likewise marked as anniversary festivals.

But the Holy Land, the promised refuge of his prayers and dreams, proved a bitter disappointment. The Jewish communities were sparse and scattered, there was no vestige of learning or culture. Maimonides and his aged father and family moved southwards – to Egypt. And it was in that corner of the Moslem world, at first under the Fatimid dynasty and later under Saladin, that they found the peace and security they had not known for twenty years.

Here, as in the splendid years of Cordova, Jewish traditions were respected, Jewish lives and property were safe. Yet there were differences. In Egypt the level of Jewish culture and scholarship was at a low ebb and two rival sects had split the community down the centre. Within twenty years Maimonides was to transform the situation completely. At first in Alexandria where he lived for some two years, then in Fostat, the old city of Cairo, he set out to restore peace to a spiritually divided community and to give a new sense of dignity and purpose to their lives.

A new Moses had arrived in Egypt, but it was not for any Messianic ambitions and delusions that he became known as the leader of the Jewish community and the spokesman for suffering Jewry in less fortunate lands. His personal needs were modest. His own small income was derived entirely from the proceeds of the family's jewellery business, run by his brother David. He absolutely refused to accept a rabbinical post, being strongly opposed to the idea of scholarship for gain, arguing that there was nothing shameful in commerce and that many of the greatest rabbis had also been carpenters, tailors, potters and builders. But unofficially he was regarded as the community's Nagid – prince – the highest authority on all spiritual, legal and moral problems. To his friends and pupils, and to the scholars and dignitaries who wrote to him for guidance, he was the Sage of Fostat. To the countless devout Jews of Europe, Africa and Asia who only knew his name, he was a prophet, the true follower of his Biblical namesake.

Shortly after his arrival in Egypt he published the great work which had occupied him during his years of exile – the *Saraj* (The Luminary), or *Commentary on the Mishna*. The Mishna comprised the oral teachings of the great rabbis from Hillel to Judah Hanasi over a period of 250 years, and formed the basis (as it still does) of Jewish laws and observances. Maimonides sought to clarify the text and meaning of the Mishna for his generation.

With precision and clarity he explained the fundamental logic underlying the laws, even the apparently meaningless ones. Strict observance of them provided a reasoned basis for a life built on sound ethical and moral principles. The section known as *Eight Chapters* was a masterly survey of ethics, theology, philosophy and science. There was nothing heretical in the *Commentary*, but the rational approach to religion which Maimonides was to develop in his later writings was revolutionary. His wide study of Greek literature and philosophy enabled him to balance the claims of Aristotelian science against traditional beliefs. In many places he showed that there was no fundamental disagreement. His recommendation of the 'Golden Mean', for example, of moderation in all things, including diet, exercise and sexual activity, was Greek in origin but skilfully interwoven with traditional Jewish teaching. And where contradiction was unavoidable Maimonides came down on the side of tradition. Any doubts as to the orthodoxy of his beliefs were allayed in the section in which he formulated his famous Thirteen Articles of Faith which were later, though not without argument, incorporated in the daily service of the synagogue.

It was a phenomenal task, considering the circumstances in which it was written. As he pointed out: 'I have explained some chapters whilst on my wanderings, and others on board ships, in inns, on roadsides, and without any access to books.' He begged his readers' indulgence in case of errors.

Yet he was far from satisfied. For practical purposes he felt that the entire complex body of Jewish law needed re-codifying. In 1170 he presented his *Book of Precepts*, summarizing the Commandments under the traditional 613 headings, and embracing the whole field of secular and religious law. Ambitious though this was, it was merely an introduction to the much vaster work which occupied him for the next ten years, the so-called *Mishneh Torah* (The Second Torah), usually referred to as the *Code*.

Meanwhile, however, life had not been kind to him. His father had died shortly after his arrival in Egypt. His own health was none too good. And in 1174 came a disaster which left him shattered for many years. His brother David was drowned at sea during a business trip, together with the entire family capital in the form of money and jewels. Moses' deep sense of grief was vividly expressed in a letter written many years later to Rabbi Japhet ben Eliahu, his former host in Acre:

'In Egypt I met with great and severe misfortunes. Illness and material losses came upon me. In addition, various informers plotted against me. But the most terrible blow which befell me, a blow which caused me more grief than anything I have experienced in my life, was the death of the most perfect and righteous man who was drowned while travelling in the Indian Ocean. Many goods that belonged to me, to him and to other people, were lost with him. He left with me his widow and a little daughter.

'For nearly a year after I received the sad news, I lay ill on my bed struggling with fever and despair. Eight years have passed, and still I mourn, for there is no consolation. What can console me? He grew up on my knees; he was my brother, my pupil.'

This was not the whole story. Faced with the problem of caring for his brother's family, he now turned to medicine, a subject of which he had extensive theoretical, but no practical, experience. Despite being a foreigner and a Jew, he achieved fame and prosperity, and eventually became one of the physicians to the royal court. Circumstances were in his favour. Under the enlightened rule of Saladin and his vizier, Alfadhel, Egypt now emerged as an oasis of progressive government and stability in an encircling wilderness of barbarity and bloodshed. Though poignantly aware of the sufferings of the Jews of North Africa under Moslem extremists and the massacres in Europe perpetrated by the Crusaders, Maimonides had to content himself with dispensing spiritual advice to those beyond the reach of physical assistance.

The care of the body and the care of the soul were now his twin concerns, basic concepts of Jewish ethical teaching and focal points of his own philosophy. The purpose of religion was to promote the well-being of both body and soul. The traditional laws were designed for this purpose, once rightly understood; and it was this immense field of law and custom that Maimonides dealt with in his second great work, the *Mishneh Torah*, or *Code*.

It was the only one of his three major books to be written in Hebrew and in many ways it was his most important work. It was to influence Jewish life and thought for centuries, to arouse heated controversy, and to establish him as unquestionably the foremost rabbinical authority of the age. A masterpiece of orderly and systematic presentation, it was divided into fourteen chapters and discussed the true meaning of all the private and public observances demanded of a Jew. These covered every aspect of a man's life – the principles of Judaism, the recital of prayers, the observance of Sabbath and the festivals, marriage and divorce, forbidden foods, purity and impurity, the treatment of neighbours, business associates, servants and animals, damage to person and property, sale and transfer, trustees and debts, civil and criminal law, the death penalty. But it was no mere recital of laws. As always, Maimonides' aim was to instruct, to explain, to clarify and to guide. It was the work of a deeply devout man, keenly responsive to the intellectual ferment of his time, to the pressures and influences of alien philosophy

Top: Maimonides. Plaque in the
Capitol, Washington, D.C.
Above left: Moses bringing down
the Tablets of the Law from Mount
Sinai (from the Sarajevo Haggadah).
Right: At the court of Murad III,
in whose reign Don Joseph Nasi's
influence waned (*The Chester Beatty
Library*).

Top: Manasseh ben Israel presents his *Humble Addresses* to the Protector Oliver Cromwell at Whitehall in December, 1655, requesting permission for the Jews to return to England after four centuries of exile. From the painting by Solomon A. Hart, R.A. *(by permission of the Chairman and Council of the Jews' College, London). Left:* Sabbatai Zevi, the 17th-century pseudo-Messiah, blessing the congregation of Smyrna. (Title-page of *The Counterfeit Messiah or False Christ of the Jews,* written by "an English person of quality".) *Below right:* A portrait of Manasseh ben Israel by his famous contemporary, Rembrandt.

and culture, but confident that the discoveries of science could be reconciled with the precepts of faith. Tolerance, moderation, right behaviour, charity, honesty – these were the virtues he preached; and through it all emerged the author's kindliness, generosity and wisdom.

The immediate response to the *Code* was overwhelming. Though attacked by die-hard traditionalists, it was hailed as the final authority, and copyists were kept hard at work to cope with the demand both in Egypt and from abroad.

Letters flowed in, thanking him, congratulating him, beseeching his advice. To all of these he replied in warm, personal terms. These letters, or *Responsa*, of which he wrote hundreds, were often miniature treatises on specific subjects – points of ritual, treatment of converts, tolerance towards Moslems, the perils of astrology, the uses of music, aids to health – never excuses for abstract rumination, but always rooted in personal experience and familiar situations. For its time it was a most effective and powerful means of mass-communication. As one contemporary remarked, 'By his letters he made Israel again one people and brought one to the other so that they became one flesh.'

It was such an exchange of letters which inspired the last, and probably the most influential, of his works, the *Guide for the Perplexed*, which he published ten years later, in 1190. It consisted of a series of essays, in Arabic, answering questions posed by a devoted pupil, Joseph ibn Aknin. Aknin had studied mathematics and philosophy under Maimonides, and it was as a father to his son that Maimonides dedicated the book to him. 'If I had none but thee in the world,' he once wrote, 'my world would be full.' Like many intelligent young men of his time Aknin was troubled about certain points in traditional Judaism which appeared to run contrary to Aristotelian thinking, especially the broader issues relating to God, the universe and the purpose of life itself. In his Introduction to the *Guide*, Maimonides wrote: 'Your absence has prompted me to compose this treatise for you and for those like you, however few they may be.' Thus it was expressly written, not for the non-believer, but for the doubter, for those people 'who found it difficult to accept as correct the teaching based on the literal interpretation of the Law'. The intention was 'to expound Biblical passages which have been impugned, and to elucidate their hidden and true sense'.

This is an issue which is still bitterly debated eight hundred years later and it is characteristic of Maimonides that he tackled it with his customary honesty and courage, warning his readers to study the book very carefully and not to skim the surface. If not, he said, it might appear to mean the exact opposite of what he intended. And so it proved. Although more thoughtful readers, Jews, Moslems and Christians alike, recognized it for the masterful and original work that it is, others, whether for personal or political motives, attacked it as heretical. Its opponents succeeded in persuading the Inquisition to burn it – a temporary setback, as it proved, to its enduring reputation and fame.

No summary of the *Guide* can do justice to its range of inquiry and boldness of thought. The Bible was subjected to detailed and searching scrutiny. God's existence, as Prime Mover and First Cause, was proved by Aristotelian methods of logic, but He was indefinable and incorporeal (this latter assertion giving outraged offence to traditionalists). Maimonides then considered such fundamental questions as Divine providence, the nature of evil, the role of prophecy and the function of knowledge. This last faculty was the key to man's progress towards perfection. Knowledge was the guiding principle of life. God could only be worshipped if He and His actions were correctly understood – what Maimonides termed 'the intellectual worship of God'.

He concluded his inquiry with an analysis of the purpose of life. Reason, moderation, knowledge, ethical behaviour – all these helped man to attain the perfection which only he could achieve. Of the four types of perfection commonly recognized, the first – acquisitive – in the guise of property or power, was accidental and impermanent. The second – bodily perfection – comprising health and physical strength, was equally illusory, and shared by animals. The third – moral perfection – was social and depended on a relationship with others. Only the fourth – intellectual perfection – could be held to be truly attainable by man alone. The true perfection was the possession of wisdom, and the sole purpose of life the knowledge of God as described by Jeremiah: 'Let not the wise man glory in his wisdom; nor let the mighty man glory in his might; and let not the rich man glory in his riches; but let him that glorieth glory in this, that he understandeth and knoweth me.'

The *Guide for the Perplexed* shines out like a beacon from the morass of medieval literature. As a statement of faith, an assertion of the supremacy of reason, as a handbook to moral and ethical behaviour in everyday life, it far transcends place and time.

The last dozen years of Maimonides' life were devoted to medicine. He was physician to the Vizier Alfadhel and numbered many leading dignitaries among his patients. His second wife, sister of one of the royal secretaries, had given birth to a son in 1186. The child was a great solace to him in his later years when strain of work increasingly undermined his health. He wrote now chiefly on medical topics and produced a compendium of drugs for general use by the medical profession, and eight or nine other books covering the whole field of practical medicine. His book on poisons and antidotes was particularly in demand and his opinions on the value of psychological therapy were centuries ahead of his time. Such was his reputation that King Richard I invited him to return to England with him, but Maimonides elected to remain in Cairo.

It is worth quoting at length from the celebrated letter which he wrote in 1199 to his friend Samuel ibn Tibbon who was preparing to translate the *Guide* into Hebrew. Advising him of the problems involved, Maimonides apologized for not being able to devote time to discuss the matter in person, and gave the following interesting account of his daily routine:

'I dwell at Misr (Fostat) and the Sultan resides at Kahira (Cairo); these two places are two Sabbath days' journey (about one mile and a half) distant from each other. My duties to the Sultan are very heavy. I am obliged to visit him every day, early in the morning; and when he or any of

his children, or any of the inmates of his harem, are in-
disposed. I dare not quit Kahira, but must stay during the
greater part of the day in the palace. It also frequently
happens that one or two of the royal officers fall sick, and
I must attend to their healing. Hence, as a rule, I repair to
Kahira very early in the day, and if nothing unusual happens,
I do not return to Misr until the afternoon. Then I am almost
dying with hunger. I find the antechamber filled with people,
both Jews and Gentiles, nobles and common people, judges
and bailiffs, friends and foes – a mixed multitude, who await
the time of my return.

'I dismount from my animal, wash my hands, go forth
to my patients, and entreat them to bear with me while I
partake of some slight refreshment, the only meal I take in
the twenty-four hours. Then I attend to my patients, write
prescriptions for their various ailments. Patients go in and
out until nightfall, and sometimes even, I solemnly assure
you, until two hours and more in the night. I converse and
prescribe for them while lying down from sheer fatigue,
and when night falls, I am so exhausted that I can scarcely
speak.

'In consequence of this, no Israelite can have any private
interview with me except on the Sabbath. On this day the
whole congregation, or at least the majority of the members,
come to me after the morning service, when I instruct them
as to their proceedings during the whole week; we study
together a little until noon, when they depart. Some of them
return, and read with me after the afternoon service until
evening prayers. In this manner I spend that day. I have here
related to you only a part of what you would see if you
were to visit me. Now, when you have completed for our
brethren the translation you have commenced, I beg that you
will come to me but not with hope of deriving any advantage
from your visit as regards your studies; for my time is, as I
have shown you, excessively occupied.'

Towards the end of his life Maimonides received a number
of letters from Rabbi Jonathan of Lunel, in Provence. In one
of them he compared Maimonides with his great predecessor,
which later gave rise to the proverbial saying, 'From Moses

unto Moses there arose none like Moses.' He posed twenty-four theological questions and requested a copy of the *Guide*. It took Maimonides two years to summon up the time and energy to reply and when he did he could not conceal his fatigue and depression. He was full of gloom at the dismal picture of contemporary religious learning, with the shining exception of Lunel itself. 'You, members of the congregation of Lunel, and of the neighbouring towns, stand alone in raising aloft the banner of Moses,' he wrote; and concluded, 'Therefore be firm and courageous for the sake of our people and our God; make up your minds to remain brave men. Everything depends on you; the decision is in your hands. Do not rely on my support, because I am an old man with grey hair. And know that for this not my age but my weak body is responsible. . . .'

His work was done. He died on 13 December, 1204, and the Jews of Egypt observed three days' mourning. He was buried at Tiberias in Palestine.

Although Maimonides is honoured by Jews as one of their greatest thinkers and writers, the scope of his work extended far beyond the Jewish communities of his day. His influence on later scholars and philosophers, Jewish and non-Jewish – men such as Albertus Magnus, Thomas Aquinas and Spinoza – was profound. The *Guide for the Perplexed*, translated into Latin as well as Hebrew, was studied in homes, schools and universities for centuries to come. His significance today lies in his 'modernity', the enlightened fashion in which he tackled the practical and spiritual problems of his time, the sensible and humane tone of his arguments, and their universal application. The matters he dealt with are those which have troubled men of faith at all times, no matter what their creed. The clash of faith and reason continues today, as the discoveries of modern science threaten more than ever to undermine traditional beliefs. Men are still perplexed and it is a measure of Maimonides' stature that his books and letters still have the power to persuade, to explain, to comfort and to guide.

Doña Gracia
and Don Joseph Nasi
c. 1510–1569 1520–1579

'Duke of Naxos and the Cyclades' – this was the high-sounding title conferred by Sultan Selim II on Joseph Nasi, financier, businessman and statesman, in 1566. His story is both unusual and exciting – the story of a man whose commercial and financial genius led to immense wealth and unprecedented political influence. Linked with him is the figure of his aunt and mother-in-law, Gracia Nasi, renowned for her own considerable business ability, her boundless generosity and humanitarian activities, and her patronage of scholarship and literature. Her importance in moulding the outlook and career of her famous nephew had not, until recently, been appreciated. Today she emerges as one of the most formidable and influential Jewish women of the Renaissance.

The story of the House of Nasi begins, as do so many of the narratives in this book, in the Iberian Peninsula. Among the families forced out of Spain into Portugal after Ferdinand's and Isabella's expulsion edict of 1492, was the famous house of Benveniste. Here, under the name of Mendes, they lived – outwardly at least – as Marranos, or newly-baptized Christians.

The brothers Francisco and Diogo formed a commercial and banking house, dealing at first in precious stones, then branching out into other fields. Diogo opened a branch in Antwerp where he prospered. He built up his personal fortune and that of the House of Mendes by virtually monopolizing the European pepper and spice trade and expanding the firm's private banking interests. His elder brother, Francisco, married the beautiful Beatrice de Luna, known secretly by her Jewish name of Gracia Nasi. Francisco died shortly after the marriage, leaving Beatrice to bring up one daughter, Reyna. In 1536, realizing that conditions in Portugal had become unbearable, Beatrice joined her brother-in-law in Antwerp. With her came a sister, Brianda, who was to marry Diogo, and a nephew, João – Joseph. He was probably the son of her only brother, and at this time a boy in his late teens.

Beatrice proved to be a more than adequate replacement for her late husband in the business and partnered Diogo until his death six or seven years later. Although life in Antwerp was immeasurably easier than in Lisbon, it was always precarious. They were still forced to lead a double life and Diogo had, prior to Beatrice's arrival, been arrested on suspicion of treason and imprisoned for two months. Yet, at great personal risk, both Beatrice and Diogo put their influence and fortune at the disposal of their unfortunate fellow-Marranos. Countless refugees from the Inquisition owed their lives to the elaborate underground escape-system operated by the Mendes family. Mendes money, Mendes agents, Mendes transport helped the victims of persecution in their long treks across Europe, northwards to Flanders, across the Alps down to Italy and the ultimate haven of Turkey. And while the rescue work went on, Beatrice captivated Antwerp society and the court in Brussels with her charm and personality.

She proved to be a woman of great stubbornness and determination, as the Queen Regent, Mary, discovered to her cost. Beatrice's daughter was now of marriageable age and among the many suitors who pursued her, both for her beauty and her potential fortune, was the elderly Francisco of Aragon. Although he had royal blood in his veins and enlisted the support both of the Queen Regent and her brother, the Emperor Charles V, Doña Beatrice was a match for all of them. She informed Mary quite bluntly that she would see her daughter dead rather than consent to such a union.

The situation, however, threatened to become awkward, and Beatrice rapidly concluded the plans she had confided to Diogo years previously – to leave Antwerp for healthier climes. Diogo had assented, but his death delayed matters. Now she was coming to rely increasingly on her young nephew, João. He was already well established in the royal entourage, a close friend and jousting partner of Maximilian, nephew of Charles V, himself destined to be ruler of the Holy Roman Empire. Beatrice entrusted him with most of the firm's overseas affairs, and he became a familiar figure in all the great European trading centres. When Beatrice left Antwerp for ever, ostensibly to take the waters at Aix, but bound for Venice, she left João in charge of the bulk of the Mendes fortunes.

Her sudden departure alarmed and angered the authorities who promptly accused her sister and herself of heresy, and threatened to confiscate their property. João, exercising all his charm and tactical skill, bargained with the government on their behalf, winning valuable time and apparently managing to safeguard the greater part of the family fortune. He left Antwerp shortly afterwards, but did not immediately join his relatives in Italy.

Venice, though no longer the undisputed maritime power of the Mediterranean, was still an important commercial city, a busy and colourful focal point of Renaissance art and culture. But the openly acknowledged Jews of the town were herded into the dirty, crowded Ghetto area, and the Mendes sisters, still professing Christians, took up residence in a splendid mansion in the centre of the city. Beatrice's work on behalf of the Marrano refugees continued uninterruptedly, Venice being in many ways better situated than Antwerp for practical relief work. Yet her stay in the beautiful city of lagoons was to be a short one. Her own sister, Brianda, dealt her a devastating blow. Whether she was jealous of Beatrice's undisputed family authority or simply envious of her general popularity and social standing, she suddenly demanded for her own daughter half-share in the family fortune. After a bitter quarrel, Brianda denounced her sister to the authorities as a secret Jewess who was making Venice only a temporary port of refuge on her journey to Turkey. Beatrice was arrested, her daughter and niece being removed to a nunnery. Once again, the legal and theological disputes over the Mendes property were resumed; Brianda, continuing her intrigues in France, was dismayed to find herself similarly denounced as a renegade Christian, and her own claims in France barred.

Now, due in some measure to the efforts of the ever-active João, the powerful international connections of the Mendes were stirred into action, this time on the family's own behalf. Beatrice had made it known through her friends and business colleagues that her ultimate destination was indeed Turkey, and that much of her fortune had already found its way to Constantinople. The Sultan's physician, a Jew from Granada named Moses Hamon, was induced to intervene on her behalf. Sultan Suleiman, known as the 'Magnificent', was an attested friend of the Jews and well aware of the importance and prestige of the Mendes family. He sent his special representative to Venice urging Beatrice's release and safe passage to Constantinople. How effective this action was is not certain. Probably by her unaided efforts, Beatrice had in fact already secured her release, had been reunited with her daughter, and ordered to leave Venice. By this time she needed no prompting. She made her home in Ferrara.

Here she was royally welcomed by Duke Ercole II and took her place, as by right, at the head of the city's thriving Jewish community. Assured of her personal freedom and immune, for the first time, from religious persecution, she and her family were able to live a full Jewish life. From now on she was known as Gracia Nasi, or more simply, as 'La Señora' and, to her Jewish acquaintances, by the Hebrew equivalent, 'Ha'Geveret'. Her sister took stock of her situation and joined the family circle again.

João visited them occasionally, but spent most of his time travelling throughout Europe on business. Whatever unselfish aid he gave behind the scenes, it was his aunt who still took, and doubtless deserved, most of the credit for the never-ending Marrano rescue work. Ferrara itself sheltered many of the refugees, evidently in sufficient numbers for the local publishing house to print translated works from the Hebrew for their benefit.

Doña Gracia's position in the community is demonstrated by the books that were dedicated to her. One was the so-called Ferrara Bible, the general edition of which was dedicated to the Duke, and the Jewish edition to her, 'The Very Magnificent Lady, Doña Gracia Nasi'. So was Samuel Usque's long prose-poem, *Consolation for the Tribulations of Israel*, a classic of Portuguese literature. The lengthy preamble, though somewhat flowery, was obviously heartfelt. It described her untiring efforts for her exiled fellow-countrymen whom she helped 'with a most liberal hand, with money, and many other aids and comforts'. The author continued: 'It is she who aided you . . . in the dangerous and urgent necessities which you experienced in the unexpected exile from that Italian city (Venice had finally expelled the Marranos in 1550) . . . succouring the multitude of necessitous and miserable poor, refusing no favour even to those who were her enemies, and sending boatloads of bread and necessities to all. . . . She brings them to safe lands and does not cease to guide them . . . and remains at all times a tried relief in all the miseries of the Portuguese people.'

Yet Ferrara too afforded her only temporary shelter. An outbreak of plague hastened her departure and for a while she returned to Venice. Here she appears to have been arrested once more. Again the Sultan sent his representative speeding to the rescue. Back in Ferrara briefly, she saw clear signs of the Inquisition gathering its forces for a fresh assault. Finally, in August, 1552, she left Italy for Constantinople.

Doña Gracia's entry into Suleiman's capital was in the

grand style. A contemporary writer recorded: 'One day a Portuguese lady . . . who was very rich, entered Constantinople with forty horsemen and four triumphal chariots, filled with Spanish ladies and serving-women. . . . She had her respects paid for her at Court. . . . She had arranged with the Grand Turk that she did not require any special privileges in his territories, except that her household need not wear clothes like those of the other Jews, but stomachers and coifs in the Venetian style.'

A less sympathetic observer from Germany reported: 'The Jews are very proud of her and call her Señora. . . . She is said to have intrigued with the Sultan's physician, who had a son and hoped she would give him her daughter.' This last suggestion was pure rumour. Gracia had other plans for Reyna. A year later, João joined the family in Constantinople. Shortly afterwards he became Doña Gracia's son-in-law. His arrival was no less splendid than his aunt's. The same jaundiced German resident wrote: 'This rogue . . . came to Constantinople in 1554 with over twenty well-dressed Spanish servants. They attend him as if he were a prince. He himself wore silk clothes lined with sable. Before him went two janissaries with staves, as mounted lackeys. . . . He is a large person with a trimmed black beard.'

There was no further need for him to dissemble. He too proclaimed himself Jewish and was known thereafter as Joseph Nasi. At first the newly-married pair lived with Doña Gracia in her luxurious house in the fashionable district of Galata. Later they moved to an equally sumptuous mansion overlooking the Bosphorus, suitably named *Belvedere*. Doña Gracia's house, in particular, became a centre of fashion and culture, and was open also to anyone in need. She still insisted on feeding eighty paupers at her table every day, and her generosity was unabated. In a city which had a large and active Jewish community she gave money for every worthy cause – schools, hospitals, synagogues, religious academies, libraries. There was no official hindrance. On the contrary, Turkish Jews enjoyed full rights and privileges, playing a prominent part in the nation's economic life – in trade, finance, medicine, law and all manner of arts and crafts. And the House of Nasi, in particular, was recognized as an invaluable imperial asset. Their commercial interests were enormous and many of the goods they handled – spices, grain, wool, cloth and textiles – were carried in their own ships. Little wonder that Suleiman and his son Selim encouraged the liaison between this family and their court which lasted for a quarter of a century.

Doña Gracia's personal influence is dramatically evident in the events arising out of a tragic episode of Jewish history – the Ancona executions of 1556.

Ancona is a large seaport on the Adriatic coast of Italy. Here a Jewish community, consisting mainly of Portuguese Marranos, suddenly found itself selected for martyrdom by the ruthless Pope Paul IV. It was he who introduced into Italy the Ghetto system, the Badge of Shame and other hallmarks of Jewish persecution. In July, 1555 some hundred Ancona Jews were thrown into gaol and 'questioned' by the Inquisition. Many of them managed to bribe their way to safety, but twenty-five were brutally tortured and publicly executed in a series of so-called Acts of Faith.

Gracia Nasi sprang into action as soon as she learned of the arrests, but not even a strongly worded ultimatum from the Sultan to the Pope could save the prisoners. Yet they could be avenged, and one of the fortunate survivors, Judah Farraj, suggested the answer. He appealed to Doña Gracia on behalf of the neighbouring Marrano-community of Pesaro to organize a commercial boycott of Ancona. She set the example by immediately transferring all her maritime business to Pesaro and trying to rally support for a complete business boycott, to last eight months. For a while it appeared that the economic future of Ancona would be endangered by the Jewish embargo. Unfortunately, theological disputes and material considerations prevented the unanimity of action which might have made it successful. It was perhaps the only occasion on which Doña Gracia's will was thwarted.

It was to be her last public appearance as lay leader of Turkish Jewry. Increasingly troubled by ill-health, she gradually retired into the background, leaving Joseph to carry on her work. He was already referred to in the capital as the

Court Jew, enjoying special commercial privileges and acting as confidential adviser to the Sultan on foreign affairs. His knowledge of European political developments, relayed by his offices and agencies abroad, was invaluable both to Suleiman and to his successor, Selim II. Joseph had, even during Suleiman's lifetime, allied himself securely to Selim's cause in his bid for the succession against his brother Bajazet, and Selim rewarded him in full measure when he came to the throne.

Yet it was Suleiman the Magnificent who first acknowledged Joseph's services in 1561 by giving him the lease of the Palestinian town of Tiberias, together with the surrounding areas, to be developed as an autonomous Jewish colony. The Nasi family, in common with their Jewish ancestors and contemporaries, had never relinquished their vision of Palestine as the ultimate refuge of the Jewish people. Doña Gracia never lived to visit Palestine, but her husband's remains were re-interred outside Jerusalem and she herself laid to rest at his side. The Tiberias scheme was initially conceived by her, but it was Joseph who developed this, the boldest and most ambitious Jewish colonial experiment until Rothschild's, three hundred years later.

Compared with the other Jewish centres of Jerusalem and Safed, Tiberias was sparsely populated and impoverished. With the aid of his representative, Joseph ibn Ardut, the new Lord of Tiberias set about reconstructing the city, attracting new immigrants and developing local crafts. The town walls were rebuilt, houses sprang up among the palms and citrus trees, the deserted synagogue was reopened. Local farmers and fishermen were subsidized, mulberry trees were planted as a basis for a silk-weaving industry and wool was imported from Spain for cloth manufacture. And an invitation went out to the oppressed Jews of Italy to come and find refuge in the thriving town on the shores of Lake Galilee.

It was a brave and enlightened experiment, but it failed. The practical difficulties of financing and transporting large numbers of refugees across the Mediterranean were too immense. The support of wealthier Jewish communities was not forthcoming. Small groups fortunate enough to find ships were attacked and enslaved by the Knights of Malta. Moreover, Joseph Nasi himself appears to have lost interest, particularly after the death of Doña Gracia in 1569. But although the Palestinian dreams of the Nasi family remained unfulfilled, the foundations were firmly laid. A century later Tiberias was to emerge as one of the four great centres of Jewish learning in Palestine.

When Suleiman died on campaign in 1566, the new Sultan Selim II conferred the title of Duke of Naxos on Joseph Nasi. His domain included not only the fabled island on which Theseus had deserted Ariadne, but a group of other small islands, among them Melos, Paros and Andros. Nor was it a mere sinecure. The new Duke and Duchess visited their island home infrequently, but Joseph kept closely in touch with his deputy governor, Francisco Coronello, on all administrative matters. Coronello was kept fully occupied. Despite comparatively lenient taxes, the Greek inhabitants chafed at Turkish rule and there was no effective method of repelling the frequent raids by pirates. In the war for Cyprus the Venetians recovered the island for a time and Coronello was taken prisoner. But the Turks regained control and Joseph remained Duke of Naxos until he died. Then, since he had no heir, Naxos was annexed by the Sultan.

With Selim's succession Joseph's commercial concessions were further extended. He enjoyed a virtual monopoly in the wine trade, being permitted to keep for himself the customs duties on all wines imported through the Black Sea. His own agents boarded the incoming vessels, inspected the cargoes and collected the taxes. He did an enormous business in wines and spirits with Poland, and his personal relationship with King Sigismund Augustus was close enough for him to make Sigismund a large loan on one occasion and to be greeted in letters from Warsaw as 'Illustrious Prince and beloved friend'. William of Orange was another of the many European statesmen who realized that an approach to the Duke of Naxos was often the best way to win the Sultan's favour, although Joseph was able to assure him only of Turkey's moral support for the Netherlands' rebellion against Spanish rule – not, as William had hoped, her armed intervention.

For Joseph Nasi, France was second only to Spain as Turkey's most hated enemy. The memory of previous humiliations still rankled. For years he had been pressing his claim against the French crown for the huge sum of 150,000 ducats due to the family. He managed to involve the Turkish treasury in his dispute, professing himself unable to settle his tax debts unless the French reimbursed him in full.

After protracted negotiations and repeated French repudiations of the claim, the Sultan took the unprecedented step of allowing Joseph to waylay French merchant vessels in Turkish waters and to seize a third part of their cargoes, until such time as the total value of the debt had been paid. French ships bound for Alexandria were promptly intercepted by the Duke of Naxos' fleet and trade was thrown into a turmoil. The French protested at this breach of an existing commercial treaty, and normal relations between the two powers were shortly resumed, but not before Joseph had recovered his money. Nor, one suspects, was the operation unprofitable for the Turkish exchequer. For the second time in a decade the commercial power of the House of Nasi had ruffled the political waves of Europe.

But the Duke of Naxos was not having things all his own way. The new Grand Vizier, Mohammed Sokolli, resented his influence and did everything in his power to advance the interests of his own favourites. Sokolli was a formidable rival and a very able politician. They clashed on foreign policy in particular, Sokolli favouring an alliance with France, Nasi opposing any link with his ancient enemy. The last occasion on which Nasi's advice prevailed was in 1569 when he persuaded the Sultan to declare war on Venice.

It was on 13 September of that year that an explosion occurred in the arsenal at Venice. The damage was exaggerated, but Joseph's agents convinced him that now was the opportunity for Turkey to deal her maritime rival a death blow, as a preliminary to challenging the might of the mortal enemy, Spain. Moreover, the island of Cyprus lay there as a tempting prize. Personal ambition may have been a partial motivation, for Joseph was under the impression that he would become the ruler of Cyprus should the campaign be successful. It seems probable that this was merely a drunken promise on the part of Selim, but Joseph took it seriously. It was said that he had standing ready in his palace at Belvedere a standard with the inscription 'Joseph Nasi, King of Cyprus'.

The Sultan agreed to the campaign against Venice and Cyprus was indeed captured. But the reward, to Joseph's dismay, went to his rival, the Sultan's son-in-law, Sokolli. And this proved to be Turkey's sole gain. The venture ended in disaster. The joint power of the Pope and of Spain was thrown into the arena and the outcome was the shattering naval defeat at Lepanto where fifty Turkish ships were destroyed and eight thousand men killed.

Although the Duke of Naxos could hardly be held responsible for the tragedy of Lepanto, the opposing faction at court stood vindicated. With Selim's death in 1574, and the accession of Murad III, Joseph's own influence waned, and a reversal in official policy towards the Jews heralded the end of their golden age. Joseph retained his titles and his property, but spent the last five years of his life in retirement in his magnificent palace overlooking the Bosphorus. Like his aunt before him he continued to dispense charity on a huge scale and to patronize scholarship and literature. He died in 1579, on the fast of the ninth of Av, and was survived by his widow, the Duchess Reyna. She continued the Nasi tradition of generosity and patronage and opened a Hebrew printing press at the Belvedere palace. But with her death, twenty years after her husband, we hear no more of the name of Nasi which for a brief and glorious period had been such an inspiration to the Jews of sixteenth-century Europe.

Manasseh ben Israel
1604–1657

'Wherefore I humbly entreat your Highness, that you would with a gracious eye have regard to us, and our Petition, and grant us, as you have done unto others, free exercise of our own Religion, that we may have our Synagogue, and keep our own public worship, as our brethren do in Italy, Germany, Poland, and many other places. . . .'

These words, addressed to Oliver Cromwell, Lord Protector of England, were part of a document entitled *The Humble Addresses of Manasseh ben Israel, a Divine and Doctor of Physick, in behalf of the Jewish Nation.* The date was September 1655, the author a young rabbi from Amsterdam, the subject under discussion the re-admission of the Jews to England after 365 years of expulsion.

It was in 1290, on the anniversary of a solemn Jewish day of fasting, that Edward I decreed that all Jews in the kingdom should be banished by all All Saints Day under pain of death. This royal proclamation was a desperate attempt to solve the medieval 'Jewish problem', the climax to one of the most agonizing periods in Jewish history.

The earliest records of organized Jewish settlement in England go back almost to the Norman Conquest. For a time the Jews prospered. To put it at its simplest, when things were going well for the nation, when an uneasy state of truce existed between king and barons and when there were no foreign escapades to drain the exchequer, the Jews were tolerated and well treated. When civil strife flared up or when scapegoats were required to explain away a local or national misfortune, then the Jews were among the prime sufferers.

They were mainly engaged in moneylending, both on a private and public level, and many of them became extremely wealthy. One such man was Aaron of Lincoln, reputedly the richest man in the realm, whose money and possessions were confiscated by the Crown upon his death. The practice of moneylending, however, inevitably aroused hatred and enmity, and despite the relative freedom which the Jews enjoyed, storm clouds were beginning to gather at the turn of the twelfth century. The irrational passions whipped up by the First Crusade found responsive echoes at home, and although there was no English counterpart to the terrible continental massacres in which some 12,000 Jews were said to have lost their lives, the fateful seeds were being sown. Between 1130 and 1183, a period of outward calm and toleration, there were a number of unpleasant episodes including, in 1144, the first example anywhere of the slanderous accusation of Ritual Murder. In Norwich that year a young skinner's apprentice died, probably accidentally, and Jews were accused of the crime. There were further occurrences in Gloucester, Bury St Edmunds and Bristol.

The tide was indeed turning and in 1190 came the horrifying York massacre when over 150 Jews, led by Rabbi Yomtob of Joigny, took refuge in the keep of York Castle, finally killing themselves and setting fire to the keep rather than face the fury of the mob. The very next day fifty-seven Jews were murdered at Bury St Edmunds. These sinister events were merely a prelude to the disasters of the next hundred years.

In 1206 England's last French possessions were lost and the English Jews were isolated from the continent – a severe economic and spiritual setback. There followed a period of strict repression as succeeding kings milked the Jewish community dry by means of excessive taxation. Jews were expected to make exorbitant contributions to the treasury and little excuse was needed to impose harsh fines for trivial or non-existent offences. To religious persecution was now added political suppression. Following an edict of Pope Innocent III in 1215, all Jews were now forced to wear the Badge of Shame – in England this took the form of a yellow taffeta emblem in the shape of the Tablets of the Law. In an atmosphere of increasing hatred more anti-Jewish riots erupted in London. In 1255 came the episode of Hugh of Lincoln, a child allegedly slaughtered by Jews for nefarious ritual purposes; the child was canonized and his story passed into national folklore, even Chaucer making use of it in the *Canterbury Tales*. The year 1263 saw more London riots, the Jewry district sacked and 400 Jews killed. In Winchester a similar uprising resulted in 1,500 reported dead.

By now Edward I was on the throne and under pressure from clergy and the merchant class to act decisively to restore order and security. His answer, in 1278, was to arrest all the Jews in the land. Next year no fewer than 293 were hanged in the capital, simply for refusing to be converted. In 1283 all London synagogues were destroyed and seven years later, urged on by the Papacy, Edward took the climactic step of expelling the Jews. Amid general rejoicing 16,000 Jews left England for France and Flanders. It was a bitter prelude to similar official action in later years in France, the Holy Roman Empire, Spain and Portugal.

So for nearly 400 years there was to be no organized Jewish community in England. Ironically it was in Spain and Portugal that Jews were now living in complete harmony with their non-Jewish neighbours. Here they were welcomed and honoured for their contributions in many fields, finance, law, medicine, scholarship and the arts. Yet here too the pendulum was finally to take another swing and after centuries of peaceful existence, persecution – in an uglier and more bloodthirsty guise than ever before – forced the Jews out on to the roads of southern, central and northern Europe, refugees once more. In Spain, under Ferdinand and Isabella, and in neighbouring Portugal, spearheaded by Torquemada's ruthless Inquisition, Jews were arrested, tortured, forcibly converted, murdered or finally expelled. The survivors fled to Italy, to North Africa, to Turkey and northwards to the Netherlands, now, at the close of the sixteenth century, free of the Spanish yoke.

Among the families who had settled in Amsterdam was one of Marrano extraction, named Soeiro. 'Marrano' – literally 'pig' – was the title given to converted Spanish and Portuguese Jews, many of whom privately observed the traditions of their faith. But whether Jews or Marranos, all had been equal in the eyes of Torquemada and his heirs. Joseph Soeiro was one such victim of the Inquisition. After terrible torture he had managed to escape, first to Madeira, then to La Rochelle, and at last to the haven of Amsterdam – popularly called the Dutch Jerusalem. His eldest son, Manoel – known by his Hebrew name of Manasseh – was probably born in Madeira.

He was a brilliant child, reared in an atmosphere of piety and tolerance, in a city which now housed some hundreds of orthodox Jewish families. Manasseh's progress at school was remarkable, and though he excelled at most of the secular subjects in the curriculum, it was evident that his inclination was towards a religious career. He studied under Rabbi Isaac Uzziel of Fez and at the astonishingly early age of 18 succeeded his teacher, on his death, as Rabbi of the famous Neveh Shalom congregation.

It was as preacher of this synagogue that Manasseh gained a reputation, among Jews and Christians alike, for the power and skill of his oratory. He was evidently a man of simple tastes. His sincere and purposeful manner, coupled with his extensive learning and broad range of interests, commanded attention and respect far beyond the confines of his own community. Speaking six languages, he was a prolific letter-writer, though only a handful have survived of the hundreds which he wrote to eminent men and women both at home and abroad. The great Rembrandt painted him, and Queen Henrietta Maria of England once came to his synagogue to hear him preach. In time he came to be accepted as one of the most informed spokesmen for the Jewish people and their problems.

Yet he lived in no ivory tower and was deeply conscious of the tragic plight of the Jews outside Holland. His link with the Marranos in particular was close, for he had married the great-grand-daughter of the celebrated statesman Don Isaac Abrabanel, former chancellor of the exchequer to Ferdinand and Isabella. He felt keenly responsible not only for his own congregation, but for the Jewish people as a whole. Those of his letters that survive reveal him as a man of vision, of deep spiritual fervour, yet with a firm practical grasp of everyday life and national affairs.

This practical sense had already convinced him that preaching alone was not enough to make a living and to support a growing family. In 1628 he set up the first Jewish printing press in Amsterdam and took an active interest in its progress. He had his own books printed there in Hebrew, Latin and Spanish. His responsibilities to Amsterdam Jewry assumed a new dimension when, in 1629, he was appointed as one of the rabbis of the unified Dutch Jewish community. For the next decade he devoted himself to his writing, especially his monumental work *Conciliador*, reconciling contradictory passages in the Bible, which enhanced his international reputation in theological circles.

Yet it seems that this was not the complete answer to his problem and it is surprising to discover that at one time he seriously considered emigrating to Brazil to launch a business career. Fortunately he was persuaded otherwise by a pair of wealthy friends who in 1640 set up a Yeshiva – a school devoted to the study of rabbinic literature – and offered Manasseh the post of Principal. From now on he could apply himself freely to his studies, his writing and the problems of his fellow Jews.

This problem was daily assuming greater urgency. In 1648 Poland, thus far a refuge for Jewish immigrants, erupted in revolution. The Cossacks, led by their brutal *hetman*

Chmielnicki, rose against their Polish rulers and massacred entire Jewish communities. Once again the unhappy refugees trailed southwards and westwards through Europe.

At about this time Manasseh happened to meet a Marrano traveller, Antonio de Montezinos, who had just returned from South America. It proved to be a significant encounter. Montezinos claimed to have stumbled across a tribe of Indians near Quito who recited Jewish prayers and practised Jewish rites. The fanciful, mystical side of Manasseh's nature responded immediately to this strange – and obviously unverified – report. He was convinced that these Indians were in fact the Lost Tribes of Israel. Furthermore, study of certain passages in the Old Testament led him to the conclusion that the Jews, apparently scattered over the whole earth, were ready for the advent of the Messiah, provided only that they were resettled in England, the only country from which, as far as he knew, they were excluded. He brooded much on this problem and then wrote his much publicized book *Spes Israelis* (*Hope of Israel*), in which he outlined his theory. The book attracted much interest and went into three editions. The author was besieged with correspondence, much of it from England. From the tone of these letters Manasseh deduced that the time was ripe to make a direct approach to Cromwell for the readmission of the Jews into England.

There were solid and encouraging reasons for such an approach at this particular moment of hiatus in the English Civil War. Cromwell's newly proclaimed Puritan Commonwealth seemed to Manasseh to provide a sympathetic political and spiritual milieu for Jewish aspirations. After all the Puritans were God-fearing, Bible-imbued people. They gave Old Testament names to their children and the more extreme among them believed fervently in the approaching Millennium.

Cromwell himself seemed to favour Jewish readmission, although his motives were commercial rather than spiritual. He knew that in many parts of Europe, Amsterdam not least, the concentration of Jewish wealth, culture and business acumen had contributed notably to local and national prosperity. England's chief commercial rivals were Spain and

Holland so that an influx of Jews from the Continent, bringing with them their wealth and their trading connections in the West Indies, would combine religious toleration with political shrewdness.

Manasseh therefore resolved to make an official plea to Cromwell to reverse the edict of 1290. He knew he could expect support both in government circles and among the tiny Marrano community which already existed in London. Isolated groups of Marranos had reached England in Henry VIII's reign, and although they had been banished in 1608 they had reappeared to lead an active, though necessarily secret life as Jews. They were now led by one Antonio Carvajal, and he, together with other members of the Marrano community, pledged support for Manasseh's petition.

Unfortunately, illness and the outbreak of war between England and Holland intervened and prevented Manasseh from coming in person. He therefore dispatched his agent, Manuel Martinez Dormido, together with his own son Samuel, beseeching Cromwell, in a written petition, to re-admit the Jews, 'granting them liberty to come with their families and estates, to be dwellers here with the same equalness and conveniences which your island subjects do enjoy'.

The plea did not fall on deaf ears and Cromwell was determined to get the support of his Council of State. The Council's reaction, however, was lukewarm. Clearly no progress could be made without Manasseh's personal advocacy. Cromwell urged him to visit London as soon as possible. In September, 1655, he arrived, accompanied by three rabbis, and installed himself in lodgings in the Strand. He drafted his eloquent *Humble Petition,* together with a personal request that all laws against Jews should be repealed, that synagogues and Jewish cemeteries be permitted and that Jews should enjoy all the private and commercial privileges granted to their non-Jewish neighbours.

Cromwell once again acted with commendable speed. On 12 November he brought the Petition before the Council and a motion was tabled that 'the Jews deserving it may be admitted into this nation to trade and traffick, and dwell amongst us as providence shall give occasion'. The Council promptly appointed a conference of leading jurists and theologians to debate the matter. It met at Whitehall on 4 December, presided over by Cromwell himself. Authorities differ as to whether Manasseh was present – it seems likely that he was but that he did not speak. Then, as happens on so many similar occasions, the debate dragged on fruitlessly through four long sessions. There appeared to be no legal reasons for excluding the Jews any longer, but no great enthusiasm for their return. Clerical and mercantile interests were united in opposition and once again popular prejudice was inflamed by means of all the traditional arguments. Fantastic rumours circulated, the most ludicrous being that the Jews had offered half a million pounds to buy St Paul's Cathedral and convert it into a synagogue, this wicked plot being forestalled by an astute government raising the price to £800,000, which was evidently unacceptable to the Jews.

The inveterate trouble-maker William Prynne was among the most vitriolic of the anti-Jewish propagandists and did much to inflame popular feeling. Manasseh, unable to endure such vile accusations, systematically refuted the age-old slanders of Jewish blood ritual in his *Vindiciae Judaeorum*, one of his boldest and most forthright pieces of writing: 'I cannot but weep bitterly and with much anguish of soul lament that strange and horrid accusation of some Christians . . . when they say that the Jews are wont to celebrate the feast of unleavened bread, fermenting it with the blood of some Christian whom they have for this purpose killed. . . . But how far this accusation is from any semblable appearance of truth, your worship may judge by these following arguments:

'It is utterly forbid the Jews to eat any manner of blood whatsoever . . . and the Jews eat not the blood of any animal. And more than this, if they find one drop of blood in an egg, they cast it away as prohibited. . . . Since then it is thus, how can it enter into any man's heart to believe that they should eat human blood which is yet more detestable, there being scarce any nation now remaining upon earth so barbarous as to commit such wickedness?'

It was in vain. The conference crawled disconsolately on until Cromwell, exasperated, marched off the dais announcing that he would take matters into his own hands, and abruptly terminated the proceedings.

Manasseh waited patiently for the next development but nothing happened for several months. News then came of renewed hostilities between England and Spain, and this proved to be a blessing in disguise. The government decreed that money and property belonging to Spaniards in England should be confiscated. Among those whose property was seized – and it included two ships – was a London resident Marrano, Antonio Rodrigues Robles. Manasseh, together with the leaders of the Marrano community, protested against this decision. The Marranos publicly confessed their Jewish origin and formally demanded recognition and the right to remain. Surprisingly the Council supported Robles' claim, admitting his legal rights as an English subject. It was a great victory – the first expressly stated readmission of an openly professing Jew.

So what the Whitehall Conference had failed to countenance had come about, almost accidentally. Cromwell let it be known that he did not oppose the resettlement of the Jews provided they did not worship in public or make religious propaganda. Yet even this condition was to be waived as further concessions were made over the years. Permission was granted in 1656 to open a synagogue in Cree Church Lane, then to lease land in Mile End for a Jewish cemetery. Gradually, without undue publicity, the revolution which Manasseh had fought for took place – by tacit consent; and curiously it was under the Stuart Charles II in 1664 that official authorization for readmission came. From that time immigration from the continent increased steadily and the structure of the modern Anglo-Jewish community began to take shape.

Manasseh ben Israel, however, did not live to see his dreams fulfilled and believed he had failed in his mission. His last years were clouded by personal tragedy and sickness. His son Samuel died after a long illness and Manasseh, broken-hearted, appealed to Cromwell for funds to transport the coffin home. Although Cromwell had treated him generously and granted him an annuity of £100, Manasseh was destitute and the Treasury refused this last request. Nevertheless he left for Holland with his son's coffin, only to die himself at Middelburgh on 12 November, 1657. He was buried at Oudekirk, near the graves of his father and his teacher.

Manasseh ben Israel certainly judged himself too harshly. History has marked out the vital role he played in laying the foundations of a Jewish community in England which was to enrich the nation's fortunes both in the material and spiritual sense. His personal qualities of loyalty and integrity won him the devotion and respect which enabled him to bring about one of the most significant, though inconspicuous revolutions in Jewish history.

Sabbatai Zevi
1626–1676

Of all the pseudo-Messiahs in history – and there have been many – none had as strange a career or as dynamic an appeal as Sabbatai Zevi. The eldest son of a poor poulterer of Spanish descent, he was born in the Turkish seaport of Smyrna in 1626, proclaimed himself the Messiah at the age of twenty, set every Jewish community in Europe, Asia and Africa aflame with spiritual fervour and expectation, and died miserably, thirty years later, in a prison in Albania.

Marked out by custom and inclination for a life of study, this handsome, solitary, unusually intelligent boy had mastered the complexities of the Bible and the Talmud by the time he was fifteen. At the remarkably early age of eighteen he was hailed by the elders of the community as a *Chacham* – wise man. But dissatisfied with orthodox teaching, and already displaying signs of the manic-depressive tendency which was to torment him throughout his life, young Sabbatai immersed himself in the semi-secret lore and literature of the *Cabala*, the mystical strain of Jewish religious tradition. The theory and doctrine of *Cabala*, as expressed in its holy book, the Zohar, and in a profusion of books, treatises and commentaries, was a strange compound of theology, philosophy, superstition and magic, relying on obscure permutations and combinations of the Hebrew letters of the alphabet and occult signs and symbols for its prophecies and divinations.

It was preoccupied with the basic problems of the universe, the meaning of creation and man's close communion with his creator, the mysteries of good and evil, and the role and destiny of the Jewish people. Central to its teaching and belief, however, was the prospect of imminent redemption through the Messiah – the constant focus of Jewish hope and faith through the ages – but now, according to the intricate calculation of *cabalists*, to be realized in the miracle year 5408 (1648).

As a practical road to purification the *Cabala* demanded of its adherents severe penance and fleshly mortification. Spurred by the vision of redemption and salvation, the young scholar embarked on a routine of extreme asceticism – prayer, fasting, flagellation, mid-winter bathing in the sea – and easily attracted a group of similarly ardent followers who regarded Sabbatai, with his persuasive voice and flashing dark eyes, as a seer and a prophet. Such adulation might have turned the head of any young man already well aware of his singular gifts. In his case the effect was even more startling, and ultimately disastrous. He succeeded in convincing himself, and them as well, that he was the Lord's Anointed – the Messiah.

As it happened, all the circumstances were in his favour. The Jews of the world were ready to respond to just such a call. Exiled from Spain, Portugal, France and England, persecuted and pent up in ghettos in Eastern Europe and North Africa, orthodox Jews were fortified and kept alive only by their unswerving faith in eventual redemption. Nor need the day be far off. Miracles were a daily fact of life. Their prayers, their history and their literature all sustained them with the promise of salvation in the return to the homeland. In the blackest days of their suffering they knew the brightness of hope. Now, more than ever, after a terrible war which had raged for thirty years, in which Jewish communities had been decimated, and which would culminate in the ghastly Polish massacres of that very miracle year, 1648, Jewish expectations rose high. Surely there had to be a meaning for this great burden of suffering. Surely their Redeemer was at hand.

The Jews were not alone in their Messianic dreams. There was widespread interest in the Jewish question, and many books and pamphlets in England, Holland and France freely discussed the deliverance of Israel and the advent of the Messiah. The German ambassador in Constantinople wrote a letter reporting the birth in 1641 of a Jewish child believed to be the Messiah. There were rumours of a great army, descendants of the twelve tribes, gathering in Arabia behind the river Sabbation, a raging torrent which subsided only on the Sabbath – an army ready to march and conquer the world bloodlessly for their God.

The English Puritans believed fervently in the forthcoming Millennium, the establishment of the Kingdom of God on earth after the ingathering of the twelve tribes. True, they differed in their conception of the Messiah, prayed for the ultimate conversion of the Jews, saw 1666 as the Annus Mirabilis, but they were motivated by the same spiritual longing. Manasseh ben Israel, infinitely more practical than Sabbatai Zevi, was to take advantage of this concurrence of beliefs in achieving his more limited, but lasting, political objective.

This overheated atmosphere, in which faith, fantasy and superstition all lent support to the confident predictions of the *Cabala*, undoubtedly influenced Sabbatai's thinking and confirmed him in his delusions. His father had now fallen on happier times as an agent for a firm of English merchants. Smyrna's close political and commercial links with Western Europe also enabled him to keep abreast with developments abroad.

As the apocalyptic year of 1648 approached, Sabbatai awaited a sign. He continued to lead his joyless life of self-imposed penance, but in accordance with custom and parental prompting, went through the marriage ceremony with a

wealthy Jewish girl. Then, either refusing or being incapable
of consummating it, he divorced her. A second marriage
shortly afterwards had a similar outcome. Clearly his mind
was on higher things.

The year 1648 ran its course without the promised happening. In Poland, Chmielnicki's Cossacks were destroying the
Jewish community in an eight-month period of horrible
massacres. Refugees began to throng the streets of European
capitals. Pious Jews saw it as a certain forerunner of the
Messianic age. Sabbatai was quite convinced of his divine
mission, but his handful of followers was not enough. Now
he had to go out and proclaim it to the multitude.

One Sabbath, in the synagogue, the congregation was
stupefied to hear the young man reciting the traditional
blessing over the Law and loudly pronouncing the full name
of God, forbidden to all save the High Priest on the Day of
Atonement. His act of defiance created pandemonium and
split the community into warring factions. He was thrown out
of the synagogue and eventually banished from Smyrna
under a solemn ritual curse. But the Rabbis of Smyrna who
exiled the blasphemer had no idea of the trouble they were
storing up for the future.

Sabbatai was undeterred. Financed by his father and
brothers he set out on many years of travels, to seek new
disciples overseas. Authorities differ widely, at this point, on
dates and sequence of events, but it matters little. One of his
first ports of call was Salonica, a city with a large Jewish
population, and an active centre for *Cabala* enthusiasts. Here
he made yet another dramatic gesture. Inviting his friends
and all the Rabbis of the town to a banquet, he appeared
clasping the sacred Torah in a mystic marriage ceremony –
he, the bridegroom, Israel, taking as his bride the holy book.
The effect once more was instantaneous. Denounced by the
orthodox as a madman he was again sent on his way.

Yet there were many who were impressed by the pretensions of this eloquent and pious young man – influential
and wealthy men as well as simple, uneducated people. In
Constantinople he was joined by a well-known *Cabalist*,
Abraham Iachini, who produced an ancient parchment (a

palpable forgery) purporting to have been written by a hermit of old, and entitled *The Great Wisdom of Solomon*. 'I, Abraham,' it announced, '. . . shut up in a cave for forty years . . . wondering why the age of miracles had not yet come, heard a voice proclaiming: "In the year 5386 (1626) a son will be born to Mordecai Zevi, and he will be called Sabbatai. And he will overthrow the great dragon . . . and shall be the true Messiah and sit upon My throne." '

This was precisely what Sabbatai and his adherents wanted to hear, and it attracted a growing number of credulous supporters, reviving his flagging spirits and strengthening his cause in practical fashion. Henceforth Sabbatai was never to lack skilled propagandists and financial aid. He appeared to his faithful in Athens, in Rhodes, in his home town of Smyrna, and inevitably in the Holy Land itself. He was seen to pray with great devotion at the Wailing Wall in Jerusalem and at the Patriarchs' Tomb in Hebron. He was followed through the streets by adoring crowds, resplendent in his robe and brandishing a silver fan.

Around the year 1660 he arrived in Cairo, where he captured the imagination of a very wealthy and pious Jew named Raphael Joseph Chelebi. Beneath his luxurious garments Raphael was known to wear the penitent's hair shirt, and at his table fifty wise men dined each day. The attraction was evidently mutual. He provided a home for Sabbatai for two years and became one of his most fervent supporters.

Here the order of events becomes somewhat hazy again. Sabbatai appears to have returned to Palestine for a time, preparing the faithful, distributing alms to the needy, scattering sweets to the children, leading his followers in singing psalms and crude Spanish love songs, to which he attributed mystical meanings. And Chelebi helped him to perform a 'miracle' which lent even more power to his elbow. The governor of Jerusalem had imposed a heavy tax on the impoverished community. Sabbatai took it upon himself to raise the necessary money. Returning to Cairo he easily persuaded his rich patron to provide the necessary funds. He was hailed as a saviour on his return.

But two important events took place during his second

visit to Cairo. The first was his marriage – and this time to no ordinary girl. Her name was Sarah, apparently born in Poland, a survivor of the Cossack massacres, and raised in a convent in Amsterdam. She had then led a nomadic existence, wandering through Europe, living as a prostitute, but mystically convinced that she was destined to be the bride of the Messiah. Chelebi heard of her when she was in Leghorn and brought her to Cairo. Sabbatai needed no urging.

In Chelebi's house, with great pomp and splendour, the Messiah married his Queen: and to those who were shocked by his choice of a bride he quoted the example of the prophet Hosea, whom God had enjoined to marry a harlot. Her outstanding beauty and sensual appeal may not have had any bearing on his decision, but Sarah was undoubtedly a great asset to the cause, a most persuasive and alluring disciple.

Then, on his way back to Palestine via Gaza, he met a pale young *Cabala* student named Nathan Gazati – Nathan of Gaza – who already had a reputation for piety and visionary powers. He too was devoting his entire time and attention to the impending Messianic arrival, and had persuaded himself that he was the Messiah's chosen prophet. He only awaited his master. Each knew of the other's activities and felt that their meeting was predestined.

Nathan was convinced Sabbatai was the true Messiah. He, as his prophet Elijah, would spread the good tidings far and wide. He was a welcome addition to Sabbatai's retinue, which already included men of more questionable sincerity – men like Samuel Primo, Sabbatai's 'secretary', and Abraham Cardozo, his 'treasurer' – who exploited all the weaknesses of Sabbatai's own character and had no scruples in making as much capital as possible out of the hopes and yearnings of the credulous masses.

It was these men who persuaded Sabbatai that his efforts in Palestine, a poor disorganized community, were largely wasted. In any event, he was under strong pressure to leave, for the orthodox needed more evidence than displays of piety and ecstatic seizures to be convinced that the Messiah was in their midst. Their opposition so angered Nathan that he

Left: A View from the Royal Exchange. An impression of the banker Nathan Mayer Rothschild by R. Brighton, drawn in 1817. *Bottom:* The "Green Shield" house in Frankfurt, where Amschel Mayer Rothschild and his sons founded their international banking business, is in the centre of this row of buildings – the sixth, counting from right to left. *Below:* Daniel Mendoza, the first Jewish prize-fighting champion, in the second of three contests against his arch-rival Richard Humphreys, fought at Stilton, Huntingdonshire, on 6 May, 1789 (from an original painting).

Right: The handsome young Disraeli was all the rage in fashionable London drawing-rooms, as this painting by A. E. Chalon, R.A. attests. *Insert:* A photograph of Benjamin Disraeli, Earl of Beaconsfield, in 1872. Disraeli became Prime Minister in 1868, at the age of sixty-three, but did not consolidate his position until his second term (1874–1880). *Below:* With his eccentricities of dress and manner, Disraeli was a natural butt of contemporary cartoonists. Here is a typical collection from *Punch*, ranging over a period of forty years.

decreed that henceforth Gaza, not Jerusalem, would be the Messiah's headquarters.

Out went the envoys, as the year 1665 drew to a close, to Europe and to Egypt, bringing the joyful news by word of mouth, while Nathan and Primo busied themselves in dispatching letters and leaflets farther afield. Sabbatai himself was sent back to Smyrna, pausing for a brief while in Aleppo, where he stood before his adoring followers in a prayer shawl. Then, fifteen years or so after his humiliating departure under curse, he returned to his native city like a conqueror.

The Rabbis and sages were now powerless to touch him. The tense, expectant atmosphere, the propaganda, the eyewitness accounts of miracles performed, the aura of the man himself, all outweighed any rational response. As he rode regally into the town, with his beautiful wife at his side, the seething crowds cheered him as their King and Messiah. But, with a keen sense of the dramatic, he secluded himself in his house, where he was reported to be resting and fasting.

Then a delegation arrived with letters. Two of the messengers were famous scholars, and after paying homage, they handed over a letter from Nathan of Gaza. That young man had experienced another vision. In a widely circulated message to the 'brethren in Israel' he proclaimed that next year, 1666, would indeed be the year of deliverance, when the Messiah, Sabbatai Zevi, would gather the armies of the twelve tribes beyond the river Sabbation, and ride at their head into Jerusalem on a lion, whose bridle would be a seven-headed serpent. He would rout all his enemies without bloodshed. The princes and kings would relinquish their sceptres and the Lord's Anointed would rule the world in glory. In more practical terms, it committed Sabbatai Zevi to deposing the Sultan, as a preliminary step to ushering in the Messianic age.

The crowds could no longer be held back. Sabbatai renounced his fast and authorized the faithful to indulge in an orgy of feasting, drinking, singing and dancing. The way was now clear for his great public declaration, his formal acceptance of his divine duty. Two days later, in a synagogue crowded to capacity and congregants flowing out into the street, he rapped on the doors of the Holy Ark, and to the braying accompaniment of the *Shofar* – the ram's horn – proclaimed himself the Messiah. And this time, to his gratification, came back the exultant roar of the people: 'Long live our King, our Messiah, Sabbatai Zevi!' Then he led a procession back to his house and held royal court, his Queen by his side, the populace milling past him, paying homage to their saviour until well into the night.

Now he cast caution to the winds. In a series of edicts he and his lieutenants reversed the entire pattern of orthodox Jewish observance and ritual. Fast days were abolished and turned into feasts. The full name of God was to be pronounced in the daily service. His own name was to be substituted for the Sultan's in the customary synagogue blessing. Women were to be permitted to participate in the services and to mingle socially with men. These and similar edicts were circulated to Jewish communities abroad.

On a more personal level, he announced that he had received a divine command to cohabit with his wife, and next morning the traditional proof of his wife's virginity was produced for the benefit of the gaping crowd. It was a strange and unconvincing demonstration, in the light of his past performance and her past history, but it was received rapturously by his half-crazed adherents. Then he proceeded to divide up his kingdom among his closest colleagues, appointing twenty-six kings, with names derived from the ancient rulers of Israel and Judah. Thus Chelebi was dubbed King Joash, Iachini King Solomon, and his brother Elias nothing less than King of the King of Kings.

There were still isolated outposts of opposition in the city, led by the Chief Rabbi, Aaron de la Papa, and his colleagues, Benveniste and Algazi. Yet although they agreed half-heartedly to pronounce sentence of death on the pretender, none of them was prepared to martyr himself by carrying the sentence out. De la Papa and Algazi were forced to flee for their lives, while Benveniste, in reward for a change of heart, was graciously appointed Chief Rabbi instead.

Other tokens of resistance were handled more forcefully. A wealthy merchant, Chaim Pegna, who had openly challenged the Messiah's credentials, barricaded himself in his house and was only saved from the fury of the mob by the fortuitous arrival of the Sabbath. Next day, praying in the Portuguese synagogue, he had to escape over the roof as Sabbatai, at the head of his rabble, broke the door down with axes. Sabbatai stormed into the pulpit to deliver a hysterical, hate-ridden sermon. Eventually, Pegna too saw the light, apparently as a result of his daughter going into a trance and seeing Sabbatai enthroned as the Messiah.

The excitement spread from Smyrna to Salonica and gradually to every town in Europe where a sizeable Jewish community existed.

In a frenzy of spiritualism Jews indulged in fantastic penances, beating themselves with rods and nettles, burying themselves up to the neck in water or snow, selling their houses and property, giving their money away to the poor, and marrying off their children so that the souls of the yet unborn could share in the coming redemption.

A German scholar wrote to the philosopher Spinoza: 'All the world is talking of a rumour of the return of the Israelites to their own country. Should the news be confirmed, it may bring about a revolution in all things.'

Spinoza, excommunicated by the Jewish authorities for his unpopular views, was forced to admit that the day of redemption might be near.

The French ambassador in Smyrna reported: 'It is said that the Sultan has agreed to hand over the whole of Palestine to the Messiah. The majority of Jews have stopped work and are preparing to migrate to Jerusalem.'

In Holland the printing presses turned out special prayer books, showing Sabbatai Zevi enthroned, flanked by lions, while angels held a crown over his head. Hamburg was similarly hypnotized by the news of miracles and visions from Turkey.

Only the learned Jacob Sasportas, friend of Manasseh ben Israel, rejected him as a fraud and condemned the whole movement. But such men were in a minority.

As for England, Samuel Pepys wrote in his Diary: 'Certainly this year of 1666 will be a year of great action; but what the consequences of it will be, God knows.' Bets were laid in the City on the probability of the Messianic event occurring; and to round off the crop of miracles, there were reports of a ship which had been sighted off the coast of Scotland, with silken sails and ropes, manned by a Hebrew-speaking crew, and flying a flag bearing the inscription 'The Twelve Tribes of Israel'.

But back in Smyrna Sabbatai could not simply sit tight and hold court indefinitely. Nathan and Primo had sent his message round the world. Now he was forced to prove his worth. Leaving Sarah behind in Smyrna, and without the haziest idea of what he was going to do, he embarked for Constantinople as the new year of 1666 dawned.

His small ship ran into heavy storms and the journey to the Dardanelles took over five weeks. When he finally stepped ashore he was immediately arrested on the instructions of the Grand Vizier.

Unresisting, he was thrown into a debtor's prison in Constantinople. Now the authorities were in a dilemma. No Mohammedan was prepared to put to death a potential Messiah. Yet the man had designs on the Sultan's life and throne. An officer was sent to interview him in prison. He was asked whether he was in fact the Messiah. At this crucial moment his courage failed him completely and he replied that he was merely a humble alms-collector from Jerusalem. This may have satisfied the Sultan but it in no way deceived his own followers. By bribing the Turkish officials he managed to obtain comfortable living quarters in the prison itself together with privileges including daily visits in procession to the seashore and a constant stream of homage-paying visitors. And the stories continued to circulate of the miracles which he was performing and the sufferings which formed an essential part of his master plan.

Clearly, this could not be allowed to continue. Trade was virtually at a standstill, the danger of rioting was ever present. The authorities, still uncertain what to make of him, decided, after two months, to remove him from the scene. They transferred him to the fortress of Abydos, on the Hellespont. Here he continued to live in regal splendour and comfort, joined by his Queen. Among the faithful the castle became known as Migdal Oz, Tower of Strength. Thousands of visitors turned it into a pilgrims' shrine. Money and gifts flowed in, local inns and hostelries did a roaring trade, the guards waxed rich on bribes, and the prison governor saw fit to charge a nominal entrance fee.

It was a ludicrous state of affairs and Sabbatai made the most of it. He issued new edicts, the boldest of which abolished the solemn fast of the 9th of Av, anniversary of the destruction of the Temple. Henceforth, since it happened to be Sabbatai's birthday, it would be celebrated as a feast. Meanwhile the faithful secretary formulated new psalms and blessings to his master's glorification. 'Bless our Lord and King, the holy and righteous Sabbatai Zevi, the Messiah of the God of Jacob' rang out from the synagogues of Europe.

One day Sabbatai was confronted by a rival 'prophet' – a learned scholar, named Nehemia ha-Cohen, who had travelled all the way from Poland to meet him. He came with an open mind, but in the course of his debate with Sabbatai, lasting three days, he became convinced that he was facing an impostor. This man could bring forward not one iota of proof that he was truly descended from the House of David and he denounced him as a false Messiah. Rushing from the fortress, he was pursued by a bloodthirsty mob, and saved himself by grabbing a turban and embracing Islam on the spot, rendering himself immune from attack.

Nehemia refused to keep silent. He informed the governor of Constantinople, who broke the news to the Sultan. The administration's relief was unbounded. Here was no Messiah, merely a common rabble-rouser. But it was still a delicate situation. To make a martyr of him would lead to worse trouble. He had to be converted to Islam.

Sabbatai was taken to Adrianople where the last act of the extraordinary drama began. The instrument of his humiliation was the Sultan's own physician, Guidon, himself a converted Jew. He found Sabbatai alone in his cell, utterly dejected and exhausted. He was easy prey. Guidon warned him of the unimaginable tortures and lingering death in store should he be found guilty of treason. He pointed out, however, that he could prove his claim by submitting to the test of being shot at with poisoned arrows, which assuredly could not harm him if he were the true Messiah. Sabbatai was terrified out of his wits. The only safe way, Guidon urged, was for him to embrace Islam.

Next day, prostrate at the feet of the Sultan, Sabbatai threw off his Jewish headgear and donned the turban handed to him by an attendant. The delighted Sultan hailed him as Mehmed Effendi, presented him with a new wife, a slave-girl from his *harem*, and appointed him royal door-keeper. Sarah joined her husband in embracing the new faith.

The great fraud was over, yet the repercussions lingered on. Though Sabbatai announced openly that he had become an Ishmaelite, his supporters either refused to believe him or held it to be a further and necessary step in the Messianic progress. After all, the *Zohar* itself said that the Messiah would be good within, yet evil without. Nathan continued to pour out letters, announcing new miracles, in a frantic attempt to rally the faithful, travelling through Europe on a now hopeless mission. Abraham Cardozo perpetuated the myth by claiming to be Sabbatai's successor, and the Sabbataian movement tottered on for a number of years, giving rise to several other eccentric and misguided sects founded by other false prophets and Messiahs.

But for the masses it was a shattering disappointment, a mortal blow to their hopes. Apart from their own misery and sense of shame, they were derided by their Christian neighbours for having fallen victim to such an elaborate hoax.

As for Sabbatai, he continued to play an equivocal role in public affairs, meeting his Jewish friends, conducting services, even briefly attempting to revive his Messianic claims. He was suspected by both sides of double dealing and was finally banished, in 1673, to the remote village of Dulcigno on the Albanian coast. Two years later, on the Day of Atonement, he died in solitude.

The fault had not been entirely his. Once he had given

way to his own fatal weaknesses of vanity and ambition he became the dupe of others more unscrupulous than he. Had the spirit of the age and the self-deception of the masses not inflated his own boundless sense of self-importance, he would have been unmasked much sooner. For he was totally unfitted to be a leader. He had no political flair, no coherent plan of action. Yet the fact that he was responsible for causing so much distress is not to denigrate the mystical beliefs and teaching which motivated him. This mystical vein of Jewish thought, with its emphasis on spontaneous, joyful religious experience, was to find expression in the great *Chassidic* movement, while the yearning for a Jewish home-land took on practical guise in the political work of the Zionists.

As for Sabbatai himself, he remains little more than a historical curiosity, a testament to man's credulity and a classic instance of mass suggestion. It is sobering to think that the demagogues of the twentieth century evoke similar responses. The modern parallels are not hard to find.

Daniel Mendoza
1764–1836

Sport does not figure prominently in these pages, but space must be found for Daniel Mendoza, who holds an honoured place in the history of boxing – the one sport in which Jews have traditionally excelled. Nor is Mendoza unworthy of inclusion among the more cerebral personalities in this collection, for he was not only a sportsman of note but a writer as well.

Pugilism, or prize-fighting, was a pretty brutal business until the opening years of the eighteenth century, despite the fact that it had a history going back to the times of the ancient Greeks. The first English champion, James Figg, was typical of the pugilists of his day. He was as expert in fencing, duelling and cudgelling as he was at bare-fist fighting, and the fact that he held the championship for thirty years testifies to his supremacy – one hesitates to say skill. His tactics consisted in placing himself firmly in the centre of the ring, parrying the blows of his opponents with his strong left arm, then grabbing them round the waist and hurling them to the floor.

It was the next champion, Jack Broughton, who in 1743 drew up the first set of pugilistic rules, thereby removing much of the brute force and physical danger from the game, and making it a fashionable spectacle and pastime for the sons of gentlemen. Among the innovations he introduced was a form of padded glove, called a muffler, which was to be worn in training and sparring, though not yet in the ring itself. He also laid down a rule whereby a man should be allowed thirty seconds to recover from a fall or a knockdown. In those days a round ended if one of the contestants fell, so that when we read of those fantastic contests going a hundred rounds or more, this does not necessarily mean a three- or four-hour affair, although many of them were marathons by modern standards. Even under Broughton's Rules, fighters were permitted a wide variety of attacking techniques – wrestling, kicking, gouging, biting, tripping, etc. Rule VII, however, did make it illegal for a fighter to be grabbed below the waist or to be hit once down.

So when Daniel Mendoza, a Jewish boy of Spanish origin, appeared on the scene in the 1780s, pugilism was becoming more scientific, though still regarded as the undisputed domain of the heavyweight. Mendoza, with his delicate features and long hair, was relatively light in build, about 160 lbs, equivalent to a modern middleweight. Yet he beat the strongest and heftiest men in the country by using novel techniques. Where they lumbered in, fists flailing – or one fist, to be accurate, because the two-arm method was not yet recognized – he would dance out of reach, using his feet to advantage, teasing them with sharp left-handed jabs, catching them off balance. He proved conclusively that grace and skill were more than a match for crude strength, as many a street brawler was to discover to his cost. What is more, he passed on the secret of his success in his book, *The Art of Boxing*, written when he was champion at the early age of 24. In order to supplement his income he opened a famous boxing academy to teach the sport to the sons of nobility and tradesmen alike, and exhibited his skill in a series of highly successful country-wide tours.

Most of our knowledge of Mendoza's career is derived

from his own colourful *Memoirs*, written at the age of 52 when he had relinquished the championship. It is an intriguing and unusual story of a rapid ascent to fame and popularity and an almost equally rapid decline. Fighting was in his blood, though, if we are to believe him unreservedly, he never got involved in a brawl without good reason. Although he does not spell it out, the boy from Aldgate must have taken a lot of teasing on account of his religion, and his father sensibly did not reprimand him if he could prove he had acted in self-defence or on somebody's behalf.

Before he was thirteen he was sent out to work, as apprentice to a glazier. For various reasons, most of them rather vague, Mendoza never seemed able to hold a job for any length of time, but there was good reason for his losing this one. He beat up the glazier's son for being habitually 'abusive and scurrilous'. In his next job with a greengrocer he evidently spent much of his time defending the owner's wife from the insults of neighbourhood rowdies. At sixteen, while working for a tea-dealer, he became involved in the first pitched battle of his life. He threw a surly customer out of the shop, challenged him in the street, and whipped him soundly in a fight lasting three-quarters of an hour. He managed to attract a large audience, including a celebrated boxer of the day, Richard Humphreys, who offered to act as his second.

Mendoza's private feud with Humphreys is related at length in the *Memoirs*, but at this early date Humphreys was so impressed by the boy's fighting prowess that he seconded him again the following Saturday in a contest in the Mile End Road, rejecting a spectator's proffered advice on the grounds that 'there is no need of it. The lad knows more than all of us.' His opponent this time was a professional. He won the match and the prize money as well.

Mendoza knew he was a better than average boxer, but he knew equally well that he could hardly earn a living from the odd five guineas to be picked up from street fights. So he became a tobacconist's assistant in Whitechapel. One day, when travelling with samples in Kent, he got into a fight with an army sergeant who had insulted him. Spurred on by an admiring group of sailors, he thrashed the sergeant, won five guineas from a sympathetic officer, and was carried in triumph by the sailors to Gravesend – eight miles away.

Leaving the tobacconist he found himself caught up in a more dubious occupation – smuggling – which he abandoned after a few days. 'I am not aware,' he writes, 'of ever having wanted resolution and courage upon proper occasions, but was not desperate enough to disregard entirely the consequences of such a dangerous profession, and having learnt that one of our party had, but a few weeks previously, lost his life in an affray with some revenue officers, I quitted my employment in disgust.' Being out of a job, he wandered about the town, won himself a few pounds in casual fights – three in one day – and then made his way, with his brother, to Northampton in quest of a job in the confectionery business. Needless to say, he ran into a young man who hinted that he ought to go back to Jerusalem. The gleam of battle again in his eye, Mendoza challenged him on the spot and beat him so severely that his opponent was confined to his room for more than three weeks.

At the age of nineteen he was ready to challenge all comers, including the professionals. He fought the formidable Tom Tyne at Leytonstone, lost, but had his revenge at a later date. He beat another professional, Matthews, at Kilburn Wells, at which 'several distinguished characters were present, among others a personage of the highest rank'. This was no other than the Prince of Wales (later George IV) himself, who decided to make Daniel his protégé and build him into a champion. This was the turning point in his career, for royal patronage brought him wealth and fame in the space of a few years.

Mendoza the Jew, as he was known in boxing circles, was becoming a power in the land. Locally he was a hero, nicknamed by his East End supporters the 'Light of Israel'. Now the Prince of Wales matched him with the redoubtable Martin the Butcher. It was Mendoza's first stage contest, and he beat the Butcher into submission in twenty minutes. He came away with more than £1,000 in his pocket, enough to get married and, as he promised his wife, to retire – a resolution he was unable to keep. He writes: 'I had now so completely established my reputation for a thorough knowledge of the theory and practice of the art of pugilism, that my friends as well as myself were desirous that instead of seeking fresh contests, I should avail myself of the fame already acquired, and make such a use of my skill as would enable me to derive from thence a regular and liberal income; and being now applied to by several gentlemen to teach the art of self-defence, I was induced . . . to open a school for that purpose in Capel Court.'

It was a wise decision. With royal patronage a steady stream of pupils was assured. Now he even rode to hounds with the aristocracy, though he was not experienced enough to know that one had to ride behind the pack, not in the middle of them. His Grace (whoever he was) was understandably incensed and threatened the upstart with horse-whipping. Mendoza, not knowing his identity, prepared to settle the matter in the traditional way. But on this occasion it ended with smiles and handshakes all round.

So all boded well, except for one cloud on the horizon. Richard Humphreys, once his friend and second, was now an implacable and disgruntled enemy. The reason is undisclosed, probably pure jealousy. At any rate, Humphreys was dying to teach Mendoza a lesson; and Mendoza, despite his vow not to fight again, was eager to make an exception of this one.

They met for the first time at Odiham, in Hampshire, on 9 January, 1788. The match received much prior publicity and there are commemorative mugs of the occasion, showing the two fighters, with their seconds, shaping up to each other. The contest took place in an inn yard, and spectators were charged half a guinea admission. Mendoza reported that the odds, at first 3–2 against him, changed to 5–2 in his favour as the match proceeded. Yet Humphreys won. Mendoza alleged later that his rival had broken the thirty-second rule while changing a shoe, and that one of his seconds had warded off what would have been a decisive blow. Mendoza was thrown, or fell down, apparently injuring himself internally, and was unable to carry on. Mendoza also discovered later, and mentioned in a footnote, that the umpire had bet on Humphreys' victory. It was all very sinister and Mendoza was bent on revenge.

This was to be delayed, however, for Mendoza, evidently under doctor's orders, was in no state to engage immediately in a return bout. So they continued their feud, to the immense delight of the public, in the newspaper *The World*. For a month accusations and counter-accusations flew back and forth, Humphreys accusing Mendoza of being a coward and a malingerer, Mendoza replying with heat, and some dignity, that he was genuinely injured and that the previous result had been accidental. He would certainly fight, but on his own terms and at a time of his own choice. It was all excellent fun and publicity. Six months went by and suddenly it all flared up again. Mendoza was a spectator at a fight in the Croydon area when Humphreys hauled him into the ring and publicly challenged him. Next month Humphreys ventured into Mendoza's Capel Court academy and challenged him again, in front of his pupils. Mendoza pleaded ill-health and lack of funds, but grudgingly agreed to a date six months ahead. Humphreys retired huffily, with Mendoza having the last word by politely returning him his shilling entrance fee.

There followed another contest of words – and insults. Mendoza was apparently well enough to give three profitable exhibition bouts at Covent Garden Theatre that winter. The academy also continued to flourish despite the shock of threatened suspension for staging illegal sparring exhibitions for money. Mendoza evaded this by selling half-crown engravings of himself to spectators and waiving the entrance fee.

The day of reckoning came, however, on 6 May, 1789, in a specially built arena accommodating 2–3,000 people, at Stilton, in Huntingdonshire. Mendoza trained at the home of one of his patrons, Sir Thomas Price. The arena was packed and the fight itself was something of an anti-climax. Forty minutes was enough to exhaust Humphreys, who fell without being struck. After an interval they continued the fight and after ten minutes Humphreys again fell, this time the decision going to Mendoza. He was now undisputed champion, at the peak of his popularity. Across the channel the shouts of the Paris mob were to bring an Empire to ruin; in London the cry was simply 'Mendoza forever!'

But the defeated Humphreys was still seething, writing open letters once more and complaining that he had been suffering from rheumatism at the time. So Mendoza offered him a third, but absolutely final, contest in September, 1790. They fought in an inn yard at Doncaster, and five hundred half-guinea tickets were quickly sold. The odds were 5–1 in favour of the champion, and after a gruelling 72-round contest, lasting as many minutes, Humphreys admitted defeat. Mendoza could afford to be gracious in victory, writing of his opponent:

'With whatever reason I might conceive myself entitled to complain of his conduct towards me at different periods, his general conduct and demeanour were such as reflected great credit on him, and deservedly gained him the esteem of the public, by whom he was always considered and treated as a respectable member of society. I feel a satisfaction in rendering this justice to the memory of a powerful though unsuccessful opponent.'

Nobody could touch him. He was wealthy – though he managed to spend money as soon as he had earned it. He was received at Windsor by King George III, and he drew full houses wherever he chose to appear. For one night's appearance, between variety acts, he could earn from 25 to 50 guineas, good money for those days. He was as popular in Scotland, Ireland and Wales as in his native England. In Glasgow he saved the life of a fellow pugilist, Fewterell, by tossing a table out of the window on the heads of his assailants. In Dublin he and his brother sparred to packed houses in Peters Street, though the season was marred by 'the ferocious conduct of the lower orders of the Irish' who threatened his life and forced him to resort to disguise after the performance. He was able to afford an academy at the Lyceum Theatre in the Strand.

Now he confined his fights to the odd corner brawl and the exhibition ring, but in June, 1791, he fought the powerful

William Ward whom he beat in twenty-six minutes. It took him only seventeen minutes to beat Ward in a return bout. Clearly the old skill was there, but his popularity was now on the wane. He spent money so freely and thoughtlessly that former friends of social standing began to avoid him. He was continually running himself into debt, and although he pleaded ill-health, which was to some extent true, he admitted himself to 'costly and extravagant pursuits'. The pupils dwindled away, the creditors hammered on the door and in 1793, unable any longer to maintain the charade, he was confined within the rules of the King's Bench. This was a form of probation, and a humiliating situation for a young man who had recently rubbed shoulders with royalty. But he bounced back, joined the army as a recruiting sergeant, and in 1795 ventured on what was to be his last fight, with the popular and very talented John Jackson, known as 'Gentleman Jackson'.

Mendoza had lost much of his popular following and now the shouts of 'Mendoza forever' had changed to 'Beat the foreigner'. So Jackson's victory in a mere seventeen minutes was wildly acclaimed. But the way in which the new champion won the fight reflected little credit either on himself or on the existing rules. Jackson simply grabbed Mendoza by his flowing locks and pounded him mercilessly into submission. To Mendoza's own credit, his *Memoirs* simply record: 'The contest between Mr Jackson and myself took place at Hornchurch in Essex the following week, and after lasting seventeen minutes terminated in his favour.'

And that was that. He was still only 31 years old and was to live – with his family of eleven children – until he was 73. But the rest of his life was undistinguished. He went on teaching – by all accounts he was very good – he continued his tours, he tried many lines of business, including management of a public house in the Whitechapel Road. He still managed to run up huge debts, once spending six months in prison in Carlisle, and on another occasion being forced to pawn his gloves. And he looked back on his short, brilliant career in the *Memoirs*, published in 1816.

He had done much to raise boxing from the level of a

crude and somewhat disreputable spectacle to that of a skilled and respectable sporting entertainment. He was the first of a long line of talented Jewish boxers, many of them East End boys with a very similar background to his own. Nobody reading the *Memoirs,* or even reading between the lines, would pretend he was a paragon of virtue. But, apart from the fact that he was quick-tempered and irresponsible where money was concerned, there is little to condemn and much to admire in his meteoric career. He was high-spirited, courageous and honourable; and his sense of humour and zest for living prevented him from going into a decline after he had been toppled from the social and sporting heights. Not many members of his profession have been able to write so fluently nor look back on their lives with as much pleasure and as little rancour as did Daniel Mendoza.

Nathan Mayer Rothschild 1777-1836

Look in the London telephone directory and you will find the modest entry, N. M. Rothschild and Sons, Merchants and Bankers, New Court, St Swithin's Lane. The initials stand for Nathan Mayer, founder of the House of Rothschild in England at the turn of the eighteenth century, the third of the five amazing sons of Mayer Amschel Rothschild, a coin-dealer from the ghetto of Frankfurt-on-Main.

Rothschild – the name evokes a sense of awe and mystery, a suggestion of fabulous wealth and power. There has always been something legendary about the Rothschilds – an absence of reliable information about their beginnings and the air of anonymity and exclusivity which, even today, masks their gigantic financial activities. The family name is derived from the sign of the Red Shield which once adorned the house in Judengasse – Jew Street – in Frankfurt where Mayer Amschel's ancestors lived from the sixteenth century onwards. The house which Mayer bought when he eventually became prosperous bore a green shield in place of the original red one, and this narrow, three-storey building is where Mayer and his wife Gudula brought up their ten children. From this overcrowded house in the main street of the ghetto Mayer, assisted by his sons, built up a private financial empire of unbelievable dimensions.

In the nineteenth century the Rothschilds were bankers to dukes, kings and governments, they amassed individual fortunes, they influenced the course of political events. Today their power in the political sphere has declined, but their precedence in the world of high finance is still unchallenged, their stakes in the fields of business, industry, scientific research, the arts, sport and entertainment are incalculable, their philanthropic activities a byword.

It is a fantastic success story and merits a volume to itself. If we concentrate here on the figure of Nathan Mayer, it is not because he was the most attractive, popular, generous or most highly cultured of the clan. He wasn't. But of Mayer's five sons he was certainly the most gifted, intellectually and commercially; and whilst we should remember that the Rothschild rise to power was essentially a brilliant piece of team-work, with five brothers playing an indispensable role in five key cities, it was undoubtedly Nathan who directed operations from his base in London. It was Nathan's early commercial dealings and stock-exchange manipulations which laid the firm foundations of the family's wealth and influence.

Mayer Amschel, Nathan's father, was himself the son of a merchant and was given a traditionally orthodox Jewish education with a view to a rabbinical career. But commerce was in his blood, and when his parents died he obtained a clerical post with a firm of Jewish bankers in Hanover. The experience gained there decided him to set up in business on his own, and he trailed back to the ghetto of his childhood, to the second-hand store run by his two brothers. He himself specialized in antique coins and in this field he patiently built up a thriving trade, with a distinguished clientèle reaching far beyond the confines of the ghetto. One of his Hanover connections, General von Estorff, was the friend and confidential adviser of the young Prince William of Hanau. Mayer obtained an introduction through Estorff. According to legend the Jewish coin-dealer found the prince engrossed in a chess game and made an immediate impression by suggesting the winning move. It sounds a bit too simple, but it is known that William became one of Mayer's regular customers. The occasional sales of coins and medals from Mayer's catalogue initiated the vital association between ghetto and royal court which set the Rothschilds on the road to fame.

The business flourished. Mayer married Gudula Schnapper, a shopkeeper's daughter, and proudly set up the sign 'Court agent to his Serene Highness, Prince William of Hanau'. Fortune was to smile on him now. William, grandson of George II and cousin of George III, was also related to the Kings of Sweden and Denmark. He was enormously wealthy and in 1785 succeeded to the title of Landgrave of Hesse-Cassel. A large part of his fortune was derived from the sale of Hessian mercenaries to the British crown for policing their North American colonies. It was a link which the Rothschilds were to exploit to the full. Meanwhile Mayer had purchased the Green Shield house in the better part of the ghetto, where five boys and five girls were to grow up. He was branching out too. One of his brothers had died, the other was retired. Mayer now controlled a respectable grocery and cotton goods business and was on the way to being a private banker, discounting drafts (cashing cheques) for clients, and numbering among such clients the Landgrave of Hesse-Cassel himself.

It was the Landgrave's financial adviser, Carl Buderus, who forged the crucial link between Mayer Amschel and his master. Buderus grew to like and respect the businessman who frequently visited the court with a new batch of rare coins. No doubt it turned out to be as profitable to Buderus as to Mayer when William was persuaded to present Rothschild with some bills for discounting – not many, but it was a start. By 1789 Mayer was handling William's drafts to the tune of some £8,000, and this source of income increased steadily with the years.

Mayer's elder sons were now grown boys. They received the same strict religious training as had their father – and as for business, they were more than adept, they were inspired.

Soon Amschel, Salomon and Nathan were all in the business, running messages, conducting negotiations, gaining commercial experience. Before long the Rothschilds in Judengasse were handling a large portion of William's financial affairs, first as agents or brokers, later unequivocally as his court bankers.

The importation of English cotton goods was a highly profitable branch of the business and it was in this connection that Nathan, at twenty, found his way to Manchester. Later, when he had made his own fortune, Nathan told his friend Sir Thomas Buxton, in his clipped, matter-of-fact way, how he arrived in England.

'There was not room for us all in Frankfurt. I dealt in English goods. One great trader came there, who had the market all to himself. He was quite the great man, and did us a favour if he sold us goods. Somehow I offended him, and he refused to show me his patterns. This was on a Tuesday. I said to my father: "I will go to England." I could speak nothing but German. On the Thursday I started. The nearer I got to England, the cheaper the goods were. As soon as I got to Manchester I laid out all my money, things were so cheap, and I made a good profit. I soon found out there were three profits – the raw material, the dyeing, and the manufacturing. I said to the manufacturer: "I will supply you with material and dye, and you supply me with manufactured goods." So I got three profits instead of one, and I could sell goods cheaper than anybody. In a short time I made my £20,000 into £60,000. My success all turned on one maxim. I said: "I can do what another man can, and I am a match for the man with the patterns and all the rest of them." I had another advantage. I am an off-hand man; I made a bargain at once.'

This is the root of the matter, the secret of Nathan's phenomenal progress at the top. Ambition, determination, commercial ruthlessness, unlimited self-confidence. Mayer Amschel knew what he was doing when he entrusted the English side of the business to Nathan. For in 1798 England was where Nathan could be of most value. The continent was in turmoil. Napoleon was soon to set it ablaze. England was emerging as the hub of the financial and business world, and the Rothschilds were determined to be at the centre of things. So partly by accident, partly by design, the international firm of merchant-bankers, N. M. Rothschild, came into being six years later, when Nathan moved to London and set up his office in New Court.

This same year, 1804, saw the House of Rothschild erupt in earnest on to the European financial scene. Mayer, described now as Superior Court Agent to the Landgrave, had taken his two elder sons into partnership. They were handling all William's loans, debts, bonds and mortgages. It happened that Denmark's treasury was almost empty and a large loan was requested. William, the dutiful nephew, was ready to help, but wanted it kept quiet. Buderus and Rothschild supplied the answer. The loan was handled not by William's official Frankfurt bankers, but by the Rothschilds, discreetly, anonymously, cheaply. It gave them a foothold in the field of state loans which they never relinquished. During the next eight years they negotiated further big loans to the Danish court, and by 1806 they enjoyed the complete confidence of the Landgrave William.

Europe was now at war. Napoleon's armies were advancing and Prussia was invaded in October, 1806. William, whose sympathies and interests were quite naturally with the allies, fled north to Denmark. What happened then is enshrouded in legend. Some say William entrusted his entire fortune to Mayer before leaving and that considerable amounts of money and quantities of jewels were buried in the Judengasse cellar, together with Mayer's files and documents. In any event, the French troops who searched the Green Shield house some years later found nothing. The Rothschilds were probably far too astute to risk leaving a fortune on the premises. Nathan, in London, was doing a profitable trade to the continent in contraband goods – cotton, tobacco, sugar and foodstuffs – and much of William's vast wealth, as Nathan himself revealed, found its way to New Court. 'We had no time to lose,' he explained, 'and my father sent the money to me in England. On one single occasion I received £600,000 from him by post, and I invested this so profitably that the prince afterwards sent me his entire stores of wine and linen.'

In fact, William was to send much more. Once the French troops had departed, while William still sat helplessly in exile, the Rothschilds toiled diligently and profitably on his behalf, combing Europe to collect his debts before the French Finance Ministry arrived on the scene, transferring funds to London, getting Nathan to invest it, and gradually amassing the fortune which was to launch the House on its extraordinary career. William was delighted, on his return home, to find so much of his fortune intact – exact accounts could not possibly be rendered – and was promptly persuaded to entrust Nathan in London with all his affairs. Nathan was in his element, purchasing government securities with William's money, speculating on a scale never previously known, playing the market coolly, unerringly, with all the cunning and wizardry at his command. As the international reputation of Rothschild grew, so did Nathan's in London. Wealth and social prestige went hand in hand. He married Hannah Cohen, daughter of the richest Jew in England. At the age of thirty, Nathan, short, balding, completely lacking his father's ease of manner and social graces, was a power to be reckoned with.

In 1810 the Rothschilds intervened again on the political scene. Nathan trimmed the story of a fantastically complicated operation down to its bare essentials, when he recalled it later in life. He wrote:

'When I settled in London the East India Company had £800,000 worth in gold to sell. I went to the sale and bought it all. I knew the Duke of Wellington must have it. The government sent for me and said they must have the gold. When they had got it, they did not know how to get it to Portugal. I undertook all that and sent it through France. It was the best business I have ever done.'

The British army under the Duke of Wellington was pinned down in Portugal during the Peninsular War, cut off from home. To pay his troops Wellington was forced to issue drafts on the treasury which were cashed by Spanish, Maltese and Sicilian bankers and moneylenders at stupendous discounts. Nathan stepped in, purchased Wellington's bills, and with the aid of his brother James in Paris and a host of well-paid agents, smuggled this enormous quantity of bullion through enemy France, converted it into paper money and emerged with Wellington's receipts. In one operation, not without risk but completely without commotion, the Rothschilds had played a vital role in the war effort and made themselves a handsome, undisclosed profit. And as the war progressed they came repeatedly to the aid of the government by organizing huge loans to the allies Austria, Prussia and Russia. With London, Frankfurt and Paris as their key points they had no rivals for operations of this size and delicacy. If they could do this in wartime what could they not achieve when peace was finally restored?

In 1812, Mayer Amschel, the founder of the House, died, summoning his sons to his bedside, charging them to carry on the business together, to consult their mother in all matters of importance and to remain firm in the path of orthodox Judaism. Male Rothschilds would be expected to marry wives from within the family and only the sons, not the daughters, would be permitted to have a stake in the business. Mayer's dying injunctions were to be observed, almost to the letter. His fierce sense of family loyalty and exclusiveness was to permeate Rothschild thought and activity in the generations to come. The involved family tree, the repetition of first names, the clannishness, the continuation of the business through male descendants only, the instinct for making money, the tradition of giving money – all stem from the personality of gentle, devout, hard-working Mayer Amschel Rothschild.

Nathan was now in virtual control of the expanding Rothschild empire. His methods were envied, admired or condemned – depending on whether you were a bystander, a competitor or a victim. But his activities were followed with breathless interest, often as a weather-vane to political events. One secret of his success was his ability to obtain information before anyone else. This was not mere luck.

The Rothschild information service was a master-stroke of organization. Contrary to legend, it was not all done by carrier pigeons, although he did run a pigeon-post service to and from the continent. Basically, however, it was done by human messengers. He paid for information at courts, embassies, government offices and in private drawing-rooms. His agents picked up news in all the capitals of Europe. On foot, by sea and by road, Rothschild couriers roamed the continent for information. For news, before it became official, was a saleable and profitable commodity.

The famous Waterloo 'scoop' is the best-known single example of the Rothschild shrewdness, opportunism, initiative – call it what you will. The Rothschilds never lost faith in the eventual defeat of Napoleon, and the return from Elba was as much of a shock to them as to the rest of Europe. On the result of the battle of Waterloo hinged not only their own fortunes but perhaps the fate of the nation. England waited breathlessly for the outcome, but it was Nathan who received the news first, thanks to one of his agents. The story that he himself followed the army to the battlefield, watched until the decision was no longer in doubt, then rushed back to Ostend, crossing the Channel in a storm in order to convey the glad tidings to the capital, is just romantic nonsense. But he certainly knew the truth long before Wellington's own envoy arrived. Whether he informed the government and was not believed, or whether he concealed it, is also a matter for conjecture. But his face and pose as he slumped tiredly against his favourite pillar in the Stock Exchange seemed to indicate the worst. Dejection was written on his brow. As if in confirmation, he began selling consols. It was sufficient to cause panic. The value of government securities plunged. He went on selling. The surrounding gloom and depression deepened. Waterloo was obviously a disaster. Then, shortly before the official news came through, he secretly bought them all back. Waterloo was a great victory. Prices reached new peaks, joy was unconfined, and nobody could have been more pleased than the impassive Nathan, who had quietly made a fortune in a day.

An anonymous writer described him as he leaned against his 'pillar': 'There is a rigidity and tension in his features that would make you fancy, if you did not see that it was not so, that someone was pinching him behind, and that he was either afraid or ashamed to say so. Eyes are usually called the windows of the soul. But in his case you would conclude that the windows are false ones, or that there was no soul to look out of them. There comes not one pencil of light from the interior, neither is there one scintillation of that which comes from without reflected in any direction. The whole puts you in mind of a skin to let, and you wonder why it stands upright without at least something in it. By and by another figure comes up to it. It then steps two paces aside, and the most inquisitive glance that you ever saw, and a glance more inquisitive than you would ever have thought of, is drawn out of the fixed and leaden eye, as if one were drawing a sword from its scabbard. The visiting figure, which has the appearance of coming by accident and not by design, stops but a second or two, in the course of which looks are exchanged which, though you cannot translate, you feel must be of most important meaning. After these the eyes are sheathed up again, and the figure resumes its stony posture. During the morning numbers of visitors come, all of whom meet with a similar reception and vanish in a similar manner. Last of all, the figure itself vanishes, leaving you utterly at a loss as to what can be its nature and functions.' It was an elaborate act, of course, part of the Rothschild mystique, shrewdly and deliberately fostered.

The family business boomed after the Napoleonic Wars. The Rothschilds were courted by all the rulers and statesmen of Europe. Their foreign loans rocketed into millions of pounds. The loan to the Prussian government, in 1818, was alone worth five million. Austria and Russia followed suit, as did the kingdom of Naples (where brother Carl opened a branch in 1821), the German principalities, Belgium and even Brazil. Rothschilds now operated on a world-wide scale, master-minded by Nathan in London. The revolution in banking, set in motion by their international clearing-house system, opened up new opportunities for business and investment; and it was Nathan himself who popularized the idea of foreign loans by arranging for dividends to be payable in London, and in sterling. It marked the beginning of the great wave of nineteenth-century investment overseas.

Nathan was indeed a remarkable character, though hardly a popular one. Not that he cared. It was hardly surprising that the portly little man, with his coarse features and thick foreign accent, should earn the enmity of many staunch upholders of British tradition and behaviour. Though his business methods were unorthodox, few dared to condemn them as unethical. He simply enjoyed making money – not possessing it – and his ambition was unlimited. Yet his code of conduct, both on the private and public levels, was unexceptionable. Like all the Rothschilds to come, he was a man of peace, and generous to a fault. His motives may not have been as humanitarian as were those of his descendants. Possibly he had so much money that he did not miss it. There was the cynical remark he once made to Buxton: 'Sometimes to amuse myself I give a beggar a guinea. He thinks I have made a mistake, and for fear I should find it out, off he runs as hard as he can. I advise you to give a beggar a guinea sometimes; it is very amusing.' But whatever his motives, he fostered the tradition of charitable work which has since won the Rothschilds international renown.

Although he was the butt of caricaturists, he was not one for private ostentation. He alone of all the brothers refused to adopt the baronial title conferred on them by the Austrian monarch in 1816. But he kept it up his sleeve. Once, at a ball, the Duke of Montmorency was boasting of his long line of eminent ancestors. With a rare gleam of humour, Nathan announced: 'You call yourself the first Christian baron. Well, I am the first Jewish baron, but I make less fuss about it.' He lived in luxury, yet, unlike many of his descendants, he was not a connoisseur of the arts nor did he care for the refinements of life. He refused to spend money on expensive paintings which he could not appreciate, and when a friend once asked him what sort of music he liked, he jingled some coins in his pocket, and replied: 'That's the only sort of music I like.'

He was pursued by all the celebrities and titled names of the day, but he would never defer to them, as many an embarrassed hostess learned to her cost. The story is told of a

German duke who was ushered into his private room one day and was motioned to a chair. Enraged at the slight, the duke thrust his card under Nathan's nose and reeled off his full title. Unperturbed, and scarcely bothering to glance up from his desk, Nathan murmured: 'Very well, take *two* chairs.'

One final story. He was once obliged to send to the Bank of England a bill for payment of a considerable sum which he had received from Amschel, his brother in Frankfort. The bank returned it on the grounds that it did not cash the notes of private individuals. Infuriated to be labelled a private individual, Nathan took his revenge. One morning he presented himself at Threadneedle Street and demanded gold for a five-pound note. The teller, somewhat surprised at this petty request from a Rothschild, handed over five gold sovereigns, which Nathan carefully counted and dropped into his bag. He then drew out another note, then another, and another, filling his bag with sovereigns. He kept it up for hours, as did nine of his clerks at other windows. By the end of the day the Bank of England's gold reserves were depleted by some £100,000. Threatening to resume operations the next morning, he was confronted by one of the managers, much agitated, who demanded to know what he was doing. Nathan replied that if the Bank of England doubted his notes, he was entitled to doubt theirs. Moreover, he was prepared to go on changing notes for gold for two months, if need be. A directors' meeting was hurriedly convened, and it was decided that henceforth any Rothschild draft would be cashed, with no questions asked.

Nathan Rothschild died in 1836, from a fever contracted at the wedding of his eldest son Lionel to his niece Charlotte. Tradition relates that a flock of pigeons was released on the night of his death, destined for all the Rothschild offices and agencies in Europe, each bird bearing the simple message *Il est mort*. His body lay in state at New Court and the funeral procession, which stretched for miles, included the Lord Mayor and the ambassadors of all the leading European powers. The running of the business was left to his four sons, in conjunction with their uncles abroad. His daughters, in accordance with tradition, were simply left £100,000 apiece.

The subsequent fortunes of the Rothschilds must be briefly told. Amschel, the eldest brother, remained in Frankfurt presiding over the original branch, living in splendour, becoming treasurer to the German Confederation and a pillar of the Jewish community. His mother died in the Green Shield house at the venerable age of 96; before her death all new entrants to the Rothschild clan were expected to pay a pilgrimage to the Judengasse to receive her blessing. The Frankfurt branch of the firm was wound up at the close of the century.

Salomon, the second son, built up the Austrian branch of the business and became a great landed proprietor. He was adviser to Metternich and treasurer to the court, and later pioneered the first railway network in central Europe. The Austrian branch flourished until the Nazis came to power, when Salomon's descendants found refuge in America.

Carl wielded the same degree of power in Naples, opening an office which only went into decline when Italy was reunified later in the century. James, the youngest son, opened the branch in Paris in 1817, and became the *eminence grise* of French finance, trade and industry for over fifty years, triumphantly surviving every change of régime. He too played a significant part in the development of the railway in France and, like the others, he was a noted philanthropist. James' son was the Baron Edmond who played such an important role in the early history of Jewish settlement in Palestine, despite the fact that he never announced his formal allegiance to the Zionist cause. But it was Rothschild money which financed the early colonists, drained swamps, surveyed land, built houses and factories, just as it was Rothschild money which later flowed into the modern State of Israel in such profusion – into industry, agriculture, business, science, scholarship and the arts.

In England, Nathan's eldest son Lionel lobbied for ten years for the right of Jews to enter Parliament and finally took his seat, against frenzied opposition from the Lords, in the House of Commons. Two Prime Ministers graced the wedding of Lionel's daughter, and it was he who, with Disraeli, organized the purchase of the Suez Canal shares. Lionel's son Nathaniel became the first Jewish peer – Disraeli, remember, had been baptized – simply adopting the title of Lord Rothschild.

The English Rothschilds lived as luxuriously as their European cousins, buying splendid town houses and country mansions, entertaining nobility and royalty. Alfred, younger brother of the first Lord Rothschild, was perhaps the most eminent of the art connoisseurs in the family and became the first Jewish director of the Bank of England. And so it went on. They bred horses, won Derbies, bought art treasures and vineyards, organized charities, founded trusts, built up the Rothschild empire – until the First World War. Thereafter the political influence of the Rothschilds declined, though not their financial importance. Today their assets are as incalculable, their devotion to Judaism is as strong, their sense of family unity as unshakeable, their work for good causes as energetic as ever. Mayer Amschel would have been proud of them.

Benjamin Disraeli, Earl of Beaconsfield 1804–1881

Heckling is a common enough parliamentary weapon and there have been many more violent and unruly episodes than the one which occurred in the House of Commons on 7 December, 1837. This one, however, had a sequel. The government benches erupted in a frenzy of laughter, hooting and catcalling as the speaker for the Tory opposition struggled to make himself heard. With his pale features set off by black ringlets, his bottle-green coat and white waistcoat hung with gold chains, he did, to be sure, cut an unusual figure. Nevertheless, he continued his maiden speech, unperturbed. Finally he thundered above the din: 'Though I sit down now, the time will come when you *will* hear me!'

Benjamin Disraeli's confident prediction came true. Soon he would rebel against his own leader, Sir Robert Peel, reorganize and lead the Tory party himself, become Chancellor of the Exchequer and, as Queen Victoria's favourite statesman, Prime Minister of England.

The D'Israelis were of Spanish origin and came to England by way of Italy. Isaac D'Israeli was a quiet, scholarly man, a book-lover and author of a collection of anecdotes entitled *Curiosities of Literature*. His son, Benjamin, born on 21 December, 1804, inherited from him a passion for history and literature and a patient, tolerant disposition. Although he was taught Hebrew, the family circle was not orthodox, and when Isaac came into conflict with the officers of the Bevis Marks synagogue he severed his links with Judaism. At the suggestion of a friend, Benjamin was baptized, at the age of thirteen, a fortuitous act which made it possible for him to embark on his political career.

Disraeli considered himself a Christian in thought and deed throughout his life, but never attempted to conceal his Jewish origins. Nor did his enemies allow him to forget the fact, as they heaped him with cheap abuse – men such as Daniel O'Connell, who, in the heat of an election campaign, swore that the name of the impenitent thief on the Cross must have been Disraeli; or the actor, Macready, who talked of this 'miserable, circumcised, *soi-disant* Christian'; or Thomas Carlyle who referred to him as a 'Hebrew conjuror, monkey and mountebank'.

Not only did he look Jewish, which was, in their eyes, unfortunate, but he also looked foreign which was unforgivable; and although he managed to strike a satisfactory religious balance by adopting Christianity as the logical culmination of Judaism, he was no more accepted unreservedly as a practising Christian than he was as a patriotic Englishman.

His racial pride was never more publicly or bravely demonstrated than in the debate on the question of admitting professing Jews into the Commons. Baron Lionel de Rothschild was unable to take his seat for years, as legislation to abolish the Christian oath formula was repeatedly blocked. Disraeli incurred the wrath of the entire Tory party as he cast his vote for morality and tolerance. 'Where is your Christianity,' he hurled defiantly at the House, 'if you do not believe in their Judaism?'

His schooldays were unmemorable, though he found ample

outlet for his narrative and dramatic gifts. He hated sports but found it prudent to take secret boxing lessons to defend himself against bullies who labelled him Jew and foreigner. He read passionately on all subjects – poetry, Greek and Latin classics, the history of the Orient, religion, secret societies. As a youth he was extremely handsome, with his pale complexion, sensitive, mobile features and black curly hair. He had a reputation for witty repartee and cultivated a languid air of cynicism. The high-flown manner of speaking was exaggerated by a florid taste in clothes. These affectations, so amusing and shocking, deluded many into thinking him a mere dandy or buffoon.

In fact the velvet jackets, gaudy trousers, coloured stockings, enormous cravats, ruffs and frills, were part of his defensive armour against the hostility and sense of alienation he experienced until late in his career. It is significant that, as he assumed responsibility and gained confidence, he shed these gaudy trappings and showed himself in his true guise – as a shrewd, brilliant and flexible tactician, ambitious yet high-principled, incurably romantic yet guided by sober reason, a man of deep and serious convictions.

His formal schooling ended at seventeen when he was placed in a solicitor's office in Old Jewry. He hated the boredom and inactivity and suffered from recurrent blinding headaches. Foreign travel helped to restore his health, first a six-week tour of the Netherlands and Germany, later a three-month visit to Switzerland and Italy. He made a costly youthful mistake of speculating in South American mining shares which landed him in debt to the tune of £7,000 – money which was to have helped to finance a daily paper, *The Representative*, backed by the publisher John Murray and edited by John Gibson Lockhart, son-in-law of Sir Walter Scott. Accumulating debt was to be the albatross round his neck for the better part of his life; he never fought his way free of financial trouble until his elderly friend from Torquay, Mrs Brydges Williams, left him £30,000 in her will. But by then he was over sixty.

It is hardly surprising that, given his range of reading and interest in contemporary affairs, his romantic imagination

Above: Prince Albert playing the organ to Queen Victoria and Felix Mendelssohn during the composer's first visit to Buckingham Palace in 1842.

Top: The German composer Felix Mendelssohn-Bartholdy. This is one of many contemporary paintings of the musician who was more popular in England than in his homeland.

Top: The French actress Rachel in a scene from Racine's *Phèdre*, 1850. Critics were agreed that Phèdre was her most memorable role. *Below right:* A youthful portrait of Elisabeth Rachel Félix, known to Paris and the world as Rachel. The painting, by Auguste Charpentier, hangs in the Cómedie Française.

Below left: Sigmund Freud, founder of psycho-analysis. A photograph taken late in his life. His theories of Dreams and the Unconscious were violently attacked by traditional scientists.

and his facility with words, he should have turned to writing as an outlet for his youthful ideas and ambitions. 'My books,' he said later, 'are the history of my life.' They repay serious attention as providing keys both to his character and political philosophy. With their ornate imagery, preposterous plots and two-dimensional heroes and heroines, they do not make for easy reading. But they abound in witty, acutely observed character studies, in aphorisms worthy of Wilde, and in penetrating assessments of the political and social scene. And beneath their glittering surface shimmer is a vein of profound seriousness – affection for ordinary people, outrage against the rampant forces of materialism and exploitation, an amazing understanding of English traditions and historical currents, and a religious, almost mystical awareness of mission and destiny, applicable to himself as to the nation at large.

Vivian Grey, published anonymously in 1826, brought him in a derisory £200. He dashed it off in four months and poked fun at recognizable figures in society. It was a great drawing-room success – until the author's identity stood revealed. Then the world of fashion and respectability closed ranks and the unknown, twenty-year-old upstart was reviled as a 'paltry catchpenny' and castigated for his 'shameless bluff' and 'ludicrous affectation of good breeding'.

The ridicule was endurable but ill-health forced him into three years of inactivity at his father's country house at Bradenham in Buckinghamshire. All he managed to produce during this period was a short, Voltaire-like satirical novel called *Captain Popanilla*, which ridiculed the flimsy structure of political and economic life, made some trenchant comments on high finance and the national debt and warned against the growing menace of industrialism.

The Young Duke, which followed in 1831, was more successful – it brought him in £500 – and it created quite a stir with its exotic, though second-hand descriptions of aristocrats and noblemen wallowing in luxury and idleness. Disraeli featured as the hero who, after almost ruining himself with drink, gambling and women, is finally rescued by true love. Once again, for all its air of fantasy and frivolity, there were many flashes of political wisdom; and it had the immediate desired effect – enough to finance a trip to the East in the company of William Meredith, the young man engaged to his sister Sarah.

The journey, which lasted more than a year, made a tremendous and lasting impression and provided unlimited scope for self-indulgence and exhibitionism. The eccentric youth created a sensation wherever he appeared. In Gibraltar he sported a pair of canes, one for morning, one for evening. In Malta he emerged in full Andalusian costume and was blackballed from the officers' mess as 'a damned bumptious Jew boy'. He left the island dressed as a Greek pirate, complete with red shirt and immense silver buttons, sky-blue trousers, red cap and slippers, and an array of pistols and daggers in his sash. In Turkey he wore green pantaloons, embroidered and beribboned, and a fringed shawl round his waist, as he lounged on a divan smoking a six-foot-long pipe. He adored the indolent ease of the Turks, the simple nomadic life of Syrian tribesmen, the grandeur of Thebes.

But the week he spent in Jerusalem was an altogether different experience and the sight of the Jewish and Christian Holy Places stirred him profoundly. Sadly, the trip ended in tragedy, as Meredith died suddenly of smallpox. Disraeli returned home in mourning to his beloved sister 'Sa', who never married.

The Eastern journey inspired a romantic novel *Alroy*, based on the exploits of a medieval Jewish hero, and another autobiographical fantasy, *Contarini Fleming* which he described as 'the perfection of English prose and a *chef d'œuvre*'. Though praised by Heine, it was hardly that. The restless, passionate poet-hero, with his conflicting artistic and political ambitions, was another idealized portrait of Disraeli himself, now at the crossroads of his own career.

Literature was in itself neither profitable nor influential. He was thirsting for action. He had boundless confidence in his abilities and although he had a low opinion of the men who guided the nation's destiny, his love for England and his desire to serve her interests were burningly sincere. Politics was the only effective sphere of activity, but first he had to become accepted. He had neither money, nor background, nor connections. He had no inclination to become attached to either political party and neither opportunity nor wish to buy his way to power. But he was enough of a realist to know that little could be achieved without friends in high places.

London, as ever, was the hub of fashion and influence, so he rented a bachelor apartment in Duke Street. At the house of his friends, the Bulwer-Lyttons, he met the cream of society: Caroline Norton and her two sisters; Count Alfred D'Orsay, the prince of dandies; and the wife of the Member of Parliament for Maidstone, Mrs Wyndham Lewis. In Caroline Norton's tiny drawing-room he dazzled the ladies with his scarlet waistcoat and ring-encrusted white gloves. At Lady Blessington's sumptuous house overlooking Hyde Park he rubbed shoulders with nobility and confided to her the details of a delightful love affair with a girl named Henrietta. As traveller, author and man-about-town, he was admired and fussed over. He enjoyed it immensely.

He decided to stand as a Radical for a by-election at High Wycombe in 1832. He lost by 20 votes to 12. After the Reform Bill had doubled the electorate he tried again, telling his audience that he came 'wearing the badge of no party and the livery of no faction'. 'Rid yourselves,' he earnestly begged them, 'of all that political jargon and factious slang of Whig and Tory, used only to delude you, and unite in forming a great national party which can alone save the country.' Familiar modern overtones, but then, as now, no way to get ahead in the political jungle. Again he finished bottom of the poll. Undismayed, he confided his ambition to the then Home Secretary, Lord Melbourne, at a dinner party. 'Tell me,' inquired His Lordship, 'what do you want to be?' 'I want to be Prime Minister,' was the direct reply. 'No, no, no chance of that,' sighed Melbourne, 'It is all settled and arranged. . . . Go into politics, you will be right. . . . But you must put these foolish notions out of your head.'

The foolish notions remained fixed in his mind, but now he faced reality. Although he distrusted inherited power and privilege as much as he disliked Whig utilitarianism, he cast his lot with the Tories. The aristocrats and gentlemen farmers were more congenial than the new industrialists. But he was to develop his own radical form of conservatism, and never betrayed a principle in the interest of vote-catching or rabble-rousing. It was on that very issue of broken pledges and abandoned principles that he was to range himself against Peel and encompass his downfall.

The party label, however distasteful, did the trick, although he experienced two more defeats, one in the 1834 election at Wycombe, the other at a by-election for Taunton. In the course of this he earned the undying hatred of the fiery Daniel O'Connell who descended to scurrilous depths of personal abuse. Disraeli retaliated in an open letter, which ended: 'We shall meet at Philippi; and rest assured that, confident in a good cause, and in some energies which have not been altogether unproved, I will seize the first opportunity of inflicting upon you a castigation which will make you at the same time remember and repent the insults that you have lavished upon   BENJAMIN DISRAELI'

By now he was launched on politics in earnest and won renown and acclaim for his *Runnymede Letters* with their bitter attack on the Whig leadership, and *A Vindication of the English Constitution* in which he outlined his political creed in taut, coherent terms. He attacked utilitarianism, extolled the virtues of the House of Lords, urged a more representative House of Commons, and reminded his readers that both Houses 'are the trustees of the nation, not its masters'. He was elected to the Carlton Club, and with the death of William IV and the accession of the eighteen-year-old Victoria, he stood ready to contest one of the two safe seats at Maidstone. The other was held by Wyndham Lewis, whose wife he had so admired at the Bulwers. Voting took place on 27 July, and after the count he wrote to 'Sa': 'Dearest – Lewis 707, Disraeli 616, Colonel Thompson 412. The constituency nearly exhausted. In haste – Dizzy.'

Shortly after the election Wyndham Lewis died and the friendship between Dizzy and Mary Anne, Lewis's widow, ripened into affection. Count D'Orsay had once mockingly challenged him: 'You will not make love! You will not intrigue! You have your seat; do not risk anything! If you meet with a widow, then marry!' She already regarded him with an awe approaching hero-worship. When he proposed she asked for a year to consider the matter and his impetuous letters and attentions decided the issue. On the face of it, the alliance seemed unpromising. She was already forty-five, twelve years his senior. Moreover, she had the reputation of being a talkative, frivolous woman with no intellectual pretensions. Cynics claimed it was a simple matter of money. Dizzy's debts amounted to some £20,000. But despite her Park Lane house and her £4,000 annual income, she could hardly be described as wealthy. Still, the inheritance could not be altogether discounted. As she wrote, years later, 'Dizzy married me for my money, but if he had the chance again he would marry me for love.' He himself acknowledged it: 'When I first made my advances to you, I was influenced by no romantic feelings.'

These were early days, however, and there is no reason to doubt that romance played its part later. Mary Anne was underestimated by society gossips. Although her adoration of Dizzy may have appeared excessive and faintly ridiculous at times, she had common sense, fortitude, and humour. Their marriage was uninterruptedly happy, with absolute loyalty on either side. He would always defend her against slights and slanders and was indebted to her for thirty years of calm, selfless devotion.

The memory of the unfortunate maiden speech quickly faded, and Disraeli soon convinced members on both sides of the House that he was a force to be reckoned with. But his independent mind and impetuous nature were an embarrassment to the cautious, unimaginative Peel; and when the Melbourne ministry collapsed in 1841, he made the mistake of writing to Peel and requesting a place in his government. Peel, under the influence of such colleagues as Lord Stanley who bluntly announced that 'if that scoundrel were taken in, he would not remain himself', coldly refused. It was an indiscretion which he never repeated. From now on he would make his own way, and that his path would deviate from that of Peel and his supporters became increasingly obvious as the debates raged round the two burning issues of the day, Chartism and Free Trade.

Peel had been returned as the sworn protector of English agricultural interests against the threat of Cobden and Bright's Anti-Corn Law League. The Corn Laws dated from 1791 and, ever since, a variable rate of duty on imported foreign corn, though to the advantage of the British farmer, had left the consumer to the mercy of economic uncertainties and the unpredictable British weather. The League had been formed in 1838 after four successive poor harvests had once more created near-famine conditions. Disraeli remained unconvinced that the Free Traders, with their slogan of 'cheap bread', could provide the answer to working-class poverty. Although the landowners stood to gain from the retention of the Corn Laws, the manufacturing middle class alone, in his view, would benefit from their repeal. For him, the growing menace of industrialism to the traditional pattern of British rural life outweighed other considerations. The get-rich-quick mentality of the cotton kings and factory owners was not to his liking. When Peel showed signs of being swayed by Free Trade arguments, Disraeli resolved to oppose him to the bitter end.

'Young England' was the name of the parliamentary 'splinter group' that he formed to reinforce and rally the Tory Protectionists. The nucleus of the group consisted of a handful of young sympathizers who, weary of Peel's dull platitudes and wavering policies, responded eagerly to Disraeli's colourful personality and crusading spirit. They shared his romantic vision of a nation with a strong working-class backbone whose best interests would be served by an enlightened monarchy and a representative, predominantly upper-class government. One of the most enthusiastic members was George Smythe, who appeared as the hero in the first of Disraeli's three political novels, published in 1844.

Coningsby, or The Younger Generation proved to be a best-seller. It was a brilliant and witty lampoon of politicians and parties, election agents and riggers, place-seekers and hangers-on. Disraeli himself appears as the larger-than-life Jewish millionaire Sidonia, though many saw the character as

Rothschild. With typical Disraeli wit and pungency, Sidonia dispenses advice and solves all problems, 'assisted by that absolute freedom from prejudice which is the compensatory possession of a man without a country'. Parliament is seen as a hotbed of intrigue and personal aggrandizement. Government must be respected, statesmen educated, leaders men of genius. The author did not disguise the fact that his object was to influence public opinion, and the sales figures suggest that his views were finding increasing favour with the public.

Sybil, or The Two Nations, which followed in 1845 was more serious in tone, grimmer in content. Based on first-hand investigation of working-class conditions in the north, the novel depicted the immense chasm between the 'two nations' – rich and poor. Disraeli was outraged and distressed at the miserable conditions he had seen in urban slums, villages, factories and mines. One of his conclusions was that 'the people were better clothed, better lodged, and better fed just before the Wars of the Roses than they are at this moment', and that 'we have more pestilence now in England than we ever had, but it only reaches the poor'. Politically, he considered the working class impotent. Enlightened leadership was essential and the establishment of 'a free Monarchy and a privileged and prosperous people'. Despite the absurdities of plot and the flat characterization, the book still impresses with its powerful indictment of political ineptitude and social injustice. He dedicated it 'to one whose noble spirit and gentle nature ever prompt her to sympathize with the suffering; to one whose sweet voice has often encouraged, and whose taste and judgement have ever guided, their pages; the most severe of critics, but – a perfect wife!'

For a detailed account of Disraeli's political career there are history books in plenty. A brief glimpse is all we can spare here. The first phase was the formation of 'Young England' and the devastating attacks on Peel in the Corn Law debates of 1845 and 1846 when he accused the government, after its sudden reversal of policy, of being an 'organized hypocrisy'. Dropping all mannerisms, hypnotizing the House with an unrivalled flow of bitter wit and logic, he appeared as the new, undisputed party spokesman while Peel wilted and cringed under his accusations. Of Peel's *volte-face* he said: 'There is no statesman who has committed political larceny on so great a scale.' He concluded a three-hour speech on the occasion of the third reading by prophesying the end of any form of public confidence in their leaders and eventual economic disaster. It was a fruitless struggle. Peel got his way and the Corn Laws were repealed, but only at the cost of personal humiliation and party disruption. Soon he was out of office for ever, and it was to Dizzy that the shattered remnants of the party looked for new inspiration. In 1847 he was returned for the county of Buckingham, the seat he held until his elevation to the Lords. But Lord John Russell and the Liberals were back in power for the next six years.

After Peel's death, following a riding accident in 1850, Disraeli was the acknowledged opposition leader in the Commons. He was himself a landed proprietor now, with a spacious wooded estate at Hughenden, near his former country home at Bradenham. To the splendid natural surroundings he added one self-indulgent artificial touch – peacocks strutting on the terrace. The money for Hughenden had been advanced by Sir George Bentinck and his brothers. Sir George, a horse-racing nobleman, had sacrificed his sporting activities to support Disraeli in his attacks on the Peelites. Disraeli acknowledged his debt in a biography of his friend, completed in 1851.

The first stage was now completed. The second was to reform the Conservative Party and equip it for office – long years of patient waiting, during which his pen was not idle. The third of the political novels, *Tancred, or The New Crusade*, appeared in 1847. It was the story of a noble Englishman who travels to Jerusalem to seek spiritual guidance and inspiration from the East as an antidote to European materialism. All Disraeli's slightly ambivalent views on Judaism and Christianity were aired in this strange work. The hero defends Jewish traditions and principles as later enshrined in the Church and sees himself as destined to lead a spiritual crusade to save Western civilization. This upsurge of faith coincided with his campaign for Rothschild in the House.

Now he had to reconcile himself to the effects of Free Trade and to concern himself increasingly with the pressing problems of electoral reform and foreign affairs. A brief taste of office came in 1852 when he became Chancellor of the Exchequer under Stanley, now Earl of Derby and evidently reconciled with the man he had once labelled a scoundrel. Disraeli's painstaking, five-hour budget speech was howled down by an opposition which included the former Peelites and led to the formation of Lord Aberdeen's coalition of 'all the talents'. The folly and inept prosecution of the Crimean War brought about the overthrow of that ministry. Derby threw away the chance of power by allowing Palmerston to take over. True, Disraeli got a second chance as Chancellor in 1858 when he tried to introduce a modified Reform Bill, but the Tories were discarded yet again and Palmerston continued as premier until his death in 1865.

In the Liberal ranks the imposing figure of William Ewart Gladstone emerged as Disraeli's most formidable antagonist. A lapsed Peelite, Gladstone was now irrevocably committed to the other side, and during the next fifteen years the House of Commons was to be dominated by these two men, so completely opposed in background, temperament, belief and method. For all their occasional gestures of reconciliation, there was never any love lost between the self-righteous, humourless Gladstone and his sardonic, mercurial rival. Gladstone considered Disraeli diabolical; Disraeli thought Gladstone a maniac.

In 1866 Gladstone introduced a new Reform Bill to replace the obsolete measure of 1832. He was defeated by a combination of Tories and a section of his own party, and Russell's Liberal government collapsed to the background of rioting in Hyde Park. Derby formed his third ministry with Disraeli as Chancellor and it was he, against violent opposition from his own party ('a Conservative surrender'), who steered a Reform Bill through the House by 21 votes. Gladstone was livid at the spectacle of his hated rival assuming the credit for a measure which, by enfranchising borough householders, doubled the electorate. But at least democracy had taken another faltering step forward.

Derby, crippled by gout, retired in February 1868 and recommended Disraeli as his successor. At last the dream was realized. At Osborne he kissed hands with a delighted Queen Victoria. He was by then sixty-three. 'I have climbed to the top of the greasy pole,' he remarked, but never ceased to regret that it had happened twenty years too late. Nor was he firmly in the saddle even now. Gladstone struck back with a proposal to disestablish the Irish Church. Dizzy was defeated and had to wander in the political wilderness for yet another six years.

He was far from idle, but being increasingly plagued by gout and asthma, was no longer the debonair, cosmopolitan favourite of the dinner-table and garden-party. His closest society friends were either dead or divorced. He was becoming increasingly gloomy and introspective, obsessed with religious problems which found expression in another novel, *Lothair*, a satire on society and an assertion of faith in the Anglican Church. Although the Conservative rank-and-file were shocked that their leader should have descended again to romantic novel-writing, the book was enormously popular; 80,000 copies were sold in America within six months.

The same year saw the outbreak of the Franco–Prussian War. Disraeli, always more discerning than his contemporaries, warned against the 'German revolution . . . a greater political event than the French revolution', with its 'new world, new influences at work and the destruction of the balance of power'. In the popular estimation Russia was the arch-enemy. Disraeli was equally wary of the threat posed by Bismarck and his Prussia.

Mary Anne, who had been ailing for years, died of cancer in 1872. Dizzy was shattered. Hughenden was empty and comfortless, Grosvenor Gate cold and unwelcoming. He stayed with friends and spent much of his time in the years to come with two sisters he had first met in London, Lady Chesterfield and Lady Bradford. Although he wrote incessantly to Lady Chesterfield, who was a widow, it was the married Lady Bradford whom he loved. At times his attentions became embarrassing. Finally he was forced to admit defeat, wistfully remarking, 'I have lived to know the twilight of love has its splendours and richness.'

Another lonely widow showered him with condolences on Mary Anne's death and his relationship with her was to affect the nation's destiny. Queen Victoria's friendship for Disraeli had ripened into affection in the years following Albert's death when she had retired into a prison of private grief. Then he had extended sympathy and advice – now he was a warm and understanding friend and counsellor. True, he knew how to flatter her ('I never refuse, I never contradict, I sometimes forget,' he once replied when asked the secret of his success with her), but there is no reason to doubt his sincerity. She opened her heart to him, took him into her complete confidence, showered him with letters and gifts, worried over his health, sending him her own doctor, the renowned Sir William Jenner, when he was ill. Thanks to him she recovered a large measure of the popularity she had forfeited when the Prince Consort died, and it was her support and encouragement that strengthened him when, after Gladstone's defeat in 1874, he was returned to power with a strong mandate.

Undoubtedly, his greatest single act of statesmanship as Prime Minister was to purchase, with Rothschild money, the 177,000 shares in the Suez Canal which opened up a short trade route to India and the Far East. Proudly he announced to his 'faery queen' that the Canal was now hers, and followed it up by introducing the controversial bill that conferred on her the title of 'Empress of India'. Victoria rewarded him by creating him Earl of Beaconsfield. 'I can't forgive him,' muttered Gladstone, 'for not having himself made a Duke.' But he was still a realist. 'Power!' he mused. 'It has come too late. There were days when, on waking, I felt I could move dynasties and governments; but that has passed away.'

After his elevation to the House of Lords, trouble loomed in the Balkans. Fanned by Gladstone's revelation of Turkish atrocities in Bulgaria, England was in danger of being dragged into the war which broke out between Russia and

Turkey in 1877. Popular anti-Russian feeling was reflected by the song on Londoners' lips:

> *'We don't want to fight,*
> *But, by jingo, if we do,*
> *We've got the ships,*
> *We've got the men,*
> *We've got the money too!'*

One of the main issues – how topical it still sounds – was Russian access to the Mediterranean which Disraeli was determined to block, but not at the expense of another Crimean fiasco. Fortunately war was averted. It was Bismarck who convened a Congress in Berlin where Disraeli showed himself a hard bargainer. Russian demands were whittled down, Turkey's prestige was upheld, and Disraeli was able to announce to cheering crowds in Downing Street that he had brought back 'peace with honour'. In fact, he had something more concrete to show from the back-room negotiations. A secret agreement with the Turks ceded the island of Cyprus to Britain in return for a defensive alliance against Russia. Even Bismarck was impressed by Beaconsfield's uncompromising nature. 'The old Jew,' he remarked admiringly, 'that is the man!'

The remaining years in office were overclouded by violence and bloodshed in distant Afghanistan and Zululand, accompanied by trade depressions and poor harvests at home. Gladstone, sensing his chance for a comeback, rallied support in Midlothian and, in the 1880 election, romped home. For Beaconsfield it was the end of public life. He resigned, yet still found time, between bouts of illness, to complete his last novel *Endymion*. Returning to London in the winter of 1881, he took a house in Curzon Street. A few months later he caught a severe chill and he died on 19 April, 1882. The Queen, from the Isle of Wight, sent two wreaths. One consisted of newly-gathered primroses – 'his favourite flower' – and attached to the other was a hand-written message: 'A token of true affection, friendship and respect'. He was laid to rest in the family vault at Hughenden.

Benjamin Disraeli, Earl of Beaconsfield

The literature on Disraeli is considerable and the extent of his achievement still much debated. The novels alone, for all their fantasy and prolixity, remain invaluable for their insight into the social and political realities of the age. As for the forty years of service which he gave to the country – a country which he loved dearly and which only recompensed him late in life, and even then incompletely – the solid achievements are admittedly few, largely because he was a man who towered above the undistinguished ruck of party politics. Conceited, proud, ambitious he may have been on occasion, yet in public life a man without such qualities would be a liar or a saint – and almost certainly a failure. Such 'defects', in his case, were tempered by his honesty, his humanity and the purity of ideals impossible to attain in this world. 'Dreams! Dreams! Dreams!' he was heard to murmur as he sat before the fire, late in life. In an age of hard-headed realism and materialistic preoccupations, dreamers of his calibre were, sadly, all too rare.

Felix Mendelssohn-Bartholdy 1809–1847

In the records of the watch at Berlin's Rosenthaler Gate the following terse entry appeared for an October day in 1743: 'Today there passed through the Rosenthaler Gate six oxen, seven swine, one Jew.' The Jew who was admitted among such distinguished company was a fourteen-year-old hunchbacked boy named Moses Mendelssohn, or, more correctly, Moses son of Mendel of Dessau. He had trudged on foot from his home town to visit his teacher Rabbi Frankel in the Prussian capital. He was eager to acquire knowledge and the first lesson he learned was that in Germany, under Frederick the Great, the Jews were still an oppressed minority forbidden to travel or engage in any trade save old clothes and moneylending, confined to certain sections of towns, denied opportunities of secular education and regarded by their compatriots as, at best, a necessary evil.

Moses, bearer of a proud name, starved and scraped in Berlin and rose to be no more, professionally, than a bookkeeper in a silk factory. But although crippled in body he had an alert, active mind and a delightful personality. The years of study resulted in his becoming one of Germany's most distinguished writers and philosophers, a close friend of Gotthold Lessing who immortalized him as the hero of his play *Nathan the Wise*. This remarkable man was the grandfather of the composer, Felix Mendelssohn.

Moses Mendelssohn's books on literature and religion were widely read, but perhaps the most influential of his works was his translation into German of the Pentateuch and other parts of the Bible. He had taught himself German, for although an orthodox Jew, he realized that by confining itself to Hebrew and Talmudic studies, the Jewish community was acquiescing in its isolation and sowing the seeds of its own social and cultural decay. It was largely due to his spirited defence of Jewish values and his liberal interpretation of the role of Jews in society that by the time his grandson was born, persecution – though not necessarily prejudice – was a thing of the past. True, the seeds were only lying dormant, ready to burst out in a more ghastly harvest of hate a century later; but Felix was born into a more fortunate age, and the fact that religion was no longer a burning issue made it simpler for the descendants of Moses Mendelssohn to exchange Judaism for Christianity.

Moses was happily married and was survived by six children. One daughter, Dorothea, married the poet and critic Friedrich Schlegel, brother of the famous August Wilhelm Schlegel, the poet and translator of Shakespeare. Another daughter, Henrietta, Felix's favourite 'Aunt Jette' who was an accomplished linguist, never married and lived for many years in Paris, where she was tutor to the daughter of General Sebastiani. She, like Dorothea, became a Roman Catholic. The eldest son Joseph founded a banking-house and was later joined by his brother Abraham. Abraham married the wealthy Leah Salomon, became director of the Hamburg branch of the bank, and bought a comfortable mansion in which three of his children were born – Fanny in 1805, Felix in 1809, Rebecca in 1811. The fourth child, Paul, was born in Berlin in 1813. By that time, the Mendelssohns, under pressure from Napoleon's Continental Blockade, were permanent residents there.

The children were all brought up as Protestants, although in deference to their Salomon grandparents, the conversion was kept more or less secret. Leah's own brother had also become a Christian and had adopted the surname Bartholdy and Abraham was persuaded to follow his example. This explains the complicated Mendelssohn-Bartholdy title.

Felix, a handsome child with a sunny disposition, turned out to be a musical prodigy, beginning piano lessons at six and composing by the age of eight when he could play all the Beethoven symphonies on the piano – from memory. He took violin lessons as well, and studied harmony and composition with Carl Zelter. By the time the eminent pianist Moscheles took him in hand at fifteen he was already something of a virtuoso, appearing in recitals and chamber music performances. His sister Fanny was almost as gifted – when she was born Leah had remarked that she had 'Bach-fugue fingers' – but being a girl was not encouraged to the same extent as her brother. It is not surprising that the relationship between brother and sister should have been so close. They were fortunate to possess all the advantages of a comfortable, cultured family background, understanding parents, enlightened teachers, and a large circle of sympathetic and talented friends.

November 1821 was the first landmark in Felix's life. Zelter arranged for him to travel to Weimar to meet the great Goethe, then seventy years old. The old man was enchanted by the personality of this boy with his delicate features, sparkling eyes and soft, black shoulder-length hair. A slight stammer did not prevent him expressing himself with assurance and yet without precosity. And his piano-playing, both technique and interpretation, were extraordinary. His brilliance at improvization amazed Goethe, who commented that he would not have thought it possible at such an age, 'And yet,' remarked Zelter proudly, 'you heard the young Mozart play in Frankfurt in 1763.' Goethe agreed that this boy appeared to be no less remarkable.

Felix's own letters from Weimar are bursting with exuberance and pride. 'Now listen, all of you,' he wrote to his family, 'today is Tuesday. On Sunday the Sun of Weimar, Goethe, arrived', and he proceeded to relate in detail the marvellous events of the next four days:

'He does not look like a man of seventy-three, rather of fifty. After dinner, Fräulein Ulrike, Frau von Goethe's sister, asked him for a kiss, and I followed her example. Every morning I get a kiss from the author of *Fasut* and *Werther*, and every afternoon two kisses from father and friend Goethe. Think of that! In the afternoon I played to Goethe for over two hours, partly Bach fugues and partly my own improvizations. . . . You cannot fancy how good and kind he is to me.'

Thus began a 'Saul and David' friendship which only ended with Goethe's death in 1832; and at the age of sixteen Felix dedicated to his friend his Piano Quartet, Op. 3.

He already had the gift of expressing himself vividly in words, as these early letters show. The most typical and engaging 'Jewish' virtue which he retained was his strong family feelings, especially for Fanny and his father. The Mendelssohn-Bartholdys were all tireless, prolific correspondents – Felix reporting on his latest concert or impressions of Paris and London; Fanny, both before and after her marriage to the artist Wilhelm Hensel, eagerly following her brother's progress and keeping a careful diary of her journeys to Italy and Switzerland; Abraham dispensing firm, sensible advice in all directions. The letters conjure up a picture of a closely-linked, carefree family, particularly when they lived in Berlin at 3 Leipziger Strasse, which Abraham bought in 1825.

This splendid house, well set back from the street, had a huge hall – large enough to hold two hundred people – with a magnificent view over the seven-acre garden, a miniature park in effect. Here family and friends gathered to make music together, and at the table in the garden, one balmy August evening, Felix sat listening to the rustling of the breeze and watching the darting flight of the fireflies, as he put the finishing touches to his gossamer-light overture to *A Midsummer Night's Dream*.

By now he was seventeen and already the composer of a symphony, three quartets, a fine string octet and an opera, *The Wedding of Camacho*, based on the Don Quixote saga. It was produced in Berlin but ran for only one night, receiving poor notices. Opera, quite clearly, was not his natural sphere and he shied away from it after this initial setback, persevering with songs, piano pieces, chamber works and short orchestral compositions. Meanwhile his musical tastes and judgements were being formed. He adored church music and revered Bach, then out of fashion in Germany.

In Paris he had already met Cherubini ('an extinct volcano'), Hummel, Meyerbeer and Rossini. But French music was one of his blind spots and Paris a city which, unaccountably, he hated all his life. When Fanny chided him for intolerance, he replied in a testy letter showing the flash of stubborn temper which now and then disturbed his normally equable temperament. 'You talk of prejudice and bias,' he wrote, 'about being morose and grumbling, and about the "land flowing with milk and honey", as you call this city. Do think a little. Are you in Paris, or am I?' This *allegro feroce*, as he termed it, was only semi-serious, but his views on France and French music, towards which he displayed a rather prudish attitude, never changed. Berlioz, though a personal friend, was a particular *bête noire*.

Two of Goethe's poems inspired the composition, at the age of nineteen, of the serene and attractive overture *A Calm Sea and a Prosperous Voyage*, giving promise of the even finer 'seascape' overture *The Hebrides* which followed his visit to Scotland. But he was far from immersing himself in his own compositions and spent the winter of 1828–9 preparing, with his actor-friend Eduard Devrient, a full-scale revival of Bach's neglected masterpiece, the *St Matthew Passion*.

Accounts vary as to how Felix came across this score. Some say his mother gave him a copy for a birthday present, others that Zelter kept it jealously hidden in a cupboard and that Devrient persuaded him to release it. Whatever the truth, he was captivated by this sublime oratorio with its tranquil arias and dramatic choruses. The two friends put on their most elegant clothes when they called on the eminent soloists they planned to engage – blue jackets over white waistcoats, black trousers, black cravats and yellow gloves; and Felix worked at fever-pitch editing the score, reorchestrating some passages and rehearsing the huge orchestra and four-hundred-strong chorus. On 11 March, 1829, it was performed at the Berlin Singakademie, with such success that a second performance had to be given ten days later; and directing this huge array of vocal and instrumental forces was the young Mendelssohn, supremely assured, Berlin's celebrity of the season.

Barely twenty years old and he had already made his mark as pianist, composer and conductor. But now he ventured abroad to extend his reputation and experience. His dearest friend, Karl Klingemann, had settled in London a few years previously and wrote enthusiastically of the wealth and variety of musical activity there. Italian and German music were equally appreciated; the German-born Handel was still a legend in London. Felix was eager to confirm Klingemann's reports. On 10 April, 1829, with Abraham and Rebecca accompanying him to Hamburg, he set out on the first of ten journeys to England.

His expectations were more than fulfilled, despite a stormy crossing, and his letters home convey his sense of exhilaration.

'It is fearful! It is mad! I am quite giddy and confused. London is the grandest and most complicated monster on the face of the earth. How can I compress into one letter what I have been three days seeing? I hardly remember the chief events, and yet I dare not keep a diary, for then I should see less of life, and that must not be. On the contrary, I want to catch hold of whatever offers itself. Things roll and whirl round me and carry me along as in a vortex. . . . Not in the last six months in Berlin have I seen so many contrasts and such variety.'

He was taken in hand by Klingemann and by Moscheles and his wife, visited the opera, went to concerts and wrote, a few weeks later: 'I am in good health: London life suits me excellently.' On 25 May he conducted a Philharmonic

Society concert introducing his own Symphony in C minor and substituting for the minuet an orchestrated version of the scherzo from his Octet, which was promptly encored. It was an auspicious first public appearance. Thereafter England was to take Mendelssohn to its heart with a spontaneous warmth that he was never to encounter in his native Berlin. 'The public here is good to me and likes me,' he wrote after a concert in which he played Beethoven's Piano Concerto in E flat, and he joined Moscheles in a performance of his own unpublished Double Concerto.

Then he set off with Klingemann to the north. Scotland was another revelation, even in the rain. But when the sun shone, Felix was really in his element. From Arthur's Seat he looked down on Edinburgh with its castle, the Forth with its shipping, like black and white insects. 'Why need I describe it? When God Himself takes to panorama-painting, it turns out strangely beautiful. Few of my Switzerland reminiscences can compare to this.' Then they travelled to Abbotsford to meet Sir Walter Scott. Klingemann described the meeting vividly, but in a postscript Felix glumly remarked: 'This is all Klingemann's invention. We found Sir Walter in the act of leaving Abbotsford, stared at him like fools, drove eighty miles and lost a day for the sake of at best one half-hour of superficial conversation.'

On fine days Felix sketched – he was a talented amateur in this field – while Klingemann jotted down verses on the places they visited. They continued up into the Highlands and to the Hebrides, whose wild, barbaric splendour moved him profoundly. In one letter he wrote: 'In order to make you understand how extraordinarily the Hebrides affected me, the following came into my mind there –' and he sketched twenty bars of music, the opening of what, three years later, developed into the wonderful *Hebrides* or *Fingal's Cave* overture. And the memory of those happy weeks in Scotland was stored up for more than ten years, culminating in the *Scottish* symphony completed and performed in 1842, and dedicated to Queen Victoria.

Towards Wales he was unfairly scathing, writing from Llangollen: 'No national music for me! Ten thousand devils take all nationality! Now I am in Wales, and, dear me, a harper sits in the hall of every reputed inn, playing incessantly so-called national melodies; that is to say, most infamous, vulgar, out-of-tune trash, with a hurdy-gurdy going at the same time! It is distracting, and has given me a toothache already.'

But he received some warm Welsh hospitality from the musician John Edward Taylor at Coed-Du, and brought away pleasant memories of his host's three daughters, to whom he dedicated three Piano Fantasias.

Back in London an accident to his knee kept him indoors for some weeks and to his dismay he was unable to attend Fanny's wedding on 3 October. Klingemann, who was nursing him, devotedly joined him in an exuberant letter of congratulation. At the end of November he was well enough to sail home, describing his last fortnight spent at the Norwood home of the composer Attwood as the happiest and richest he had yet enjoyed.

Next year his strong Protestant fervour found expression in the powerful, but uneven *Reformation* symphony which was not published during his life. At about this time he was offered the post of Professor of Music at Berlin University, turning it down in favour of his friend Adolf Marx. He himself now set out on his first and only trip to Italy, halting at Weimar, where Goethe presented him with a manuscript sheet of *Faust*, with the inscription: 'To my dear young friend Felix Mendelssohn-Bartholdy, the strong and gentle ruler of the piano, in friendly recollection of glad May days in 1830'.

Mendelssohn's *Reisebriefe* – Letters of Travel – vividly convey the emotions and impressions of that extended holiday in Italy. He was away from Berlin for two years. Interspersed with detailed accounts of his visits to Florence and Venice and of his daily life in Rome, where he stayed five months, are letters to Zelter on purely musical matters. The Italian landscape, church music and art treasures impressed him deeply, though the antiquities left him indifferent. He witnessed the ceremonies connected with the coronation of the new Pope and met new and influential friends, including the sculptor Thorvaldsen and the painter Vernet. He began work on the *Scottish* and *Italian* symphonies, completed his G minor Piano Concerto and set to music yet another Goethe poem, *First Walpurgis Night* – a powerful choral work pointing ahead to Wagner and far removed from the Mendelssohn of *Songs Without Words* and *A Midsummer Night's Dream*.

Italy was undeniably a refreshing and rewarding experience, yet for all its warmth and colour he was not drawn irresistibly towards the south in later years. As he confessed to Zelter in a letter from Paris on his way home: 'Having enjoyed the wonderful sights and experiences of Italy and Switzerland, I came back to Germany . . . and realized that here was the climax of my journey. Here I became aware that I am a German, and I knew that I want to live in Germany as long as possible.'

During the next few years he was much in demand as pianist and conductor, giving concerts regularly at the Düsseldorf and Cologne spring festivals. He spent the summer of 1833 pleasantly in London with his father who was scathing about the English climate – his hairdresser referred to a misty dawn, with a watery sun barely visible, as a 'very fine morning'! – and who was then laid up with an ankle injury for a month, while the family fretted in Berlin. Finally he returned home with a young painter he had met, one Alphonse Lavie, as he told his family in advance. The painter turned out to be Felix, who received the customary affectionate welcome.

That autumn Felix accepted the job of musical director in Düsseldorf. His plans to reinvigorate the town's musical life were not entirely successful, mainly because he fell out with Karl Immermann, who ran the local theatre and opera house. His father sensed, and bluntly said so in a letter, that it was probably because he was not getting things all his own way. Yet the two years in Düsseldorf were busy and creative. He started on another volume of his *Songs Without Words*, wrote a fine overture *The Fair Melusine* and plunged into an ambitious choral composition based on the life of St Paul.

In 1835 a better opportunity beckoned from Leipzig. He was invited to conduct the famous Gewandhaus concerts and to become the orchestra's director. Here he was visited by Chopin, and the two men played for each other their compositions. Here he also met another great pianist-composer, Robert Schumann, and Clara Wieck, who later became Schumann's wife. Everything augured well, when he was brought unexpected news of his father's sudden death. He felt the loss deeply, writing to Julius Schubring, who had written the text of *St Paul*, of the 'crushing blow that has fallen on my happy life . . . a trial under which I must either strive to bear up or go down utterly'. Abraham had always been one of his son's most searching critics. Shortly before his father's death Felix wrote: 'I often cannot understand how it is possible to have so acute a judgement towards music, without yourself being technically musical; and if I could express what I undoubtedly feel, with as much clearness and intuitive perception as you do, as soon as you broach the subject, I would never make another obscure speech all my life long.'

Mendelssohn's oratorio *St Paul* was performed at the Lower Rhine Festival at Düsseldorf in May, 1836, but although it was played extensively in the years that followed, it has never achieved the fame or popularity of *Elijah*. Its success at the time, however, helped to lift Mendelssohn's depression and during a visit to Frankfurt he met someone who was to restore his happiness completely – Cecile Jeanrenaud, daughter of a Protestant clergyman, living there with her widowed mother.

There was something deliberate about Felix's courtship – almost as if, after his father's death, it was his duty to follow his sisters' examples and get married in order to raise a family. Nor did he propose to the girl until he had imposed on himself a period of absence at the Dutch seaside resort of Scheveningen. What is more, among all the family letters there is not a single one addressed to her. We cannot doubt that he wrote to her, or that he was deeply fond of her, but this enormous gap in the Mendelssohn correspondence still remains to be filled.

Cecile, though an enthusiastic oil-painter, was not exceptionally cultured or intellectually inclined. But she was pretty and gay, and the serene, gentle domestic background which she provided was the perfect antidote to the frenzied routine of conducting, composing and teaching which was slowly undermining Felix's health. And perhaps he knew exactly what he was doing. Where feminine intellect was concerned, he had encountered it in plenty with the women who had so far dominated his life – his mother, his adoring sisters and his formidably gifted aunts. He was undoubtedly happy with Cecile. She bore him five children, three boys and two girls, and as husband and father he could not be faulted.

As the years passed his reputation increased as he shuttled between Leipzig, Düsseldorf, Frankfurt and Berlin. The compositions flowed rapidly – too rapidly at times – from his pen: songs, psalms, piano pieces, trios and quartets, choral works, overtures and concertos. In 1838 he began the sparkling Violin Concerto in E minor, completed six years later (another Violin Concerto was recently discovered in manuscript and added to the repertoire by Yehudi Menuhin). And he planned a new oratorio on the theme of *Elijah*.

Then he was tempted by the new king of Prussia, Friedrich Wilhelm IV, to return to Berlin as head of the music department of a projected Academy of Arts. The salary was good but the duties vaguely defined. He moved temporarily to Berlin and the negotiations dragged on interminably for several years. At the king's request he composed the music for Sophocles' *Antigone* which was performed at the royal theatre at Potsdam. The king commissioned more works and awarded him an Order of Merit, but a permanent post in Berlin still failed to entice him. He decided to remain in Leipzig. It was a wise and fortunate decision, for it enabled him to complete a long-cherished plan – the foundation and virtual directorship of the great Leipzig Conservatoire which was ceremonially opened in the spring of 1843. One of his earliest pupils there was a boy named Joseph Joachim, of whom Mendelssohn wrote in glowing terms to the English composer Sterndale Bennett: 'Of all the young talents that are now going about the world I know none that is to be compared with this violinist.' His judgement was correct, as Joachim's subsequent musical career proved.

London still drew Mendelssohn back regularly, and it was in the summer of 1842 that England's favourite foreign composer paid a call on the young Queen Victoria and her husband at Buckingham Palace. It was a delightfully informal occasion. Albert played a chorale on the organ and Felix reciprocated with a passage from *St Paul* while Albert managed the stops. The queen then instituted a search for the scores of Mendelssohn's first set of songs, and after removing a pet parrot from the room she sang to Felix's accompaniment. She happened to select one of Fanny's compositions which she performed 'quite charmingly, in strict time and tune, and with great feeling'. Only when she came to one line, reported Felix, 'where it goes down to D and then comes up again by semitones, she sang D sharp each time; and because I gave her the note the first two times, the last time she sang D where it ought to have been D sharp. But with the exception of this little mistake it was really charming, and the last long G I have never heard better or purer or more natural from any amateur.' She then obliged with one of Felix's own songs, and the session ended with the composer improvising on the piano on themes played during the afternoon. He received permission to dedicate to the queen his *Scottish* symphony and walked away in the rain, well satisfied.

Leah Mendelssohn died that winter, just after the foundation of the Conservatoire, and in its first season Berlioz was one of the honoured guests. Fanny wrote in her diary: 'When the time came for parting, Berlioz offered to exchange batons, "as the ancient warriors exchanged their armour", and in return for Felix's pretty light stock of whalebone covered with white leather, sent an enormous cudgel of limetree with the bark on, and an open letter beginning, "Le mien est grossier, le tien est simple!" A friend of Berlioz who brought the two translated this sentence, "I am coarse and you are simple", and was in great perplexity how to conceal the apparent rudeness from Felix.' They parted good friends, though Felix was still not reconciled to the French composer's music.

He returned to Frankfurt at the end of 1844, the Berlin situation being resolved, but he was physically exhausted.

1845 proved a fertile year for composition and in the summer the family settled again permanently in Leipzig. *Elijah* was completed and performed for the first time in August, 1846 at the Birmingham Festival. Felix wrote to his brother Paul: 'No work of mine ever went so admirably at its first performance, nor was received with such enthusiasm by both musicians and audience. . . . No less than four choruses and four arias were encored.' At the first London performance, Albert sent a warm message to 'the noble artist who, though encompassed by the Baal-worship of false art, by his genius and study has succeeded, like another Elijah, in faithfully preserving the worship of true art'.

Next year he returned to England for another six performances of *Elijah* and a tiring succession of concerts and social functions, including a visit to Buckingham Palace. His health was strained to the limits and friends remarked that he seemed to have aged prematurely. Shortly after his return home he received the news of Fanny's sudden death of a stroke during a rehearsal of her choir. He fell to the ground, unconscious, and although he recovered his health a little during a holiday in Switzerland, was a broken man physically and spiritually. He sketched half-heartedly, put the finishing touches to some compositions, but became seriously ill in that autumn of 1847. On 4 November he died peacefully, six months after his sister. Cecile survived him for only six years.

His had been a short and crowded life, and he had made his rightful mark as one of the greatest piano virtuosi and romantic composers of the nineteenth century. If he fell short of the achievements of Mozart and Beethoven it was possibly because he composed with too much ease and some lack of discrimination. Ironically, a life which was almost entirely free of care and suffering prevented him from striking the note of profundity and achieving the range of emotional expression that less happily circumstanced composers brought to their music. His happy, extrovert temperament, which endeared him to his family and to innumerable friends and colleagues, rendered him immune to personal hostility during his lifetime.

Curiously, it was Richard Wagner, whose music he so admired, who launched the first vicious attack on his reputation and memory in a pamphlet entitled *Judaism in Music*. It was published a few years after Mendelssohn's death, under the pseudonym of Karl Freigedank. And so the man who had prided himself on his patriotism and his loyalty to the church, who had never considered himself a Jew or as much as mentioned Judaism in his letters, went down to posterity as a Jewish composer, and, according to Wagner, as one who had dangerously polluted the mainstream of German musical life. The Nazis, less than a century later, were not remiss in elaborating on this miserable argument, and had his music banned, his books and scores destroyed. The restoration of his reputation in Germany has been slow, and it is in England where his image remains freshest and his work most frequently performed. It is safe to predict that his songs and piano pieces, his overtures, concertos and symphonies, his Octet, and – despite some lapses of inspiration – *Elijah*, will long be played and loved. 'Blue sky and sunshine benefit my very heart; they are so indispensable to me!' he once wrote. His most enduring music has the radiance and carefree high spirits of those summer days in which he delighted.

Rachel
1821–1858

In the summer of 1842 Charlotte Brontë, having just arrived in Brussels, went to the theatre. The famous French actress, Rachel, was playing her first season in the Belgian capital. At twenty-two she was already the rage of Paris and London. It was no ordinary theatrical experience, as the staid young governess from Yorkshire was to recall later, describing Vashti, in *Villette*:

'I had heard this woman termed "plain", and I expected bony harshness and grimness – something large, angular, sallow. What I saw was the shadow of a royal Vashti – a queen, fair as the day once, turned pale now like twilight, and wasted like wax in flame.

'For a while – a long while – I thought it was only a woman, though an unique woman, who moved in might and grace before this multitude. By and by I recognized my mistake. Behold! I found upon her something neither of woman nor of man: in each of her eyes sat a devil. These evil forces bore her through the tragedy, kept up her feeble strength – for she was but a frail creature; and as the action rose and the stir deepened, how wildly they shook her with the passions of the pit! They wrote HELL on her straight, haughty brow. They tuned her voice to the note of torment. They writhed her regal face to a demoniac mask. Hate and murder and madness incarnate she stood.

'It was a marvellous sight: a mighty revelation.

'It was a spectacle low, horrible, immoral. . . .'

Charlotte Brontë, perceptive as always, was enthralled, yet somehow repelled by Rachel's tormented genius.

Out of the gutter, on to the stage of the Comédie Française, into the glittering salons of the Faubourg Saint-Germain and the royal courts of Europe – this was a genuine tale of rags to riches.

She was born Elisabeth Rachel Félix in a Swiss wayside inn in 1821. Her father Jacob was a pedlar, her mother a secondhand clothes dealer. Before she was ten, the frail, plain, underfed little girl was out on the Paris streets with her elder sister Sarah, earning money for the growing Félix family by giving dramatic recitations and singing bawdy or patriotic songs to the accompaniment of a guitar. Arsène Houssaye, Rachel's friend and later her nominee to the directorship of the Comédie Française, tells how Victor Hugo once stopped to pat her on the head and give her a silver coin. Like many of the Houssaye stories, it is probably untrue. It is a fact, however, that she was eventually discovered by Etienne Choron, director of a singing school, who launched her on what was to be a fabulous stage career.

The various teachers of drama who trained her during the next few years were quick to recognize the unusual, precocious talent of this 'ugly duckling'. Lacking any formal education, she responded eagerly to the rolling cadences of the classical tragic playwrights Corneille and Racine. On 4 April, 1837, she made her début in the tiny Théâtre du Gymnase in a melodrama called *La Vendéenne* based on Scott's *Heart of Midlothian*. In the audience was the famous critic Jules Janin who announced: 'There is a great future in store for this gifted child.' He was not put off in the slightest by her lack of inches or by the unbecoming red hat with yellow rose which she was wearing when he went round to congratulate her.

Her heart was set on the one and only Comédie Française, and she was soon to achieve her ambition, thanks to the actor and teacher Joseph-Isidore Samson who, welcoming her as a daughter into his own family circle, turned this rising young star, talented but inexperienced, into a mature, professional actress – queen of the Paris theatre at the age of eighteen.

In her début at the *Théâtre Français* on 12 June, 1938, she played Camille in Corneille's *Horace*, a part in which she won international acclaim. Recognizing Janin after the performance she reminded him, proudly and ungrammatically: *'C'est moi que j'étai t'au Gymnase.'* Smartly, he replied, *'Je le savions!'* Two days later he wrote ecstatically of 'the most astonishing, most marvellous little girl the present theatrical generation has seen . . . a lively, powerful intelligence served by a frail body; a blade of gold in a sheath of clay'.

From that moment she was made. In an age which had turned its back on classical tragedy, in a Paris riding on the crest of the new wave of Romanticism, she restored the plays of Corneille and Racine to their former peak of popularity, bringing to them a new lease of intensity and passion, breathing life and feeling into the heroic characters whom convention had represented as stilted, two-dimensional and unreal. King Louis-Philippe, a rare theatre-goer, exclaimed after seeing Rachel in Corneille's *Cinna*: 'You have brought back the great days of French tragedy.'

Paris was at her feet, and she now set about conquering the salons as well as the boards. Soon she was scandalizing society and agitating her relatives and friends with a series of notorious and well-publicized love affairs. Among the first was Dr Louis Véron, a fat, balding, scrofulous individual who had made a fortune out of selling pills, and who was now a tremendous power in the literary and theatrical world. Presumably she accepted this unsavoury character for that reason alone. Certainly she had other lovers, very possibly including the poet Alfred de Musset, and she was not unnaturally enraged when Véron set detectives on her trail and gave a public reading to his friends of her love letters. Yet this liaison had the desired effect. Despite her obvious ambition, her insolence, her common background (of which she made great capital), she was received by society with open arms. In the gilded drawing-rooms she put on performances every bit as convincing as those on the stage. Her charm, her smile, her vivacity and her passionate temperament assured the social success she craved.

News of the new star crossed the Channel and in 1841 she made her English début at Her Majesty's Theatre in Racine's *Andromaque*. The reviews were unanimous in her praise. Performances were packed out and London society, to her delight, emulated Paris. She visited Epsom with the Home Secretary, Lord Normanby, recited poetry to the Countess of Jersey and the Marchioness of Aylesbury, had dinner with Palmerston, received the Duke of Wellington, called on the Rothschilds at Richmond, and gave a private recital for Queen Victoria at Windsor. Fanny Kemble wrote:

'She is completely the rage in London now; all the fine ladies and gentlemen crazy after her, the Queen throwing her roses on the stage out of her own bouquet, and viscountesses and marchionesses driving her about, *à l'envie l'une de l'autre*, to show her all the lions of the town.'

Only one danger signal disturbed the placid scene. She had to spend four days in bed, writing to her friend and lawyer, Adolphe Crémieux: 'The name of the illness is haemorrhage.' And Fanny Kemble had also remarked, ominously: 'Her want of chest and breadth indeed almost suggest a tendency to pulmonary disease, coupled with her pallor and her youth. . . .'

But nothing could stop her now. Unconcerned by gossip, careless of her health, she threw herself frenziedly into the strenuous round of rehearsals and performances, provincial tours and foreign seasons. Life off the stage was just as frenzied, as one lover followed another. M. and Mme Crémieux had begged her to break with the odious Véron and her refusal to do so ended their friendship with her for many years. But eventually she found a worthier successor, no less than the Prince de Joinville, third son of the King himself. The indomitable Houssaye recounts – and it is a good story even if he made it up – how the handsome, popular, profligate prince simply sent up a card to Rachel's dressing-room, with the words: '*Où? Quand? Combien?*', to which she, with equal directness, replied, '*Chez toi. Ce soir. Pour rien.*'

The affair lasted, off and on, some seven years and carried her to the pinnacle of French society. It is not surprising that she made enemies too. Her acts of impulsive generosity alternated with episodes that showed her in less creditable light. For example, there is the well-authenticated story of the dinner-party when she begged her host to give her a silver centre-piece from his dinner-table. She insisted on taking it home with her in his carriage, to which he coldly replied: 'Certainly, Mademoiselle, but you won't forget, will you, to send back my carriage?' And there is the guitar which she 'borrowed' from an artist, decorated with ribbons, hung on her drawing-room wall and passed off as the very instrument she had played on the Paris streets. She then sold it to a prominent financier for one thousand louis.

There are any number of such tales, shocking or amusing, depending on the biographer's and reader's tolerance. But even the writers who professed themselves most shocked by Rachel's immorality were agreed on one thing – that throughout her life she remained loyal to her faith and to her family. Her father whose avarice increased in proportion to his comfort and security acted as her unofficial business manager and held the Théâtre Français to ransom on more than one occasion. He was a rough, uncompromising, domineering individual, while his wife, more worldly-wise, was evidently more concerned about her daughter's health and future. Rachel settled them in a magnificent country house at Montmorency. Her elder sister Sarah ran up enormous debts with her notorious supper parties, which Rachel paid. To her younger and favourite sister Rebecca she was especially devoted, presenting her with a sumptuously furnished house towards the end of her tragically short life. Thanks to Rachel's support Sarah, Rebecca, her brother Raphael and two younger sisters embarked on successful stage careers.

Above left: Samuel Alexander, the Australian-born Professor of Philosophy at Manchester University and author of the brilliant book *Space, Time and Deity*.

Above right: Theodor Herzl, author and journalist, who founded the Zionist Organization, paving the way for the establishment of the State of Israel fifty years later.

Below: In August, 1949, the remains of Herzl were re-interred at a ceremony outside Jerusalem. The site of his tomb was named Mount Herzl. Today his memory is honoured throughout the Jewish world.

Right: Rufus Isaacs, First Marquess of Reading, lawyer, judge and Viceroy of India. *Centre:* An historic picture. Frederick Seddon is sentenced to death by Mr Justice Bucknill in 1912 for poisoning his lodger, Eliza Mary Barrow. Rufus Isaacs was the prosecutor in this, his only murder case. *Bottom:* Rufus Isaacs and the Solicitor-General, John Simon, received knighthoods after appearing on behalf of King George V in the Rex *v.* Mylius case in 1911.

The family, in one guise or other, was constantly at her elbow. Although not all deserved it, she rewarded them all handsomely.

Next in line for her favours – or possibly concurrently, for nobody could keep an accurate record of number or sequence – was Count Walewski, illegitimate son of the Emperor Napoleon and the Polish Marie Walewska. A widower, not unlike his father in appearance but singularly lacking in charm or intelligence, he established his new conquest in a splendid house in the Rue Trudon. In her immense dining-room, decorated with frescoes, Rachel dined her guests off solid silver or Sèvres plates, with a gold-engraved 'R' in the centre, while in the white and gold drawing-room upstairs she continued to dazzle the cream of Parisian society. The entertaining Houssaye alleges that the menu which Rachel served to Walewski at their first encounter read as follows:

Saucisson à l'ail de Toulon
Omelette au jambon de Mayence
Andouilles à la Bonaparte
Poulet à la Marengo
Bombe glacée à la Moskowa

Rachel's devotion to the Napoleonic legend (disregarding the ambiguity of the final item on the menu) was amply demonstrated by her intimacy with two, if not three, of the Emperor's descendants.

Meanwhile her public career went from strength to strength, the critics noting new signs of maturity with every addition to the repertoire. On 24 January, 1843, she played her famous part of Phèdre for the first time. Janin, tireless in her praise, had slight doubts and Rachel herself was dissatisfied. Ten years later she was the jealous, lustful, tragic queen incarnate. But even now Théophile Gautier, eccentric high priest of the Romantic movement, was fascinated and awed by her 'fatal, sinister air of a victim devoted to some horrible expiation'; and G. H. Lewes wrote: 'It was terrible in its vehemence and abandonment; eloquent in its horror; fierce and rapid, as if the thoughts were crowding upon her brain in tumult, and varied with such amazing compass of tones, that when she left the scene our nerves were quivering with excitement almost insupportable.' Yet amid the enthusiastic reviews and public acclaim Rachel still found time to write to her old teacher Samson: 'I've studied my sobs. I don't dare to boast about the second performance, but I'm sure they'll come to me. I didn't see you in the wings, but I will look out for you when I come on stage, to see whether you are satisfied.'

Rachel, as she had the wit to realize, was unchallenged in classical tragedy, but on several occasions she succumbed to the temptation of modern melodrama. Delphine de Girardin was one of the many playwrights who longed to create parts for Paris' leading actress. Rachel consented to play the lead in her play *Judith*. The part of the Jewish biblical heroine seemed tailor-made for her, but it proved to be a wretchedly written piece, running for only nine performances, and never recovering from a disastrous first night when a small grey cat wandered on to the stage at the climactic moment of the killing of Holofernes, and set the audience in uproar. Later Rachel was to console herself with the attentions of Émile de Girardin, the unfortunate author's husband. Delphine, nothing daunted, followed up *Judith* with *Cléopâtre*, a role which Rachel played a few years later and which was equally unsuccessful, though for other reasons, as we shall see.

In her own field Rachel would stand no opposition. One young actress, Mlle Maxime, who presumed to challenge her, was vanquished on the battlefield. The climax of their rivalry occurred one night when both actresses met on the stage, Mlle Maxime as Queen Elizabeth, Rachel as Mary Stuart, in the play *Marie Stuart*. In the third act, before an expectant and violently partisan audience, the two women poured out their hatred for each other – in verse. Janin described how Maxime seemed crushed and cowered by Rachel's ferocious delivery of her lines, culminating in the triumphant cry, 'I have plunged the dagger into my rival's heart,' leaving nobody in doubt as to her real meaning. The luckless Maxime was finished as an actress.

In the spring of 1844 she found herself pregnant. She continued acting up to two weeks before the delivery. She even tried her hand in Molière, but comedy did not come naturally to her and she did not often repeat the exercise. Her first son, Alexandre, was born shortly before she parted from his father, Walewski, but at least he acknowledged the child: strange to think that the boy's grandfathers were a pedlar and the late Emperor Napoleon.

Walewski broke off the affair, probably having discovered her new liaison with de Girardin, and he married a Florentine noblewoman. He took Alexandre with him, but Rachel who was passionately fond of the child pleaded for his return, and the count complied.

Nevertheless Rachel was far from happy. She was plagued by fits of depression and prolonged bouts of poor health. She made this the excuse for cutting short a season at the Comédie Française but still managed to fulfil engagements in London – now expectantly awaiting her regular appearances – and in Holland. So she resigned from the Comédie Française, knowing well that she held them in the palm of her hand. It only needed a change of management for her to return on her own terms.

For her next lover she again turned, obliquely this time, in the direction of the Bonapartes. He was Arthur Bertrand, the dissolute son of Napoleon's former Grand Marshal. He was also the lover of Rachel's friend Virginie Déjazet, the queen of French farce. Rachel had no qualms about taking over Bertrand, but to her credit she resolutely refused to pay his enormous gambling debts. Soon she became pregnant again. The indefatigable playwright Eugène Scribe, who had written a play for her with Ernest Legouvé, wrote to his collaborator, as if it were a personal insult: 'You have probably heard the trick the wretch has played on us – she is five months pregnant. The news is official, and anyway, the comet is visible to the naked eye. I am trying to get her to play *Cléopâtre* before her confinement. After that she will be able to give us her undivided attention.' *Cléopâtre*, Mme de Girardin's second play for Rachel, was even more inept than the first, but Rachel's presence was enough to fill the theatre.

She took the opportunity of advertising her private drama in no uncertain terms, gazing up longingly from her royal couch to the box where Arthur Bertrand sat flushed with embarrassment. Gautier, among others, praised her majesty and passion to which were added unfamiliar qualities such as charm, seductiveness and humour. But Rachel, pleading fatigue, abandoned the play after a few nights.

Her second son, Gabriel-Victor, was born shortly afterwards, but was never accepted by Bertrand as his son. Well might he have had his doubts, for Rachel was soon to choose, perhaps already had chosen as his successor yet another Bonaparte – Prince Napoleon, son of King Jerome of Westphalia (a younger brother of the Emperor), nicknamed Plon-Plon. Hardly a love-match this, but Plon-Plon remained surprisingly loyal to his mistress – and to her memory.

1848 was the year of revolution in Europe. Louis Napoleon, another nephew of the Emperor, and also an admirer (if not more, as Houssaye hinted) of Rachel's, proclaimed himself Prince-President. The *Théâtre Français* changed its name to Théâtre de la République. The 'Marseillaise' was sung in the streets, and Rachel, sensing the public mood, decided to bring it to the stage. It was a fantastic success, and only she could have brought it off. After a performance of *Horace*, she moved to the front of the stage dressed in a simple white tunic, carrying the Tricolor. Passionately she declaimed the words of Rouget de Lisle's anthem, sinking to her knees amid the folds of the flag to tumultuous applause. While other theatres remained empty, the crowds flocked in to hear Rachel as Liberty.

Scribe and Legouvé soon had the satisfaction of seeing Rachel appear in their play, and its success exceeded their wildest dreams. *Adrienne Lecouvreur* was the story of the celebrated actress who, defeated by a rival in love, committed suicide by poison. Rachel ran the entire gamut of tragic emotions and the part was certainly the most popular with audiences, outside Corneille and Racine. There was a touching and revealing episode at one of the rehearsals when the actress' mask dropped long enough to reveal momentarily the loneliness and despair which were never far beneath the surface charm and gaiety. Legouvé complimented her on her performance and suggested that in the absence of an audience she had become Adrienne herself. Rachel replied quietly: 'You are wrong. But a strange thing happened. I had a sudden premonition that I, too, should die young. It seemed to me that I was in my own room, at my last hour, watching my own death. And when I came to the line, "Farewell, my triumphs of the stage! Farewell, the raptures of the art I have loved so well!" you saw me shed real tears. I was thinking that time would soon carry away all trace of my talent, and that soon there would be nothing left of her who was once Rachel.'

Another misunderstanding with the Comédie Française led to a further resignation threat, but she returned in triumph after bringing pressure on them to appoint her old friend Houssaye as Director. Yet the public mood was changing. Melodrama, farce and domestic comedy were increasingly in vogue, and her two new experiments in romantic drama, Dumas' *Mademoiselle de Belle Isle* and Hugo's *Angelo*, were not successful. The critics continued to applaud her indiscriminately, but she remained unconvinced. To Legouvé she confided wistfully: 'I haven't achieved a quarter of what I might have done. I have had talent: I could have had genius. If only I had had a different upbringing. If only I had had different people around me. What an artist I should have become.'

Yet her foreign seasons were as successful as ever. London acclaimed her again in 1850 and in the year of the Great Exhibition. In Italy and Germany she repeated her classical triumphs. And in the summer of 1852 she performed in the open air before the Czar, in Germany. He was so captivated that he invited her in the spring of 1854 to perform in St Petersburg. It was the eve of the Crimean War. The Comédie Française reluctantly gave her a year's leave of absence. Her current lover, a poet and dramatist named Ponsard, protested to no avail. Legouvé who had written a new play for her, *Médée*, was enraged. Her patriotism was questioned. But Rachel was in no mood to turn down the most glittering, lucrative invitation of her entire career and

off she went, travelling by train via Warsaw, on to her conquest of Russia.

She was received and regaled like a queen and sent long,
breathless accounts of her progress, in her disjointed, un-
grammatical style, to her mother. She revelled in every minute
of it – the banquets, the champagne, the expensive gifts, the
warmth of royal approbation, the thunder of public acclaim.
But on her journey home she received shattering news.
Rebecca, only twenty-three, was dying of typhus. She hurried
back to nurse her, but on 19 June her sister died.

It aged her overnight. She herself was now desperately ill
and her renewed threat to resign from the *Comédie Française*
was sincerely meant. Janin managed to persuade her to return for a final season, but the writing was on the wall. She
had returned from Russia to find a young Italian actress,
Adrienne Ristori, poised to topple her from her throne.
Legouvé was suing her for breach of contract, and although
she managed to retain the legal services of her old friend
Crémieux, now reconciled after many years, she lost the case
and had to pay heavy damages. A new play, *Rosemonde*,
a lurid affair of adultery and murder, repelled both critics
and public. Janin, calling at her home, was shocked and distressed at her appearance. He found her 'breathless, distraught, wordless, motionless. . . . Perplexed in soul and sick
in spirit, feeble in health, she had no more courage, no more
hope.' She summoned up enough strength to appear in
Scribe's new play *La Czarine* for eighteen performances,
followed by a few appearances in her classical repertoire.
And Paris, though it did not know it, had seen the last of its
idol.

It had not been a calculated, inevitable farewell. For she
fully intended to come back. But first she had to score over
La Ristori. An invitation had been sent to her from America.
Against her better judgement, against the advice of her doctors and friends, but egged on by her father and her brother
Raphael, her business manager, she decided to accept, promising to return to the Comédie Française the following
season. The singer Jenny Lind had recently earned a fortune
in the United States. She, with her reputation, would do

better still. She left from the Gare du Nord one July morning in 1855, played a short season – her last – at the St James' Theatre, and then boarded the *Pacific* for New York.

The American trip proved to be an utter disaster. New York gave her a royal welcome with flags, bunting and champagne, but the public never warmed to the unfamiliar convention of French classical tragedy. During that bitter winter she caught a cold and a racking cough. In Boston and Philadelphia the takings were disappointing. Contracts had to be cancelled, and her last ever performance was given in a dingy, obscure theatre in Charleston, South Carolina. Off they sailed, despondent but with a sense of relief, to the warmer climate of Cuba.

She was in no condition to carry on. Week after week she remained listlessly in her Havana bedroom, racked with pain, writing pathetic letters, knowing her days were now numbered. 'I am ill, very ill indeed,' she wrote. 'My body and mind have fallen away to nothing. . . . I am bringing back my poor routed army to the banks of the Seine; and perhaps, like another Napoleon, I shall myself come to the Invalides to die, and ask for a stone on which to lay my head.'

At the end of February 1856, Rachel sailed back to France, spending a lonely spring in a country house near Versailles, then a few fruitless months taking the waters at Ems. In October, in a desperate attempt to regain her health, she set sail for Egypt. On board she met a young naval lieutenant, Gabriel Aubaret, a pious Catholic, who though unsuccessful in converting her to Christianity devoted himself during her last year to her care and comfort. But her letters home, to Houssaye and to her mother, were poignant and despairing. In the spring she returned home, sold her mansion in the Rue Trudon and spent the summer in Montpellier, near Aubaret's home. Here she lived quietly, visited occasionally by old friends such as Houssaye and Ponsard, darting back to Paris in June on a mysterious errand. She stayed in a house in the Place Royale, attended by Aubaret, and on one misty autumn morning, took a carriage on a lonely pilgrimage. She made the driver stop twice, once before the

Théâtre du Gymnase, once in front of her beloved Théâtre Français. Then she drove home.

The last few months were spent in the south, at Le Cannet near Cannes, in a villa overlooking the Mediterranean. There, on the evening of 3 January, 1857, she died. On 11 January, her funeral procession set out from the Place Royale and she was buried in the Jewish section of the Père Lachaise cemetery. Representatives of the arts and all the leading Paris theatres were there. Only her old teacher and friend Samson was absent. Vindictive to the last, Jacob Félix refused to have him present.

The great Rachel was dead, at the age of thirty-six. She left no natural successor, founded no school, created no tradition. Yet for twenty splendid years she reigned as a queen. She lived and loved passionately and unsparingly. Her life was a mass of contradictions, but in one thing she was consistent. She remained true to her faith to the end.

It was Janin who had the last word as he delivered the oration by her graveside. He described Rachel as 'the youngest and greatest artist of our age'. That would have satisfied even Rachel.

Sigmund Freud
1856–1939

Thirty years after his death Sigmund Freud remains something of an enigma. Mention his name in polite drawing-rooms and you are likely to raise a few embarrassed giggles or to spark off the latest 'Oedipus Complex' joke. The man in the street is as ignorant of Freud's work as his counterpart was sixty years ago. Even in so-called 'informed circles' psycho-analysis is frequently regarded as a bit of a joke, the hobby of rich Americans, the last desperate resort of the defence counsel.

Freud himself would not have been a bit surprised. Controversy and opposition surrounded him at every stage of his career, and his story is one of continuous struggle – against poverty, against a hidebound medical profession, against anti-semitism, against dissenting colleagues, against illness and mortal disease. Yet it was also an epic story of single-mindedness, of an obsessional quest for knowledge, of courage and faith. Anyone who wants to delve thoroughly into the character of the man and the significance of his work is best advised to read the superb biography written by his friend and colleague Ernest Jones. This is the most accurate and fair-minded survey of Freud we are likely to get and it refutes many of the ill-informed and malicious legends which were freely circulated even while he was alive.

One other point needs making in this introductory section. We can do no more than trace the main outlines of his long career, indicating his major contributions in the field of psycho-analysis and recording certain essential aspects of his character, based on his own writings and the opinions of those who knew him. No layman is entitled to discuss his theories in detail or to compare them with those of other schools of thought. All we can attempt to do here is to convey something of the scope of his achievement as the founder of psycho-analysis, the man who revealed the vast unconscious areas of the mind, who discovered the underlying causes of adult neuroses stemming from forgotten childhood experiences, who discovered the hidden significance of dreams and fantasies, and whose scientific curiosity ranged over the fields of philosophy, sociology, theology, anthropology, literature and the arts. No matter that some of his theories have been challenged or superseded. There is enough that remains of permanent value and mankind is in his debt.

Sigmund Freud was born on 6 May, 1856, in Freiberg, a pleasant little town in Moravia, then part of the Austro-Hungarian Empire. His father Jakob was a wool merchant, but the family was not well off. The fortunes of the town itself were declining, owing to the advance of new industrial techniques, and as German-speaking Jews the Freud family were caught up in the surging wave of Czech nationalism with its unpleasant anti-semitic undercurrents.

At birth the child had a covering of black hair and was hailed by his mother as her 'little Moor'. A peasant woman who attended the birth predicted that he would one day be a great man. His mother believed it implicitly and the young Sigmund was firmly resolved to see the prediction fulfilled, especially after hearing his father remark casually, when he was still at school, that he would never amount to anything.

The family pattern was a complicated one. Sigmund was his mother's eldest child and her favourite, but she was his father's second wife. He had two elder half-brothers, Emanuel and Philipp, and subsequently five sisters and two brothers, one of whom died at eight months. Since Emanuel had two children when Sigmund was born, he was already an uncle, and his father a grandfather. There was also a Nannie, described by Freud as a 'prehistoric old woman' who was an ardent Catholic in the midst of a Jewish household. The situation proved bewildering at times for the growing boy and in later years he was to unravel the threads of childhood memories in an attempt to assess their influence on his development. For any deep study of Freud's personality these early experiences are important – the conflicting love-hate relationship with a much older father, the lavish affection of his mother, the unexplained disappearance of Nannie, the close emotional link with his nephew John, the shock of his younger sister's birth and so on. But to outward appearances Sigmund's childhood was serene and uneventful. He was a lively, alert, intelligent little boy, and if there were inner conflicts (and it was Freud who showed that these are common to us all), it is misleading to exaggerate their significance.

When he was three the family moved to Leipzig and then to Vienna. Here he was to live for the next seventy-nine years. Emanuel and his family went to Manchester and Sigmund only saw them at rare intervals, often envying their good fortune in finding refuge in a relatively enlightened country. Vienna was a gay, stimulating city, but strongly anti-semitic in feeling despite a ten per cent Jewish population. Although he worked here all his life, it was among the last of the major capitals to recognize the importance of his work and it was from abroad that he received his main inspiration and encouragement.

Sigmund worked hard and was head of his class at the *Sperl Gymnasiun* for six years running, finally graduating *summa cum laude*. He was a voracious reader, spoke French, Italian, English and Spanish in addition to the classics, had a phenomenal memory and showed an indiscriminate interest in science, literature, history and the arts. He considered law as a profession and then settled on medicine. He claimed that it was partly fascination with Darwin's theories and partly his discovery of Goethe's *Essay on Nature* which led to this decision; and although he was not yet attracted towards any particular branch, science was unquestionably his chosen path. 'I was moved,' he wrote, 'by a sort of curiosity, which was, however, directed more toward human concerns than toward natural objects.'

He tried zoology and chemistry at University before deciding to concentrate on physiology. He spent six happy and rewarding years under the renowned Ernst Brücke and his brilliant assistant Ernst von Fleischl–Marxow, but the practical problem of a permanent career was no nearer solution. 'The various branches of medicine proper, apart from psychiatry, had no attraction for me. I was decidedly negligent in pursuing my medical studies, and it was not until 1881 that I took my somewhat belated degree as a Doctor of Medicine.'

It was Brücke who eventually persuaded him to begin doing practical work at the Vienna General Hospital, and he acquired a wide range of experience in several departments. He became junior resident physician, worked for six months on cerebral anatomy, and in 1885 was appointed Lecturer in Neuropathology. Having made an intensive study of the nervous systems of invertebrates and humans he now turned his attentions to the field of nervous diseases, a largely unexplored area of medicine. Gradually he built up a reputation for his researches and publications on this subject.

Yet he was still much concerned about the future. He was not earning a comfortable living, hospital work failed to absorb him, his health was indifferent, and he had fallen in love. Martha Bernays whom he met in April, 1882, was a gentle, gay, intelligent girl from Hamburg. It was undoubtedly a love match. During their long four-year engagement Freud poured out his heart in some 900 letters, revealing a depth of feeling which, prior to their publication, many biographers had denied. But it was a difficult period, what with opposition from Martha's family, pressure of work, jealousy of her men friends, antipathy towards her brother (who was married to Sigmund's sister), doubts about his true feelings towards her and vice versa, and continual worries about his health and his future. They became secretly engaged in June, 1883, but it was to be three years before they married. There were long periods of separation during which he continued to work feverishly at the hospital, on his research, and on the nature and properties of cocaine. Despite the claims of a colleague, it was Freud who was largely responsible for discovering the pain-killing properties of the drug, using it to relieve his own father's eye trouble, but arousing a storm of protest when cases of cocaine addiction came to light. Finally, in Freud's laconic words: 'In the autumn of 1886 I settled down in Vienna as a physician, and married the girl who had been waiting for me in a distant city for more than four years.'

The previous autumn and winter had been spent in Paris and were to prove crucially important to his future. Here, for a few months, he studied at the Salpêtrière, the city's insane asylum, where Jean Marie Charcot was doing pioneer work on hysteria and hypnotic treatment. Freud was intrigued by Charcot's methods and personality. He wrote about Charcot: 'He was not a thinker, but a man of artistic temperament – to use his own word – a "seer" . . . It was his practice with things that were new to him to look at them again and again, intensifying the impression of them from day to day, until suddenly and spontaneously understanding would come. . . .' These were methods which Freud was himself to adopt, and those few months were sufficient to spur him on to study the nature of hysteria and the therapeutic value of hypnotism in greater detail. It was the key which was to unlock the gates of the unconscious regions of the mind.

Despite Sigmund's objections the couple had a traditional Jewish wedding and settled in a newly built flat in the 'House of Atonement', a building of evil omen, on the site of the old Ringtheater which had burned down with the loss of 600 lives. Freud had advertised his return from Paris and setting up in private practice in the *Neue Freie Presse*, and supplemented his income with writing, translating and working three afternoons a week as head of the department of children's nervous diseases at the Kassowitz Institute.

Yet these were still lean years and he had to rely much on the generosity of friends. His former colleague Fleischl sent him patients, and his friend and future colleague Josef Breuer lent him money. Three children were born here, two boys and a girl; three more were to follow, a boy and two girls, when they moved to their next home at 19 Berggasse. Completing the family was Martha's sister Minna who lived with them during the whole of their fifty-three years' marriage.

Freud now began to use hypnotic technique in treating his own patients. It was unorthodox but effective. In France it was already widely employed, and a visit to a clinic in Nancy where thousands of patients were being treated in this way for a variety of nervous disorders convinced Freud that this was the direction his work should take. Conventional medicine was no longer of interest. The human mind was to be his exclusive preoccupation.

Nevertheless he still had much to learn. Symptoms could be re-experienced under the influence of hypnotic suggestion but the underlying causes of hysteria and allied disorders were still a mystery. Freud tried to probe deeper, urging the patient to describe the origin of such symptoms; and gradually a pattern began to appear which led Freud to suspect underlying emotional causes.

It was Dr Josef Breuer who helped him find the answer. Breuer was a distinguished Viennese physician who, some years previously, had treated a young woman for paralysis of certain limbs as well as accompanying defects of sight, speech and nervous coughing. Breuer had placed her under deep hypnosis and induced her to relive experiences dating back to a time when she had nursed her father through a serious illness. The symptoms, which had seemed to be jumbled and disconnected, were clearly linked, stemming from emotional situations which the patient could not remember when awake but could recall and describe under hypnosis. Once the symptoms were located, claimed Breuer, they were removed for ever. The patient was almost completely cured.

Freud was fascinated by the case of Anna O., as it came to be known, and felt convinced that the key to the problem lay at hand. But hypnosis was time-consuming and inefficient. A closer and more personal relationship between doctor and patient was possibly the answer. The solution arrived in an unexpected way, as Freud wrote in his autobiography:

'One of my most acquiescent patients, with whom hypnotism had enabled me to bring about the most marvellous results, and whom I was engaged in relieving of her suffering by tracing back her attacks of pain to their origins, as she woke up on one occasion, threw her arms round my neck. The unexpected entrance of a servant relieved us from a painful discussion, but from that time onwards there was a tacit understanding between us that the hypnotic treatment should be discontinued. I was modest enough not to attribute the event to my own irresistible personal attraction, and I felt that I had now grasped the nature of the mysterious element that was at work behind hypnotism. In order to exclude it, or at all events to isolate it, it was necessary to abandon hypnotism.'

From 1892 onwards Freud began to develop a revolutionary technique, soon to become the standard procedure in the new science of psycho-analysis (a term invented by Freud himself). It was known as 'free association'. The patient simply relaxed on the consulting-room couch and talked, with Freud's gentle prompting and encouragement, about his or her early experiences. The results were astonishing. Out of these random, disordered recollections, many of them apparently unimportant, emerged a clear pattern of emotional disturbance, strikingly similar in every case. Patient sifting and documentation of the evidence led to the formulation of Freud's theories as to the root-causes of neurotic illness and the methods of curing it. The appearance of a paper in 1895 entitled *Studies in Hysteria*, published jointly by Freud and Breuer, revealed their astounding discoveries to the medical profession.

What years of research and practical treatment had made abundantly clear was that there were underlying emotional reasons for the physical symptoms displayed by neurotic patients. Experiences going back as far as childhood could be remembered and described under analysis. These were often of a shameful or painful nature, incidents which had either been forgotten or of which the patient was completely unaware. Unconscious forces were at work, described by Freud as 'resistance' and 'repression'. The patient resisted – though not consciously – the uncovering of these early experiences, and repressed impulses and desires which gave rise to neurotic symptoms. By stripping away layer after layer of hidden and buried experience the analyst was able to construct a coherent pattern of behaviour. Once brought to light the physical symptoms could be alleviated or even removed.

The revelation that there existed in everyone a vast unconscious area of the mind which affected and conditioned behaviour and health was epoch-making. 'I showed my recognition of the new situation,' wrote Freud, 'by no longer calling my method of investigation and treatment catharsis but *psycho-analysis*.'

The traditional world of medicine could no longer afford to disregard Freud's findings. With only a handful of exceptions, it was uncompromisingly hostile and more so as Freud developed his theories during the closing years of the century. Closer investigation of his case histories led him to the conclusion that most of these disturbing childhood experiences were of a sexual nature. Childhood was revealed as far from 'innocent', but instead a tangled battleground of conflicting emotions, in which the figures of a strict, authoritarian father and a weak, over-indulgent mother, assumed tremendous importance. The child, according to Freud, was a sexual animal long before puberty, passing through various stages before settling into a 'normal' adolescent pattern. His theories of infantile sexuality, the 'Oedipus Complex' and the 'libido' were developed in considerable detail over the years. As could have been predicted, they aroused violent opposition, largely due to ignorance and wilful misunderstanding, but they remained basic to Freud's own thinking and Freudian psycho-analysis. No aspect of his published work caused greater controversy and many of his colleagues, including Breuer – and, later, Adler and Jung – parted company with him as a result.

Most of these findings were described in his monumental work *The Interpretation of Dreams*, which he worked on for four years and published in 1900. He himself wrote of this: 'Insight such as this falls to one's lot but once in a lifetime.' In it he demonstrated in depth the basis for his theory of the unconscious mind and broke new ground by describing the vital part played by dreams and fantasy in providing clues to human neuroses. He had long been fascinated by dreams and saw them as expressions of unconscious, unfulfilled desires. He had shown that they could be scientifically investigated and interpreted and that they were inextricably linked with unconscious impulses of childhood. For the first time he explained his 'Oedipus Complex' theory, the delicate balance of love and hate which the child feels for his parents, and the turbulent nature of the child's emotional life which has such a bearing on his later development.

This was the high-water mark of his achievement to date and it coincided, significantly enough, with the resolution of his own inner problems and conflicts. For during the past ten years he himself had undergone a series of private crises in which unmistakable neurotic symptoms were evident. He had deep fits of depression which interfered with his work. He had doubts about the value of his research and was concerned at the hostility it aroused. He became suspicious and mistrustful of friends and colleagues. He was worried about his own health and had a morbid fear of early death.

Recognizing these and other danger signals he embarked on the bold and painful road of self-analysis, even to the extent of recording and interpreting his own dreams. His discoveries about himself reinforced his other case-book findings. He uncovered his own deeply buried feeling of hostility towards his father. The germs of an 'Oedipus Complex' were dangerously apparent in his own nature. Yet he succeeded in coming to terms with himself and thereafter the doubts were dissipated. Although there were many difficulties and disappointments ahead, he was able to face them with more detachment and determination. Always reluctant to depend too strongly on others he was now resolved to continue his chosen line of work unflaggingly, if need be alone. It had been a hard period both for him and his family, but maturity had now arrived in both the emotional and professional sense, and henceforward a new element of authority permeated his work. He was to emerge from what he called 'splendid isolation', to attract disciples and spread the message of Freudian psycho-analysis far and wide.

What of his private life during those crucial years? Much has been written, some of it malicious and uninformed, about Freud's relationship with his wife and children. Dr Ernest Jones, his official biographer and friend for over thirty years, confirms that the marriage was a happy one, and all the evidence – Freud's own reminiscences, his letters, the opinions of friends, his own children's testimony – points to a warm, lively, compact family relationship. Although Martha did not share his intellectual interests she was a devoted wife and mother, a wonderful housekeeper and a gracious social hostess. True, life revolved round 'der Papa', meals were eaten punctually, and long working hours precluded entertainment on a lavish scale. But life in the Berggasse was far from dull and joyless. Freud's affection for his children was warm and sincere, although he was not by nature demonstrative. In the long summer holidays – particularly in later years when he was in a better financial position – the family would take a villa in Bavaria, Styria or the Tyrol and he would join his children in their games, in boating and swimming, and in long nature rambles, from which they would return with pocketfuls of wild plants and mushrooms.

These were months of relaxation even when he was writing, for the rest of the year was taken up with his practice, his lectures, meetings and conferences, with one evening set aside regularly for his favourite card game of Tarock, and Sundays reserved for visits to his mother and to local art galleries and museums. Antiquities were his main hobby, theatre visits were rare, concerts anathema. All in all a comfortable, harmonious, if unexciting picture of family life.

The turn of the century brought a change in his fortunes. Within the next ten years he and his colleagues from many countries, though popularly regarded as 'cranks', had set up the International Psycho-analytical Association, with many active local branches; within twenty years the practice of psycho-analysis would be accepted and already burgeoning out in different directions. In the meantime Freud was to publish more than seventy-five papers, essays and books, ranging from his own specialized subjects – the unconscious mind, infantile sexuality and dreams – to the nature of humour, art and the creative processes, love, war and aggression, religion, anthropology, literature and philosophy. His range of inquiry was enormous, his search for knowledge limitless.

Within the next few years Freud built up a small but enthusiastic band of followers who met every Wednesday evening round the long table in his waiting-room to talk, argue, compare notes and plan for the future. Among them were Wilhelm Stekel, Max Kahane, and Alfred Adler, all to become eminent analysts themselves. Soon there were so many new recruits that they had to hold their meetings elsewhere, and eventually they formed the nucleus of the Vienna Psychoanalytical Society.

Two of the first psychiatrists to adopt Freud's methods were Eugen Bleuler, director of the Burghölzi Clinic of Psychiatry in Zürich, and his assistant, Carl Gustav Jung. Jung was a particularly ardent champion of Freudian theory and technique and Freud was greatly encouraged by the Swiss experiment.

By 1908 Freud was sufficiently confident of his following abroad to convene the first Psycho-analytical Congress in Salzburg. Pioneers of psychiatry assembled to read papers – Freud opening the proceedings, followed by a number of his Viennese colleagues, as well as Ernest Jones from London, Karl Abraham from Berlin, Jung from Zürich and Sandor Ferenczi from Budapest. At the second Congress in Nuremberg in 1910 the International Psycho-analytic Association was formed, with headquarters in Zürich and branches in a number of European capitals.

Meanwhile he was writing some of his most important books. In 1904 he published one of the most popular, *The Psychopathology of Everyday Life*. This dealt with various manifestations of unconscious processes at work in daily life, such as forgetfulness, superstitions and apparently meaningless actions. 1905 was a particularly fertile year. *Three Essays on the Theory of Sexuality* returned in detail to the theme of childhood sexuality. It created a sensation and triggered off a storm of vilification and abuse which did not simmer down until after the war. It is now considered, together with *The Interpretation of Dreams*, his most significant work.

In the same year he made public his famous 'Dora' analysis, the first of six lengthy case histories, in which he stressed the role of dreams in therapy. *Jokes and Their Relation to the Unconscious*, describing the unconscious sources of pleasure in jokes and humour, covered entirely new and uncontroversial ground.

These and other books and papers added to his reputation, though the financial rewards were meagre. But the ten years prior to the war also saw the most vicious and consistent onslaught on his theories by the enemy camp. He was considered to be a moral danger, a sexual pervert. 'Wrong', 'objectionable', 'superfluous', 'gruesome old wives' tale psychiatry', 'descent into absolute filth' – these were the types of comment which greeted Freud as he continued to explore the dark caverns of the human mind and personality. Most of them made no effort to try to understand the admittedly complicated theories of the 'libido'. It was sufficient to stigmatize him as a sex-obsessed monster – this of the retiring, soft-spoken man who was rarely known even to smile at an improper joke! Freud endured it all patiently, though stung to remark: 'For the degree of arrogance which they displayed, for their conscienceless contempt of logic, and for the coarseness and bad taste of their attacks there could be no excuse.'

He travelled a great deal now, either with his family or a companion. In the summer of 1901 a long-cherished dream was fulfilled. He visited Rome – 'the high-point of my life' he called it. He was to return to it again and again. Rome exerted an almost mystical appeal on him and was to inspire a number of important philosophical works, especially a remarkable essay on *The Moses of Michelangelo*. And he ventured farther afield, to Venice, Naples, Capri, Sicily and Greece, eager to extend his experience of classical art, architecture and archaeology.

At the pre-war Congresses the dominant figures were Freud, Adler and Jung. It was inevitable that men with such strong views and unyielding personalities should clash. Adler was irascible, temperamental and highly ambitious; he developed his own theories on the causes of neuroses and human behaviour. He placed total emphasis on man's aggressive instincts and rejected the Freudian view of sexuality. Freud and he were never close friends and the final break in 1911 was a relief to both of them. Jung, on the other hand, was one of Freud's earliest friends and colleagues, his second-in-command and heir apparent – 'Allah and his disciple' was one of the milder comments tossed out by an unsympathetic observer. Yet after four or five years Jung also began to strike out in other directions. He publicly minimized the importance of Freudian sexual theories, and his own researches, particularly his own essay on the libido, angered and distressed Freud. At the Fourth Congress at Munich there was open revolt. The movement was irrevocably split. There was to be undying bitterness between the two men and their followers. Once again Freud felt he had been betrayed and thereafter assumed full responsibility for the Association's work. He was now in complete command.

Two more important books were published before the war. In 1910 came a brilliant study on Leonardo da Vinci, displaying the extraordinary range of Freud's literary and artistic interests. Da Vinci's psychology intrigued Freud. The official title of the publication was *A Study in Psychosexuality*, but it developed into a comprehensive account of a man who, like Freud, was torn by conflicting artistic and scientific urges. In 1913 he published a massive survey of beliefs and superstitions – *Totem and Taboo* – his first of several excursions into the world of religion. Thomas Mann later described the book as 'a piece of world literature'. It discussed incest, tribal taboos relating to enemies, rulers and the dead, magic, mythology and totemism, as well as the origins and features of organized religions. The book was badly received at the time but demonstrated the new-found range and ambition of Freud's thinking, now extending far beyond individual psychology to the study of society and civilization as a whole.

The First World War was a traumatic event for Freud and his generation. The work of the Psycho-analytic movement ground to a halt and though he himself wrote steadily until 1915, the quality and scope of his work declined sharply as he lost contact with his overseas colleagues. Freud was at first sympathetic to Germany and the Central Powers, but he veered round to the Allied cause as he saw increasing evidence of Austrian incompetence and German brutality. He was desperately worried about his two sons in the army, needlessly as it proved. There were food shortages, he had difficulty in obtaining his beloved cigars, and his practice was in the doldrums. Yet even in these trying times he published three vital works. His essay on *The Unconscious*, a forty-page survey of his essential thinking in this field, was considered the most original contribution to psychology for fifteen years. He also published the remaining five of his classic case-histories including that of five-year-old 'Little Hans', the first full account of the analysis of a child. Finally, in 1917, came what was to prove his most popular work, *Introductory Lectures on Psycho-analysis*, with a brilliant section on Dreams, and covering every aspect of neurotic illness and treatment.

His practice was slow to recover after the war, but he was greatly heartened to meet his old friends and colleagues and to receive a sizeable legacy from a Hungarian friend for the furtherance of his work. In 1919 a publishing firm was founded, the *Internationaler Psychoanalytischer Verlag* of Vienna, which was to play a vital part in his life, publishing both his own works and other books and periodicals dealing with psycho-analysis. During its twenty-five-year existence it ran into financial difficulties, but Freud's son Martin, together with Ernest Jones, came to its rescue in the early thirties before it was finally destroyed by the Nazis.

The opposition was gradually dying down by this time. New groups were formed, new pupils arrived to carry on the practical work. Freud settled again into the daily routine. The children were scattering. The death of their second daughter, Sophie, was a grievous blow, alleviated by the arrival of grand-children. His books continued to explore new territory – *Beyond the Pleasure Principle* (1920) contrasted man's life and death instincts; *The Ego and the Id* again broke fresh ground, modifying and extending his earlier work on the Unconscious and introducing terms which are now standard symbols of psycho-analytical investigation – the *ego*, the *id* and the *superego*, representing the conscious and unconscious forces determining human personality and behaviour.

In 1925 Freud published his *Autobiography*, providing a full account of his scientific career, but revealing, typically, little of his private life.

A sinister development in Freud's continuing history of ill-health occurred in 1923 when he detected a small growth on his palate which restricted his swallowing. Reluctantly he took medical advice and an operation was recommended. The growth was found to be cancerous although Freud was not informed at the time. It proved to be only the first of thirty-three operations over the years, the condition becoming progressively worse, culminating in the destruction of one side of the jaw, affecting his powers of speech and causing him unimaginable pain. His last fifteen years have to be viewed against this appalling background of suffering alleviated only by stoical application to his work, the devotion of his family, particularly his daughter and disciple Anna, and the loyalty of his many friends. Birthdays came and went, the seventieth, the seventy-fifth. As the adulation increased he shrunk back into a self-imposed cocoon of privacy and isolation, interrupted by the welcome award in 1930 of the Goethe literary prize.

The storm clouds were gathering. In 1933 the Nazis burned his books. His ironic comment was, 'What progress we are making. In the Middle Ages they would have burnt me; nowadays they are content with burning my books.' It was only his reputation, his bad health and advanced age that prevented worse from happening. In 1938, after the

Nazi occupation of Austria, he was finally persuaded to leave his Berggasse home and to seek refuge in England. Here he spent the last year of his life, receiving friends, honoured by the Royal Society, and miraculously still at work on his last great book, controversial as ever, entitled *Moses and Monotheism*. In it he sought to prove that Moses was an Egyptian, using this to introduce a comprehensive survey of Judaism and Christianity, the sources of anti-semitism and the place of religion in the modern world. The parallel between the figure of Moses – teacher, leader and law-giver – and Freud himself, is obvious and revealing.

He died peacefully in Hampstead on 23 September, 1939. Ernest Jones concluded his funeral oration with these words:

'A great spirit has passed from the world. . . . His creative spirit was so strong that he infused himself into others. If ever man can be said to have conquered death itself, to live on in spite of the King of Terrors, who held no terror for him, that man was Freud. . . . From our hearts we thank him for having lived; for having done; and for having loved.'

What he was like as a man scarcely matters beside his achievements. Beset by inner conflicts and external troubles, knowing poverty, bereavement, ill-health, hostility, anti-semitism and mortal illness, who could expect such a man to go through life radiating optimism and joy? The allegations that he was cynical and unforgiving to former friends and colleagues, unfeeling towards his wife and family, coldly analytical towards all problems, human ones included, have a vestige of truth in them, but ignore the evidence to the contrary. He was often embittered and enraged by criticisms and defections and supremely confident in the powers of his own reasoning. His search for knowledge and truth in the widest sense utterly engrossed him, but he was never so deaf as to persist obstinately in a wrong course, nor to modify his views if the evidence justified it.

In private he was essentially warm-hearted, generous and tolerant, impatient of superficialities, perhaps old-fashioned in his views about women, possibly a poor judge of character in men. He was keenly aware of his Jewish origin, and

Sigmund Freud

although not observant, he thought and felt as a Jew and encouraged his children to do the same. For all the self-analysis and self-criticism, he possessed most of the virtues and weaknesses of lesser men. And it was not false humility which led him to end his *Autobiography* with the words: 'Looking back, then, over the patchwork of my life's labours, I can say that I have made many beginnings and thrown out many suggestions. Something will come of them in the future, though I cannot myself tell whether it will be much or little. I can, however, express a hope that I have opened up a pathway for an important advance in our knowledge.'

Samuel Alexander
1859–1938

In Chaim Weizmann's autobiography *Trial and Error* there is an intimate and flattering reference to Professor Samuel Alexander, of Manchester University, as a friend and neighbour who was responsible for introducing the young chemist to Lord Balfour during the war. It was to Alexander that Arthur Balfour scribbled on a postcard: 'Dear Sam: W. needs no introduction, I still remember our conversation in 1906.'

The development of that friendship, culminating in the Balfour Declaration, is the subject of another chapter of this book. We are concerned here with the rather deaf, shabbily dressed and enormously popular professor of philosophy, his long flowing beard giving him the appearance of a Jewish prophet – the man whom Weizmann described simply as 'one of the great philosophers of our generation'.

It is perhaps only in an age of Sunday-newspaper profiles and television brains-trusts that an original mind in a remote and specialized field can make any kind of impact on the community at large. But even if such opportunities for communication had existed fifty years ago it is doubtful whether Samuel Alexander would have utilized them. He could never have achieved the notoriety of Bertrand Russell or A. J. Ayer. His retiring disposition would have shunned the publicity, and the profundity and complexity of his theories would emphatically not have lent themselves to superficial popularization.

So, although colleagues, students and commentators have concurred with Weizmann in hailing him as one of the most significant and influential philosophers of the twentieth century, Alexander remains unknown outside his chosen field. He was showered with honours during his lifetime – President of the Aristotelian Society, Honorary D.Litt. from half a dozen universities, Fellow of Lincoln College, Oxford, Fellow of the British Academy, Order of Merit.

He was the first Australian philosopher of world repute, though his countrymen may be forgiven their comparative neglect, for Samuel Alexander left Melbourne at the age of eighteen and never returned. Only at Manchester was he fittingly commemorated in the bust by Sir Jacob Epstein which stands in the hall of the Arts building of the University.

Samuel Alexander was born at 436 George Street, Sydney, on 6 January, 1859. His father, a saddler, died shortly before Samuel's birth, and soon afterwards the family moved to St Kilda, Melbourne. Here Samuel attended a private school run by a Mr Atkinson who, according to his bright young pupil, was 'quite mad'. It was at Wesley College, with its outstanding headmaster M. H. Irving, that the talented boy received the broad structure of education which enabled him to matriculate at sixteen and enrol for an Arts course at Melbourne University. During his two years of study there he won distinctions in Classics, English, Mathematics and Natural Philosophy. He then left for England and won a scholarship to Balliol College, Oxford. The competition was stiff, one of his rivals being George Curzon, later to become Viceroy of India. At Oxford he also did brilliantly, achieving a First Class Honours in Classical and Mathematical Moderations and a First in Greats.

In May, 1882, he became the first Jew to be awarded a Fellowship to an Oxford or Cambridge college – in fact to Lincoln College, Oxford, where he was philosophy tutor for ten years.

Alexander was never a prolific writer and, apart from articles and reviews, had made little mark outside Oxford prior to the essay which won him the Green Moral Philosophy Prize in 1887. Entitled *Moral Order and Progress*, it was published in book form in 1889. In it he first formulated his theory of evolutionary ethics. The book went through several editions, but as he came to modify his views, he eventually let it die a natural death.

Although his appointment at Lincoln did not expire till 1893, he seems to have found both the atmosphere and subject too limiting. He became increasingly absorbed in the study of experimental psychology, a rapidly developing, though not yet entirely respectable field of research. He took up a teaching post at Toynbee Hall and in the winter of 1890–1 visited Professor Münsterberg's laboratory in Freiburg as a prelude to further practical work in the subject. After three unsuccessful attempts for a professorship he was finally made Professor of Philosophy at Manchester University in 1893, a post he occupied with distinction for thirty years.

Alexander was frequently described as the 'best-loved man in Manchester' and all his friends and students have testified to the unflagging warmth and humanity of his temperament, despite his steadily deteriorating hearing and his occasional fits of depression. In company he was invariably cheerful, his conversation fresh and stimulating. When, in 1902, he was joined from Australia by his elderly mother and aunt, two elder brothers and a sister, he began to entertain more lavishly. His sister acted as his hostess. The Wednesday evening social gatherings for students and colleagues, past and present, became celebrated.

His students admired and loved him, though bound to remark on his eccentricities of behaviour and dress. He had all the hallmarks of an absent-minded professor, wiping the blackboard with the sleeve of his raincoat, launching off into lengthy digressions during lectures, wobbling dreamily along the pavements on his bicycle. Yet these were endearing and harmless mannerisms. Though he would often hesitate for the exact word, he would talk profoundly and clearly on his chosen subject and many of his students have commented on the deep influence by his teaching.

Among academic colleagues who thought highly of him were Gilbert Murray, the Australian-born classical scholar, and the renowned philosopher, F. H. Bradley.

During the war Alexander was Gifford lecturer at Glasgow University. His lectures on metaphysics formed the foundation for his most important book, published in two volumes in 1920 under the title *Space, Time and Deity*. Professor Laird, Alexander's executor and biographer, described this ambitious work as the 'boldest adventure in detailed speculative metaphysics attempted in so grand a manner by any English writer between 1655 and 1920' – that is, since Hobbes' *De Corpore*. It was widely acclaimed; his Arthur Davis Memorial Lecture on *Spinoza and Time*, published the following year, formed an appendage to the earlier volumes.

Philosophers still speak of *Space, Time and Deity* with awe and respect, though confessing to its occasional obscurity. They praise it as being one of the most comprehensive and original metaphysical systems ever devised, in which the theories of Spinoza, Locke, Kant, Bentham, Mill, Moore, Bradley and Bosanquet are wedded to the space-time systems of Einstein, Sir James Jeans and Sir Arthur Eddington.

An attempt to *précis* the complicated theories propounded in this massive work is both an impossibility and an impertinence. Suffice it to say that Alexander's argument stems from the supposition that space-time, or pure motion, is the basic stuff of the universe, from which everything develops by a process of 'emergent evolution'. Matter, life and mind all emerge in ascending levels from this space-time matrix. The quality next above mind is 'deity', but even this is not necessarily the crown of evolution, for the universe may be striving towards yet higher qualities. On this framework Alexander builds a realist theory of knowledge or awareness based on the 'compresent' existence of the knower and the object contemplated. Random quotations from the book would serve little purpose and readers interested in delving more deeply into the subject will need no prompting to refer to what is still considered a masterpiece of philosophical literature.

Alexander retired from his Chair at Manchester in 1924 to devote himself to research, occasional lecturing and writing. Despite the growing handicap of deafness his active brain would not condone idleness. His knowledge of literature and the arts had always been extensive and in these latter years of his life he pondered much on the subject of Aesthetics. In 1933 he published *Beauty and Other Forms of Value*, in which he defined art as the expression of a constructive impulse turned contemplative. But in this he was wandering some distance from the subject which really engrossed him, and the book never achieved the success of *Space, Time and Deity*.

For the ordinary reader wishing to dip briefly into the wide-ranging thought of Samuel Alexander the best introduction is through the *Philosophical and Literary Pieces*, published posthumously in 1939, with a valuable one-hundred-page Memoir by Professor John Laird. The book contains articles on Dr Johnson, Jane Austen, Molière and Pascal, lectures and articles on the nature of Art and Value, a discussion on Theism and Pantheism, and two lectures on Spinoza.

It is not fanciful to trace a direct line of development between the three great Jewish philosophers, Maimonides, Spinoza and Alexander. He often acknowledged his debt to the seventeenth-century Spanish thinker who also strove to relate philosophy to science. In his lecture on Spinoza, published by the Manchester University Press in 1933, he noted: 'I do not suggest that Spinoza's philosophy is beyond exception either as a whole or in its parts. But it is very near to our own problems, not because it raises them explicitly, but for the lessons it carries to us, as it were, by anticipation. It exhibits the science of the physical world as one part of a system whose method applied to human affairs interprets for us morals and religion not only so as to secure their value but in an exalted expression. . . . He was too remote from common beliefs to be regarded as what he was, a devoted servant of God. But he is at least a type of a kind of philosophy which, by pursuing the method of neutrality . . . which is naturalism, establishes the ideals of good life, and maintains religion without excuse . . . and at the same time without affirming that either morals or religion, as so many suppose today, supplies us with directer knowledge of reality than physical science. For all things alike are modes of God and have both the mind which the human sciences investigate and the extension which is the subject of the physical sciences.'

Indeed, Spinoza and Alexander had much in common, an affinity of mind spanning the centuries. But in one respect they differed: in their adherence to traditional Judaism. Spinoza, as is well known, was excommunicated for heretical views, Alexander, for all his unorthodox beliefs, remained a member of the local Jewish community all his life, deeply aware of Jewish problems and especially concerned about the plight of the Jews in Hitler's Europe. As Weizmann indicated, he was an early supporter of Zionism and later Honorary Vice-President of the Friends of the Hebrew University of Jerusalem.

Professor Alexander, who never married, died on 13 September, 1938, bequeathing the greater part of his estate to the University where he had spent many fruitful years. Some of his contemporaries regretted that circumstances did not lead him to choose a more widely applicable field of study in which his influence would have been greater. But within this restricted sphere he ranks with the great.

Theodor Herzl
1860–1904

'A majestic Oriental figure . . . with eyes that brood and glow – you would say one of the Assyrian Kings. . . . His voice is for the most part subdued. . . . And yet beneath all this states-manlike prose, touched with the special dryness of a jurist, lurk the romance of the poet . . . the fantasy of the Hungarian, the dramatic self-consciousness of the literary artist, the heart of the Jew.'

This is how Israel Zangwill, the famous writer, described his friend Theodor Herzl addressing the delegates to the first Zionist Congress in Basle in 1897. Yet even Zangwill could find no rational explanation for the extraordinary effect that the tall, black-bearded young journalist from Vienna had on those who met him, from common labourers to crowned heads. All the talents he possessed, the lawyer's sharp judge-ment, the essayist's fluent prose style, the dramatist's sense of occasion, the reporter's intuitive perception – these were merely the tools he employed for the immense task which he imposed on himself. These were learned and acquired, and valuable only in so far as they reinforced the inborn qualities

– obsessional determination, unlimited resources of inner strength, unbounded self-confidence and utter dedication to an ideal. In his unflagging pursuit of this ideal – a homeland for the Jewish people – he combined the shrewdness of modern diplomacy with the power of Biblical prophecy: and he drove himself to an early grave in the service of his people.

The conception of a Jewish State as a solution to the so-called Jewish Problem struck the young Herzl with the sudden, shattering impact of a revelation. Even he was at a loss to say exactly how and when it occurred. Certainly not in his childhood and student years in Budapest and Vienna. As the son of a well-to-do merchant he received a traditional, but not intensive Jewish training – the domestic celebration of festivals, the weekly visits to synagogue, enough Hebrew tuition to prepare him for the Bar-mitzvah ceremony at the age of thirteen, but little more. There was scarcely an echo in comfortable Vienna of the agony and misery of Jewry in the East; nor was the young Herzl aware of the work of Moses Hess and Leo Pinsker advocating a national homeland. Hess had been trying to influence the Jews of Germany twenty years before Herzl was born, and his *Rome and Jerusalem*, published in 1862, developed the theme. Pinsker's *Auto-Emancipation* appeared much later, in 1882, the year of the frightful Russian pogroms. He was a member of the *Chovevei Zion*, Lovers of Zion, movement – a forerunner of Zionism, founded for the purpose of setting up agricultural settlements in Palestine. Already hardy pioneers from Eastern Europe, supported by wealthy philanthropists but with no moral or political backing from world Jewry, were staking claims in that forgotten corner of the Turkish empire, struggling against officialdom, against marauding Arabs, against cholera and malaria. The seeds were there, but as yet Herzl, having abandoned a legal career and taken up journalism, was completely uninformed and uninvolved.

As the years passed, however, he could not avoid noticing the barriers which society and public opinion placed in the path of a Jew hoping to enter the professions – law, army, public life; and even though he was successfully turning out plays, short stories, essays and topical articles, and gaining himself a fair degree of renown and approbation, he could not be insensitive to the reports of increasing anti-semitism all over Europe. Moreover, he was to receive first-hand experience of this when he was appointed Paris correspondent, in 1891, of the great Viennese liberal newspaper *Neue Freie Presse*.

Some people have linked Herzl's 'conversion' directly with the trial and conviction for treason of Captain Alfred Dreyfus, but this is too glib an explanation and not confirmed by Herzl himself. It is true that he was present on that day in January, 1895, when Dreyfus was publicly degraded in the courtyard of the Paris military school, that he was visibly shocked at the brutal attitude of the crowd, dismayed at the viciously anti-Jewish tone of the press, particularly the writing of Edouard Drumont, editor of the anti-semitic paper *La Parole Libre*. But although he was not sufficiently enraged by the affair to take up a Zola-like stance, it was in that year 1895 that he first began to study the situation seriously and to work out a solution; and once convinced that resettlement and not assimilation was the only possible solution, he had to work day and night for nine years to make the dream come true.

From the moment that he sat down in his Paris hotel preparing the notes which he later compressed into his famous pamphlet *Der Judenstaat* (*The Jewish State*), he could not be diverted from his goal. Everything was subsidiary, including his private life. He had married a lively, sociable girl named Julie Naschauer in 1889 and was now the father of two girls and a boy. She had no understanding or sympathy for her husband's Zionist ideals; as the wife of a man who was wedded to a great national vision, she must have sensed that the struggle was hopeless almost from the start.

Herzl's *Diaries* record with brilliance, poignancy and humour the sequence of events which began with his earliest encounters with the Jewish Problem, to his death nine years later at the age of forty-four. He describes his meetings with politicians, diplomats, bankers, philanthropists, religious leaders and princes; he recounts his popular successes with ordinary working people who looked on him also as a Messiah, and his failure to win the support of the wealthy, influential, complacent, narrow-minded Jews of western Europe whose practical co-operation was so vital for the success of his grandiose scheme. One is amazed at the sheer persistence of this remarkable man who, despite a chronic heart ailment of which he was fully aware, drove himself to seek out the most powerful men of Europe in an effort to negotiate by honourable and legal means a homeland for his persecuted people. How could he have endured the succession of delays, snubs, setbacks, gibes and hostile comments which assailed him from all sides? And what, in the end, did it all amount to?

Criticized during his lifetime for his methods, for believing that Palestine was something that could be bought or bartered, with little but vague promises and expressions of sympathy to show from that endless round of interviews and audiences with the men who shaped the world's destiny, nevertheless the foundations he laid were solid and enduring. He it was who, through his writings and public appearances, threw out a challenge to the Jews of the world, who gave them a sense of national pride and identity, who persuaded their leaders to come together to a great Congress where the Zionist Organization was formed, a plan of action adopted and work embarked upon to implement that plan. And it was Herzl who by unceasing discussion and persuasion so moulded opinion at high government level that the later, decisive work of men like Weizmann was greatly facilitated. All the subsequent Zionist leaders and founders of the State acknowledged their debt to him.

The order of events is unimportant compared with this broad view of his life's work. The key events were the publication of *Der Judenstaat*, the first Zionist Congress in 1897, and the stormy sixth Congress which debated the British government's offer of a homeland in East Africa.

The Jewish State, which Herzl wrote in three hectic weeks, had a tremendous impact on world opinion. Rejecting the idea of assimilation, deriding the piecemeal, philanthropic

activities of Baron de Hirsch and Baron Edmond de Rothschild, he saw the establishment of a Jewish State as the only
practical solution – an economic and political solution rather
than one based on moral or spiritual considerations. At first
he did not even insist on Palestine. What was essential was
that the Jewish State should come about by international consent and agreement. As he wrote,

'The Jewish question is a national question which can only
be solved by making it a political world question to be discussed and controlled by the civilized nations of the world
in council.' He proclaimed: 'We are a people, one People. . . .
Distress binds us together and, thus united, we suddenly discover our strength. Yes, we are strong enough to form a
State, and a model State. . . .'

The eminent writers Max Nordau and Israel Zangwill
were among the few influential Jews who responded to
Herzl's clarion call immediately. The bankers and businessmen refused their support; the orthodox Jewish leaders resented his non-religious background and his frankly national-
istic ambitions; cautious politicians, afraid of antagonizing
the Turks, palmed him off with lofty-sounding words, promising support, then shelving the matter. Herzl was perhaps
rather too innocent in his dealings with the mighty, never
really admitting to himself that what chiefly motivated them
– then as always – was self-interest, greed and expediency.

The *Diaries*, truncated though they are, afford a fascinating glimpse of the way his mind worked. Purely as literature
they merit close study; as a slice of history they form an
important document. But for the ordinary reader their appeal
lies in the very human figure that emerges – intense, passionate, bitter and intolerant at times, often vain or pompous,
occasionally aware of his own fallibility, enraged at his
physical weaknesses, generous in praise of loyal friends and
colleagues, deeply aware of his responsibility to his fellow
Jews, utterly convinced of the truth of his vision.

His sketches of events, scenes and personalities are vivid
and penetrating. His accounts of the tortuous shifts and
schemings which paved the way towards those critical meetings with Kaiser Wilhelm II and the Sultan are as entertain-

ing as the reports of the interviews themselves, and his descriptions of Constantinople and Jerusalem are quite captivating. Though never losing sight of his ultimate objective, Herzl was too much a man of the world not to be absorbed by foreign places and intrigued by the oddities of character of the many interesting people he encountered in his travels.

One of his first contacts, Baron de Hirsch, proved a waste of time, as did the English Chief Rabbi Hermann Adler who later called the Zionist movement 'an egregious blunder'. The Chief Rabbi of Vienna, Dr Moritz Güdemann, was, however, partially converted. 'I could think you were Moses,' he remarked when they first met. Zangwill, at his Kilburn home, signified immediate support, as had Nordau previously. Of him Herzl correctly observed, 'Nordau will, I believe, go with me through thick and thin. He was my earliest conquest, and so far perhaps the most valuable.'

Among these early entries is the following ominous observation: 'Dr Beck has examined me and diagnosed a weakness of the heart, caused by powerful excitement. He fails to understand why I concern myself with the Jewish cause.'

The next onslaught was on the Kaiser himself, the go-between being the Grand Duke of Baden. He in turn had to be approached by one of Herzl's closest friends and aides, the Reverend William Hechler, son of a Protestant missionary and at that point chaplain of the British legation in Vienna. He was tutor to the son of the Grand Duke, and as an enthusiastic and emotional supporter of *Der Judenstaat* introduced the pamphlet both to the Kaiser and the Sultan. The Grand Duke ('a robust, not too obese, old general') expressed sympathy for the cause and Herzl left considerably encouraged, having explained the economic and political advantages which might accrue to Germany, and eliciting a vague pledge of future co-operation, without an actual promise of a meeting with the Kaiser. He decided to continue to exert pressure both on Turkey and Britain.

There followed his first expedition to Constantinople when he was accompanied by his Polish friend Philip Nevlinski, formerly a diplomat in the Turkish capital. The prospects, as

Herzl realized, were dim. Herzl's complicated plan to negotiate a Palestine charter in return for extricating Turkey from her financial difficulties was communicated to the Sultan. The response, conveyed through Nevlinski, was chilling. The Sultan was reported as saying: 'I cannot sell even a foot of land, for it does not belong to me but to my people. . . . The Jews may spare their millions. When my Empire is divided, perhaps they will get Palestine for nothing. But only our corpse can be divided. I will never consent to vivisection.' Herzl was driven to remark, 'I was touched and moved by the truly lofty words of the Sultan, although for the time being they put an end to my hopes.' And so, with several pages devoted to the colourful *selamlik* procession where Herzl at least caught sight of the Sultan ('a wasted, sickly figure of a man'), and a moderate message that Herzl would be received sooner or later (it was to be five years), the indefatigable traveller returned to Vienna, then to London, then back to Paris.

Everything was now leading up to the great Congress where Herzl hoped to crystallize Zionist aims and policies. In June 1897, he launched the first issue of a Zionist weekly, *Die Welt*. It was distinguished by its far-ranging attitude to Jewish affairs in the context of world events and was naturally designed to spread the Zionist message yet farther afield.

The first Zionist Congress, originally scheduled to convene in Munich, but altered to Basle because of local opposition, met from 29–31 August of that year. It was an historic assembly, with almost 200 unofficial representatives of Jewry from fifteen lands. Goodwill and encouragement flowed in from all sides.

Herzl's gaunt figure dominated the proceedings. In his eloquent opening speech he defined the aims of the movement. Nordau followed with an impassioned address described by Herzl as 'a monument of our age'. Facing the speakers over the entrance to the hall hung two blue and white striped flags and beside them the six-pointed Star of David, later to be combined to form the flag of Israel.

A four-point declaration of intentions, known as the Basle Programme, was adopted by the Congress which was pledged 'to obtain for the Jewish people a publicly recognized, legally secured home in Palestine'. The four points stressed settlement, the unification and organization of world Jewry, the fostering of Jewish national consciousness, and the setting in motion of a machinery to obtain the consent of governments to fulfil Zionist aims. The Congress itself was defined as the 'chief organ of the Zionist movement' and Herzl was appointed President of the Zionist Organization, a post he held until his death.

This was undoubtedly Herzl's most triumphant achievement. Other Congresses followed, but none of them displayed the same enthusiasm and unanimity of purpose as this one. Herzl hastened on with his diplomatic approaches, his attempts to win moral and financial support from the waverers, and to translate the lofty aims of the Congress into action. In 1899 the Jewish Colonial Trust was set up, which was to play an important role in the early years in financing colonies and institutions in Palestine; and more important and permanent, the Jewish National Fund, created in 1901 to purchase and develop communally owned land in Palestine.

The success of the Congress and the publicity it received may have helped to smooth Herzl's diplomatic path at this point. The Kaiser was the first conquest. Herzl was received by Minister of State von Bülow and Imperial Chancellor Prince Hohenlohe. Despite their individual prejudices they promised him a meeting in the Turkish capital, and another in Palestine during the forthcoming State Visit. Herzl was asked to head a Zionist delegation to put his case in the Holy Land.

On 18 October, 1898, occurred the first long-awaited interview with Wilhelm II. Herzl had already propounded his suggestion, in writing, for a chartered company under German protection, and now explained it in more detail. The conversation was desultory and rambling, ending with the customary expression of goodwill and a promise to discuss matters with the Sultan. They agreed to meet again in Palestine.

The *Diaries* at this point become especially interesting.

Herzl was thrilled to be able to visit Palestine, but was much depressed by the desolate and miserable existence of the 50,000 or so Jews who lived there, only a few thousand of them on the land, in charitably maintained 'colonies'. He visited a small village named Rishon le-Zion, later to become a famous wine-growing centre, which he characterized as a 'poor little settlement'.

In oppressive heat he was driven to the agricultural training school at Mikveh Israel where the first meeting with the Kaiser took place as the royal pilgrimage proceeded on its course. This was very brief, with the Kaiser merely remarking that the country clearly had a future, but needed much water – a fairly obvious discovery.

The audience in Jerusalem was longer. (Herzl paints a vivid picture of the city as it then existed and foresees a thriving new town outside the Old City limits.) But it hardly lived up to Herzl's expectations. He had written in his diary that it might have world-consequences, but the Kaiser again urged the need for irrigation and afforestation and barely touched upon the Turkish support he had hoped to win. As Herzl ruefully remarked, *'Il n'a dit ni oui ni non'* – the too-familiar line adopted by statesmen everywhere. It did not take him long to realize that the Kaiser was not genuinely interested in the problem and that little practical help could be expected from Germany.

Passing through Paris on his return he stayed at the Hôtel de Castille and wrote: 'Out of piety I still put up at the old place where I wrote *The Jewish State* four years ago. What a road since then! And what weariness. My heart is badly strained.'

The fourth Zionist Congress took place in London where, as ever, Herzl enjoyed impressive popular support. Then, in May 1901, he went back to Constantinople where the Sultan finally consented to hear him plead his case in person. The talk was polite. *Der Herr*, as Herzl called him, was 'small, thin, with great hooked nose, full dyed beard, a weak quavering voice'. Herzl had difficulty preventing the Sultan straying from the subject, but managed to outline his plans to put the Turkish economy on a sound footing. They parted, after two hours, with no commitment on either side. He was later requested to expand his ideas, and only then, and in writing, he put forward the Palestine charter-scheme, almost as an afterthought. He left, dispirited, only to be summoned back the following February, when glittering promises were made in exchange for vast sums of money which he had no hope of raising. Settlement plans were approved provided they were not in Palestine, provided the Jews were to remain Turkish subjects – and so forth. In the end the Turks withdrew their offers. Once again Herzl's hopes were dashed, and at this stage even close colleagues such as Nordau expressed frank criticism of this apparently futile course of action.

In the meantime, energetic as ever, he had found time to complete his novel *Altneuland*, with its motto 'If you will it, it is no dream'. It described life in a future Jewish State in Palestine, and though uneven in literary quality, still grips the interest for its uncannily accurate projection of later events.

Now, as his hopes ebbed, Britain came to the rescue. On 23 October, 1902, he had a meeting with the Colonial Secretary – 'the famous master-figure of England, Joe Chamberlain'. Chamberlain was no ardent lover of Jews or Zionists, but he was not unmoved by the plight of Eastern European Jewry. He also saw the political advantages of a Jewish settlement in the Middle East. He invited Herzl's ideas. Cyprus was mentioned as a possibility, then discarded. Then El Arish and the Sinai Peninsula was suggested. This territory was under joint Anglo-Egyptian control. Herzl grasped eagerly at the straw. Surprisingly the British government gave its consent and a Commission was appointed to investigate. It returned with an affirmative report, provided Egypt was prepared to divert Nile water to irrigate the area. But despite personal representations by Herzl in Cairo, Egypt refused. Thus ended yet another scheme.

However, Chamberlain had another, and more serious offer to make. In Herzl's words: ' "I've seen a land for you on my recent travels," said the great Chamberlain, "and that's Uganda. It is hot on the coast, but the climate of the interior is excellent for Europeans. Sugar and cotton can be raised there. And I thought to myself, there's a land for Dr

Herzl, but of course he only wants to go to Palestine or its neighbourhood." '

At this stage Herzl was not disposed to take this offer at face value. In desperation he was still searching round for other solutions – Mozambique, Congo, Tripoli – all useless. The horrifying Kishinev massacre of Easter, 1903, again pinpointed the necessity for urgent action, and it surprised many people that within a few months of this event Herzl was making overtures to the man widely held responsible for the pogrom, the Russian Minister of the Interior, Vyacheslav Plehve. Herzl was under no illusions as to Plehve's feelings and described him as 'the arch anti-semite, cool, frank, a butcher'. But he clung to the hope that Russia might bring influence to bear on Turkey to open the gates of Palestine. Amazingly, Plehve promised support for Zionist aims (partly as a useful method for ridding the country of undesirable elements) and Herzl brought away in triumph a letter which he planned to show to the next Zionist Congress. But this too proved to be worthless and Russo-Turkish relations deteriorated so rapidly that clearly there was no progress to be made in that direction.

So Herzl was driven back to the only concrete and practical proposal which he had ever received – 6,000 square miles of high plateau country in East Africa, misleadingly referred to as 'Uganda'. This proposition was debated at the sixth Zionist Congress and resulted in bitter, acrimonious displays of temperament, the entire Eastern European delegation walking out at one stage, resolute in their hostility towards a proposal which they saw as a betrayal of Zionist ideals. In fairness to Herzl and his supporters, they themselves regarded it only as a temporary measure, or as Herzl put it 'an auxiliary colonization'. Nordau graphically described it as a 'night-shelter'. Palestine, they reiterated, was still the only, the ultimate objective. Despite the opposition it was resolved to investigate the area. Herzl's dilemma was expressed in his *Letter to the Jewish People*. 'If it should come to a split,' he wrote, 'my heart will remain with the Zionists and my reason with the Africans.'

The Congress petered out inconclusively and it was a sad

note on which to end. For it was to be Herzl's last Congress. Next year saw him pushing on with his negotiations – with Austria, with the King of Italy, with the Pope, while behind the scenes the 'Uganda' scheme was quietly forgotten.

It was all too much for his failing heart. It was with a deep sense of shock that the world learned of his death on 3 July, 1904, at Edlach, near Vienna. He was buried in Vienna, and in 1949, after the emergence of the State which he knew would one day be founded, his remains were flown to Israel and reinterred on a slope outside Jerusalem, fittingly named Mount Herzl.

In 1897, after the first Zionist Congress, Herzl had written: 'If I were to sum up the Congress in a word – which I shall take care not to publish – it would be this: at Basle I founded the Jewish State.

'If I said this out loud today I would be greeted by universal laughter. In five years perhaps, and certainly in fifty years, everybody will understand.' It was exactly fifty years later that the State of Israel was proclaimed.

Rufus Isaacs
first Marquess of Reading
1860–1935

Queen's Counsel, Solicitor-General, Attorney-General, Lord Chief Justice, Special Ambassador to the United States, Viceroy of India, Secretary of State for Foreign Affairs: These were only some of the official titles of Rufus Isaacs, Marquess of Reading, during a long and distinguished career. By any standards, a remarkable array. For a Jew, unprecedented.

His predecessors were of continental origin, settling in England after the readmission of the Jews under Cromwell. His father, a wholesale fruit-merchant, was an orthodox Jew, but his mother who was a much stronger character had little traditional Jewish feeling. Her family – Mendoza – was from the Spanish and Portuguese community. Rufus' great-uncle was the celebrated prize-fighter, Daniel Mendoza.

Joseph and Sarah Isaacs lived a comfortable middle-class life in the City of London, and their fourth child, Rufus, was born on 10 October, 1860, within the sound of Bow Bells.

This was no rags-to-riches story. Childhood and schooldays were normal and undistinguished. Rufus was a cheerful, volatile, mischievous child, not fond of school routine, described as 'the terror of his schoolmasters, the scandal of the neighbourhood and the despair of his father'. At the tender age of five he was sent to a school in Brussels and made his mark by memorizing a long passage of French prose and repeating it without error, the first sign of a remarkable gift which he was to use to advantage in later life. He was then sent to a Jewish school in Regent's Park – the family having moved to Hampstead – and to University College School. At fourteen, however, his formal schooling was considered to be over and he was ready to be launched on a commercial career. At fifteen he found himself ensconced, none too happily, in the family business in Eastcheap.

His father soon realized that this was not the answer. Searching round for an occupation which would instil some discipline into his restless son, he hit on the idea of a naval career. At the age of sixteen Rufus signed on as ship's boy with the *Blair Athole*, bound for South America. The story that he ran away to sea is unfortunately not true. It was done with his father's consent and active encouragement. As ship's boy he was detailed to perform the humblest and most unpleasant tasks that could be devised. It was a tough life, but he was a determined lad and despite bouts of sea-sickness and occasional brushes with fellow seamen, in which he used his fists to advantage, he arrived in Rio seven weeks later none the worse for wear but heartily sick of the sea. So he jumped ship, spent several days hiding in open country, exhausted and hungry, and eventually found shelter with a native woman who fed him for two days on bananas. When she judged him sufficiently recovered she began to make amorous advances at which the terrified boy fled back to the port area where he was promptly apprehended. After a punitive period of coal-shovelling he was relieved to be able to resume his former duties on the *Blair Athole*, now bound for Calcutta. It was a long, hot voyage, the highlight of which was a fight with the bullying ship's boatswain. The ship's boy was the victor by a knockout and his reputation was much enhanced. Fourteen weeks later they reached the river Hooghly and he caught his first glimpse of a country to which he was to return, forty years later, as Viceroy.

Back he then sailed to London, his nautical career over – back to the stool in Eastcheap, but not for long. After a brief business interlude in Holland he decided to enter the Stock Exchange. As a clerk and then a full member of the Exchange, Rufus worked for four years. The exercise ended in disaster, although the experience gained was invaluable. One day, as a result of an unexpected slump, he found himself in debt to the tune of £8,000 and was 'hammered'.

His home life in the meantime had been happy and active. He was popular with girls, spent most of his dinner hours boxing at a school behind the Café Royal, but at twenty-four was no nearer to discovering a permanent occupation. He resolved to emigrate and packed his bags to go to Panama. He got as far as Euston Station when he was summoned home by his hysterical mother who informed him that he was destined for a legal career, a shrewd decision on her part, no matter the motivation. So it was arranged for him to go into a solicitor's office for six months. It took less time than that for Rufus to discover his aptitude and liking for the work and to make the Bar his new goal. Three years later, having eaten the requisite number of dinners and passed his examinations against stiff competition, he was called to the Bar; and three weeks after donning wig and gown he married his neighbour's daughter, Alice Cohen, at the West London Synagogue.

Rufus Isaacs was now on the threshold of a sensational legal career which, in turn, was to prepare him for an equally distinguished life in government service. The years 1887 to 1914 covered his active life at the Bar, culminating in his appointment as Lord Chief Justice. During the war years and until his death in 1935 he devoted his talents to public service, when as Lord (later Marquess of) Reading he was successively Ambassador, Viceroy and Foreign Secretary. Linking his time at the Bar and his public service is the parliamentary period, beginning in 1904. Had he not entered politics it is improbable that he would have achieved high government office, but there was never any doubt that his skill and renown as an advocate would bring him the highest rewards – in every sense.

If, in this short study, we concentrate on the earlier part of his career, this is not to undervalue the very important contributions he made later in the financial and diplomatic fields. But it is as a famous advocate that Rufus Isaacs will be longest remembered, particularly for his courtroom encounters with the other legal giants of his time, Marshall Hall and Edward Carson, and for his superb handling of the most varied and complicated cases, ranging from fraud and union disputes to charges of royal bigamy and – on one occasion only – murder.

Briefs began to flow in steadily as he demonstrated his ability to absorb the most complicated and specialized details of a case, to present them clearly and concisely to a jury, to wear down the most difficult witnesses by the simple force of logic and reasoned argument and to win verdicts against all apparent odds. His remarkable powers of memory, his incredible capacity for hard work, the unfailing courtesy of his manner in and out of the courtroom, were soon bywords in the profession. A well-known solicitor, Sir George Lewis, saw him in action in the High Court during the early days, and asked, 'Who's that young man? He knows what he's talking about and I like his style.' 'That's young Rufus Isaacs,' he was told, and jotted down the name that was soon to become famous.

The contrast between his calm, suave courtroom manner and technique and that of the 'heavyweights' like Hall and Carson was revealing. Not for him the grand emotional, impassioned plea, the dramatic gesture, the lofty rhetoric, the thundering, intimidating cross-examination. His delivery was as cool, quiet and measured as his appearance was neat and impeccable. He could make an opening speech lasting five hours without once becoming excited or confused. He could confront the most truculent or confident witness and wear him down by sheer, unrelenting persistence, the subtly-angled questions building up to reveal, gradually and implacably, the essentials of a criminal design. Many a witness was to underestimate, to his own cost, the power and deadliness of his bland, disarmingly polite professional manner.

Already in his second year at the Bar Isaacs was earning £750, concentrating chiefly on commercial cases. There was much county and police court work, while the occasional High Court case also gave much-needed experience. His first big case was Chetwyn v. Durham, in which he appeared as junior on behalf of the racehorse owner Sir Charles Chetwyn who was suing Lord Durham for libel. The great Irish lawyer, Sir Charles Russell, a future Lord Chief Justice, appeared for Durham and although Isaacs took little part in the twelve-day hearing, he revelled in the atmosphere of this highly publicized case and earned himself the handsome fee of £230.

His own chance came shortly afterwards, though in less spectacular circumstances. The case was known as Allen v. Flood, which arose from a labour dispute in Millwall. It was to make legal history, for it went to the Court of Appeal and then to the House of Lords. So it came that Isaacs, appearing for the union delegate Allen, addressed the assembled peers for an entire morning, impressing them with the force of his reasoning and the confidence of his delivery. The fact that the decision went against his client was unimportant compared with the wide publicity he received.

The next step was to take 'silk' in April, 1898. By now his earnings were more than £7,000 a year and as a Q.C. he was increasingly in demand. The paper work was behind him and he now entered willingly into a more spectacular role. He was to earn more than any previous member of the Bar and was to count these years as the happiest in his life. Despite the tremendously long hours which he devoted to his legal work (he needed no more than five hours' sleep to be completely refreshed), he still found time to lead an active social life, to participate in local political work and to prepare the path for his parliamentary career.

Within five years he was the acknowledged leader of the Commercial Court and participated in a stream of notorious cases. The Beall case, which he lost, was his first major appearance as Q.C., followed by the sensational libel action brought by Arthur Chamberlain, brother of the Colonial Secretary, against the *Star* newspaper.

A series of *Star* articles had accused this eminent business-man of using political pressure to obtain government contracts for army supplies; but the attacks were clearly directed against the unpopular Joseph Chamberlain and his son Austen. Isaacs appeared for the *Star*, claiming the articles to be fair statement of fact. It was a thankless task, the verdict a foregone conclusion, but Isaacs was instrumental in having damages reduced to a mere £200. The *Star* praised the 'vast skill and the perfect discretion' with which Isaacs handled the defence.

A criminal case followed in which Isaacs defended a young South African, Dr Frederick Krause, on incitement to murder and attempted soliciting to commit murder. Krause was a barrister at the Middle Temple, with pro-Boer sympathies, and it was his association with a man named Broeksma who had been convicted and executed in South Africa for treason that led to his own arrest on a similar charge. Leading for the prosecution was the Solicitor-General, Edward Carson, and this was the first of many courtroom duels between the two men. Isaacs lost his case, but his client was fortunate to be sentenced to a short two-year term of imprisonment.

The Bank of Liverpool frauds case was less dramatic, but far more involved and interesting. Isaacs defended a man named Kelly, accused with three others of defrauding the Bank of Liverpool over a period of years of several hundreds of thousands of pounds. The central figure was a gullible young ledger-clerk in the bank named Goudie; Kelly and his colleagues had used him to accumulate a vast income based on non-existent betting 'losses' on the racecourse. Kelly was one of the minor offenders and eventually got off with two years' imprisonment with hard labour.

A series of varied cases followed, the Suffield libel case, the Hartopp divorce-suit and the Taff Vale action. In the un-savoury Hartopp case Isaacs appeared for a Mrs Sands, one of his opponents being the renowned Sir Edward Clarke. There were charges and counter-charges of adultery, ending with the somewhat surprising verdict that nothing improper had in fact occurred on either side. Isaacs made an eloquent closing speech on behalf of his client, accused of intimacy with Lord Hartopp, and was applauded by the spectators.

The Taff Vale case, centring on the question of trade union liability, was of historic importance. Although the Union lost the case to the Taff Vale Railway Co., it proved to be a stepping-stone towards the Trade Union Disputes Act of 1906 for which the unions, and Isaacs too, as a Liberal Imperialist parliamentary candidate, had long been campaigning. The case, arising out of a strike lasting eleven days, went to the Court of Appeal and the Lords, and cost the Union £23,000 in damages. But the 1906 legislation thoroughly vindicated Isaacs' courtroom arguments and won him support and admiration in trade-union circles.

In January, 1904, occurred the famous Whitaker Wright case, in which Rufus Isaacs established himself unquestioningly as one of the most able advocates of the age. The accused was a prominent financier, company promoter and former millionaire. Briefly, Wright, a popular and well-respected figure, was indicted on twenty-six counts for swindling the shareholders of his London & Globe Finance Corporation by manipulating the assets of a group of associated companies and falsely announcing comfortable profits when the company was insolvent. Wright displayed a balance sheet which showed a profit of £463,672; eleven days later this was revealed as utterly fictitious. The angry creditors, owed £2,296,000, howled for Wright's blood. Foolishly he absconded and was finally arrested in New York. He was astute enough to try to retain Isaacs' services but was dismayed to learn that Isaacs was actually leading for the prosecution.

The prosecution's opening speech lasted five hours and displayed to the full Rufus Isaacs' uncanny grasp of complex detail, all the more remarkable for the clarity and precision with which he explained the tortuous processes of big business and finance to the jury. The highlight of the trial was his masterly cross-examination of Wright himself, one of the most formidable witnesses he had ever confronted. Ebullient, self-confident, a figure of seeming respectability, his attitude when he entered the box was jaunty and patronizing. When Isaacs had finished with him he was a defeated, ruined man, his guilt evident for all to see.

Wright was forced to admit that he had published the balance sheet to conceal the true situation from his shareholders. During the judge's summing up, with the verdict a certainty, he was seen to have scribbled the figure VII on a scrap of blotting paper – the maximum sentence of seven years which he expected, and in fact received. He bowed to the Bench, protested his innocence, discussed an appeal with his solicitor, Sir George Lewis, retired to the lavatory and, returning, requested a glass of water and a cigar. Suddenly he slumped back in his chair, dead, having swallowed a capsule of potassium cyanide. It was a dramatic ending to a famous trial.

Isaacs had already fought a by-election unsuccessfully and now he entered the lists again for the Reading constituency. He was elected by a majority of 230 votes and his parliamentary career began. His maiden speech, during a debate on the Aliens' Bill, was attentively though not rapturously received. The truth is that he never excelled as a speaker in the Commons; courtroom methods were not as effective in that more heated assembly. But his reputation as a lawyer and the respect in which he was held by Liberal leaders led him steadily and surely onwards to the posts, in close succession, of Solicitor-General and Attorney-General. These he did not attain until he was fifty, and that was still six years away.

The year after entering the House Isaacs undertook the defence of the editor of the *Liverpool Daily Post*, Sir Edward Russell, later Lord Russell of Liverpool. The charge was that his newspaper had criminally libelled members of the Licensing Committee of the Liverpool Justices. Russell accused them of not trying to reduce the number of public houses in Liverpool because of their vested interests in the liquor trade. The prosecution proved unwise, for Isaacs was at his brilliant best and won an acquittal. In two splendid speeches he argued powerfully for the right of free speech and the 'not guilty' verdict was cheered in court. Sir Edward's paper paid high tribute to Isaacs' defence and his contribution to the cause of Press freedom.

In 1906 he held his seat for Reading with an increased majority and continued as busily as ever in the courts. He was opposed by Carson in a number of cases and the spectacle of these two splendid lawyers in full cry was enthralling. Their most extraordinary confrontation occurred at the end of the Lever *v.* Associated Newspapers case, when Isaacs acted for the defendants against the plaintiffs, Lever Bros Ltd, the big soap manufacturers. The *Daily Mail* and *Evening Standard* had accused Lever Bros of selling soap in a fraudulent manner to deceive the public as to its weight. Clearly it was a difficult case to defend. Mr W. H. Lever, later Viscount Leverhulme, made such a strong impression in the box and was so unruffled by Isaacs' cross-examination that the latter finally withdrew his case. Carson demanded heavy damages and after some preliminary haggling Isaacs announced airily, 'Look here, Ned, you can have £15,000.' Lever refused. Isaacs increased his offer by stages to £40,000 and then to £50,000. 'What do you say to that, Mr Lever?' asked Carson. 'That's a substantial offer,' was the reply. 'I'll take it.'

Another sensational case, again with a racecourse background, was Rex *v.* Sievier. Again Carson and Isaacs faced one another. The charge was extortion; Isaacs' client was acquitted. Carson had his revenge in the Cadbury *v.* Standard Newspapers case in which Cadbury's, the chocolate manufacturers, Quakers and social reformers, were alleged to be paying no heed to the monstrous conditions under which their raw materials were obtained, in sharp contrast to the model conditions of employment which they offered their factory workers and families in England.

The newspapers were awarded the verdict, but Isaacs, for Cadbury's, had the satisfaction of hearing damages fixed at the derisory figure of one farthing.

In the first of two elections held in 1910, Rufus Isaacs again held Reading with a slender majority of 207; and after a government reorganization, in recognition for his services to the Bar, he was appointed Solicitor-General. A few months later, prior to another election in which he was again returned, he was elevated to Attorney-General. With the accession of King George V that same year he was awarded a knighthood.

One of the first cases he handled in his new capacity was the controversial Archer-Shee hearing in which a young naval cadet was accused of stealing a postal order worth 5s. The publicity surrounding this case was out of all proportion to the seriousness of the alleged misdemeanour and Isaacs was forced to proceed with a prosecution which he found distasteful. Carson appeared for the boy defendant and Isaacs was finally compelled to announce his acceptance of the lad's innocence.

In 1911 occurred the extraordinary case of Rex *v*. Mylius, in which Sir Rufus Isaacs and Sir John Simon, the new Solicitor-General, appeared on behalf of the King to clear his name against a scurrilous charge of bigamy, circulated by a journal called *The Liberator*. This alleged that Queen Mary was not his lawful wife, as a result of a union twenty years earlier, in Malta, with the daughter of a British admiral. The prisoner, Frederick Mylius, who was the journal's agent in England, startled the court at the outset by stating, 'I wish to ask if the King is present. . . . I demand his presence.' 'You are perfectly aware,' replied Lord Alverstone, the Lord Chief Justice, 'that the King cannot be summoned here. The King is not present.' The defendant's case was torn to shreds when it was proved that there was not a grain of truth in the allegations, after Isaacs had solemnly concluded his speech to the jury as follows: 'You will . . . bear in mind this: that the King is none the less entitled to the verdict of a jury and to the protection of an English Court of Justice in any attack made upon his honour because he happens to be the King of England.' A sworn statement signed by the King was read out after the verdict and sentence (twelve months' imprisonment) to the effect that he had never gone through any ceremony of marriage except with the Queen, and that he would have given evidence to this effect had it not been unconstitutional to do so. In token of the King's appreciation both Isaacs and Simon were made Knights Commander of the Royal Victorian Order.

One more case remains to mention – the only murder trial in which he ever took part – the notorious Seddon poison case. This was in March, 1912.

Frederick Seddon and his wife were accused of murdering their lodger Eliza Mary Barrow by administering arsenic. It was a sordid story of meanness and cupidity, suspicion first being aroused after Miss Barrow's death, apparently from natural causes, by several circumstances. Seddon was discovered to be in possession of her property, he had spent next to nothing on her burial in a public grave (even extracting a commission of 12s 6d from the undertaker), and he had failed to notify the dead woman's relatives, although they lived nearby. The body was exhumed, over two grains of arsenic were found in it, and the Seddons were committed for trial. But it was all circumstantial evidence. The arsenic was supposed to have been contained in flypapers allegedly purchased by the Seddons' daughter, Maggie. Marshall Hall, for Frederick Seddon, demolished the chemist's evidence of identification and then forced the medical experts to admit that the symptoms were more consistent with chronic than acute poisoning. One of the doctors subsequently reversed this opinion but it was still very much an open case.

Seddon then elected to go into the witness-box and there followed a six-hour marathon of a cross-examination in which Isaacs, not attempting to prove conclusively that Seddon had administered the arsenic, gradually revealed him as a mean, petty-minded, greedy, heartless individual. The monster he denied himself to be stood before the Court. At the end there was no doubt in anyone's mind that this callous murder had been committed – for no other motive than money – by Seddon, possibly with the assistance of his wife.

It has been widely suggested that if Seddon had not gone into the witness-box he might have been acquitted; as it was he convicted himself by a series of damning admissions. Isaacs' opening question, delivered so quietly and innocently, was a master-stroke in itself:

'Mr Seddon,' said Isaacs, very politely, 'did Miss Barrow live with you from July, 1910 till September, 1911?' 'Yes,' said Seddon. 'Did you like her?' inquired Isaacs. The question was so unexpected that Seddon stumbled, repeating 'Did I like her?' Isaacs waited calmly while Seddon struggled for an acceptable reply. Finally he ventured, 'She wasn't a woman you could have been in love with, but I sympathized with her deeply.'

So the relentless cross-examination continued. 'Can you account for the arsenic having got into her stomach and intestines?' 'It is all a Chinese puzzle to me,' confessed the prisoner.

The verdict was 'guilty' and Seddon was hanged. Mrs Seddon, somewhat surprisingly, was acquitted. Sir Travers Humphreys, the great criminal lawyer, later described the trial as follows: 'I venture to recommend to any young barrister in search of a model cross-examination and to any medical man who aspires to become an expert witness the perusal of this interesting trial.'

At the height of his fame, having just achieved the unique honour of being given a Cabinet seat, and having been considered for (though finally not offered) the post of Lord Chancellor, Sir Rufus Isaacs' entire career and future were threatened by the exposure of the so-called Marconi scandal. It is recorded at length in all the biographies of Lord Reading and arose as a result of some shares in the Marconi Company which Sir Rufus purchased on the recommendation of his brother Godfrey, managing director of the English Marconi Company. Marconi, England, were then in negotiation with the Post Office for a contract. After the agreement was signed ugly rumours spread to the effect that Rufus Isaacs and Herbert Samuel, the Postmaster General (it was no coincidence that they were both Jewish), had engineered the deal and made a great deal of money out of the shares whose value had naturally appreciated.

The nub of the matter was that Isaacs had bought *American* Marconi shares at market value and that he had resold them shortly afterwards, showing a net *loss* of £1,300 on the transaction. The American company had no interest in the English company. It was obvious to any fair-minded observer that Isaacs would never have risked jeopardizing his honour and his future career by indulging in political corruption as was now alleged. It soon became apparent that Rufus Isaacs was not the prime target but that Lloyd George's government was under attack. At this point the entire misconception might have been cleared up had Isaacs explained the truth about his American share purchase. Unfortunately he chose to say nothing about it. As a result a Select Committee had to be set up to investigate the matter. There were protracted hearings at which all the evidence was sifted, followed by the inevitable finding that all the individuals involved were totally free of blame. The House accepted this finding unreservedly, no political capital was made of the matter, the legal profession stood staunchly behind Isaacs throughout, and the blemish on his character was removed. But it had been an agonizing eighteen months for him and his family.

Now, however, the honours accumulated ever more rapidly. In October, 1913, Sir Rufus Isaacs succeeded Lord Alverstone as Lord Chief Justice, the first Jew ever to have been accorded this honour. In the Honours List for 1 January, 1914, he was created a Baron, taking the title of Lord Reading of Erleigh. His career as judge was short and he hardly had time to prove his ability on the Bench. He did valuable work in the Court of Criminal Appeal, regarding it as more than a formality, a Court with the duty to reduce sentences and reverse verdicts if the facts warranted. He presided over the treason trial in 1916 of Sir Roger Casement, sentencing him to death after a two-hour summing-up which was as usual a model of restraint, unimpassioned but unforgiving.

It was in 1915 that the government sent him to America, leading an Anglo-French mission to negotiate a $500,000,000 war loan, and such was his success in these delicate financial discussions that in 1917 he was appointed Ambassador Extraordinary and High Commissioner to the United States. He was popular in Washington and when he returned after the war Lloyd George thanked him for 'the leading part which you played in co-ordinating the war effort of the United States and the other Allies'. Balfour, then Foreign Secretary, welcomed him back to the 'calmer labours of the Bench'.

This was not to be. On 6 January, 1921, it was announced that Lord Reading was to be Viceroy of India. During his five-year term of office he and his wife won the respect and affection of the Indian people in a difficult and violent period of history. All his tact and tolerance was required to restrain the forces unleashed by opposing political and religious passions. These were the years of the Amritsar massacre, of Gandhi's civil disobedience campaigns and imprisonment, of continuous Hindu-Moslem strife against a background of poverty, social inequality and economic under-development. Both Lord and Lady Reading were unsparing of their time and talents; both wished and worked for improved living standards and social conditions, and his message on leaving India was typically modest. 'It is the end of five great years for me,' he said. 'If it has been of any use, I am delighted.'

When he returned, to a round of civic dinners and communal receptions, he was made Marquess of Reading – the highest rank ever attained by a Jew. One appointment which he accepted with pleasure was Chairman of the Board of the Palestine Electrical Corporation. This was his only public link with Jewish affairs. Though not an active Zionist, he was strongly in sympathy with Zionist aims, and when he visited Palestine in 1931 with his second wife he was accorded a warm and spontaneous welcome.

One final honour was still in store, though it was short-lived – Secretary of State for Foreign Affairs in Macdonald's Cabinet of Ten, a post which he tackled with his customary verve and expertise. But he had suffered a grievous loss in the death of his wife in January, 1930. She had never been physically strong, but her support and loyalty had been vital at every point in his successful career. Later he married his former secretary. The last four years in semi-retirement were as quiet and uneventful as the ominous pattern of world events would allow. His wife was at his side when he died at his country home, Walmer Castle, on 20 December, 1935.

'I would always prefer to be known as a just man rather than a great lawyer,' he once remarked, and as such history will remember him.

Sir John Monash
1865–1931

In 1875 the pupils of the only school in Jerilderie, New South Wales, included a particularly bright ten-year-old lad named John Monash. Jerilderie was a sleepy little town, tucked away in the bush. John's father, Louis Monash, kept a general store there. The family had moved north from Melbourne where John had been born on 27 June, 1865.

It was the local teacher who persuaded Mr and Mrs Monash to send John back to Melbourne where he could get the quality and variety of teaching that he obviously required. It meant splitting up the family – Mrs Monash and her two daughters moved back to town with John while her husband remained in Jerilderie – but the decision was to mould the career of this unusually talented boy who grew up to be one of Australia's greatest men.

John matriculated at the age of fourteen and graduated from Scotch College in East Melbourne two years later. His distinctions included equal Dux of the school, Dux in mathematics and modern languages and an Exhibition in mathematics worth £25, a handy sum for a family always struggling to make ends meet. In 1882 he enrolled at the University of Melbourne, on the Arts side, his ambition being to become a civil engineer. He passed his first-year examinations only at the second sitting, chiefly because of the diversified nature of his interests.

Refusing to be tied down to a narrow course of study, he branched off in the most surprising directions. Reading was second nature to him and the University and Public Library satisfied his curiosity on a multitude of subjects – literature, music, science, art, architecture, archaeology, law, history, travel and technology. His thirst for knowledge was boundless and his capacity to absorb information phenomenal.

Yet he was no mere walking reference book. He listened to parliamentary debates, attended trials, wrote newspaper articles, played the piano, took painting lessons and dabbled at carpentry and conjuring. He also found time for concerts, plays and parties. He made friends easily, never flaunting his knowledge for its own sake, but already radiating a feeling of calm self-confidence.

His university career was cut short after two years for financial reasons. He was forced to go job-hunting. All this meant was that his distinguished engineering career started earlier than it would normally have done and that he continued his studies on the side. His degrees in Arts, Civil Engineering and Law came when he had already acquired a wide range of practical engineering experience with several firms of contractors. One of the first major constructional projects on which he was engaged was the Princes Bridge across the River Yarra. The late 1880s were prosperous years in Victoria and the building boom in both the private and public sectors enabled him to utilize his outstanding talents in a variety of important development schemes including the construction of the city's Outer Circle Railway.

He was earning good money and in 1891 he married Victoria Moss. Two years later a daughter was born, but by that time prospects were no longer so bright. After the boom had come a slump, bringing widespread unemployment and a virtual halt to building activities. Although John Monash had a job as draughtsman with the Melbourne Harbour

Trust, he was now supporting two sisters as well as his own family. When he lost his job in 1894 there seemed only one solution – to go into business for himself. So he opened his own office as a Consulting Engineer and Patent Attorney.

It seemed that the pattern of his life was irrevocably shaped, but in fact it was not so simple. For John Monash had another absorbing interest, going back to his college days – soldiering.

In his second and last year at University he had joined the University Company of the 4th Battalion, Victoria Rifles. When it was disbanded two years later he was a Colour Sergeant. By now he had acquired a liking for the disciplines and challenges of this part-time occupation. As a patriot it satisfied him emotionally, but more important were the opportunities to exercise his brain on tactical problems and to develop his natural qualities of leadership. Just after joining the Militia Garrison Artillery, he wrote in his diary: 'The undercurrent of my thoughts has been running strongly on military matters. I have been attached to Major Goldstein's battery with the prospect of appointment before Easter; a combination of military and engineering professions is a possibility that is before me.'

The combination was more than possible. It was to prove brilliantly successful. John Monash served first as an officer and later as commander of the North Melbourne Battery for over twenty years, gaining the theoretical and practical experience that he was later to put to such remarkable use in the First World War. As in the civilian field, he rapidly acquired a reputation for uncommon ability and imaginative flair, establishing his authority with tact, firmness and quiet assurance.

Nevertheless it was to be twenty years more before the military side of his genius was permitted full scope; it was as an engineer that he made his name at the turn of century. Slowly the practice grew, and with it the Monash fortunes. He won particular fame as a pioneer in the use of reinforced concrete. Of many constructional projects for which he was responsible one of the proudest was the three-span reinforced-concrete bridge he built in Melbourne across the

Yarra – originally known as the Anderson Street Bridge and later named the Morell Bridge. His work in this new field extended to other parts of Victoria as well as to South Australia and Tasmania.

John Monash's interest in new materials and techniques was the secret of his success in both the civil and military spheres. It helped his business to expand until the war interrupted its even and peaceful progress. And it was his study of the development and deployment of modern weapons that accounted for much of his achievement during the war years.

He had travelled abroad in 1910 and spent several months in Germany. What he had seen and heard had depressed him greatly and convinced him that a conflict was coming. In 1913 he was appointed to the command of the 13th Infantry Brigade – a year which he spent training his battalions to a high pitch of excellence. Sir Ian Hamilton, Inspector General of the British Overseas Forces, was deeply impressed by his ability.

His first appointment after war was declared was unexciting – Deputy Chief Censor – but on 15 September he was given the command of the 4th Infantry Brigade, part of the volunteer Australian Imperial Force. Within a few months he was in Egypt, his brigade a unit of the Australian and New Zealand Division commanded by Major General Sir Alexander Godfrey. In April 1915 he and his men first saw action in the ill-fated landing on the Gallipoli Peninsula.

Monash's *War Letters*, mostly written to his wife and daughter, provide a lucid and exciting account of his wartime experiences. Unlike his deservedly praised book *The Australian Victories in France in 1918*, published just after the war, they do not discuss matters of tactics and strategy. They range over a much broader field, providing an unequalled insight into the mind of an extraordinary man – a man who rose from colonel of militia to commander of the Australian Army Corps in a brief period of five years – promotion that was achieved solely as a result of his own skills and genius.

The letters chart the course of his career from the moment

the Brigade landed in Egypt until the demobilization of the Corps in 1919. Through them runs the thread of Monash's personal philosophy of war as a tragic, wasteful operation, an unlikeable job that has to be done, and to which a person is bound to devote his maximum effort and talents.

He is unsparing in his criticism of muddle and inefficiency but ready to praise bold leadership and high fighting prowess. His confidence in his own powers of command and in the unequalled fighting spirit and capacity of his Australian troops never wavers; and he attributes their success to the comradely relationship between officers and men, encouraging a pride in team-work and providing scope for individual initiative. His pride in their achievements was fully supported by their record, especially in the closing phases of the war.

Monash entered on the Gallipoli campaign with high expectations, describing it as 'the greatest feat of arms of this nature ever attempted'. A month later, writing from Anzac headquarters, he praised the magnificent quality of his troops, though grieved at the heavy toll of losses. Of 132 officers he had lost 99 killed or wounded. On 22 June he wrote that of all the Anzac brigadiers he was the only one fortunate enough not to have been disabled and to keep going since the start without a break. He pointed proudly to the fact that his men were the first to have set foot upon enemy territory and to occupy it.

The philosophic strain broke in on 18 July as he assured his wife: 'I have got over worrying long ago . . . one simply goes through one's day's work. One may get into an express train with the feeling that it might be that particular train that is going to be smashed up; but there is no use in making the journey miserable because that *might* happen.'

He had now been promoted to brigadier-general and wrote confidently: 'We have dropped the Churchill way of rushing in before we are ready, and hardly knowing what we are going to do next, in favour of the Kitchener way of making careful and complete preparations on lines which just can't go wrong.' Unhappily things did go wrong, largely due, in his opinion, to the 'cult of inefficiency and muddle and red-tape practised to a nicety'. On 12 December came this diary entry: 'Like a thunderbolt from a clear, blue sky has come the stupendous and paralyzing news that, after all, the Allied War Council has decided that the best and wisest course is to evacuate the Peninsula. . . . I am almost frightened to contemplate the howl of rage and disappointment there will be when the men find out what is afoot, and I am wondering what Australia will think at the desertion of her 6,000 dead and her 20,000 other casualties.' But he immediately applied his clear thinking and organizational skill to the tremendous task of evacuation. In a fortnight it was done and he wrote home: 'We had succeeded in withdrawing 45,000 men, also mules, guns, stores, provisions and transport valued at several million pounds, without a single casualty, and without allowing the enemy to entertain the slightest suspicion. It was a most brilliant conception, brilliantly organized and brilliantly executed, and will, I am sure, rank as the greatest joke – and the greatest feat of arms – in the whole range of military history.' The first phase was over.

The Australians and New Zealanders were now reorganized in Egypt in preparation for the greater challenge soon to come. Two Anzac corps were formed, one under Sir William Birdwood, the other under Sir Alexander Godfrey. Though passed over for the command of the 4th Division, Monash showed no petty resentment. His patience was rewarded when in July, 1916, he was promoted to major-general and given the command of the 3rd Division. The entire Anzac fighting force was transferred to the Western Front, a large part of it seeing immediate action in the Somme offensive. Monash's 3rd Division was held back for training on Salisbury Plain until November. In September it paraded before King George V. Monash was proud to be in the king's company for several hours of pleasant and often flattering conversation. Finally, on 24 November, the Division disembarked in France.

On 21 December, Haig, the Commander-in-Chief, inspected them and congratulated Monash, placing his hand on his shoulder and murmuring: 'You have a very fine division. I wish you all sorts of good luck, old man.' Haig was not the only high-ranking officer to be impressed by the Australian's dynamic personality and unconventional approach to the problems of offensive warfare. But for the time being he had little chance to show his mettle. The Armentières sector was relatively quiet and not until June, 1917 did the 3rd Division really prove its worth, in the successful attack on the Messines Ridge – three days of bitter fighting in which they helped to knock out the entire 3rd and 4th Bavarian Divisions.

A few months previously, on leave in the Riviera, Monash had written to his wife: 'You say I might take up military work as a profession after the war? I hate the business of war, the horror of it, the waste, the destruction, and the inefficiency. . . . My only consolation has been the sense of faithfully doing my duty to my country, which has placed a grave responsibility upon me, and to my division which trusts and follows me. . . . But my duty once done, and honourably discharged, I shall, with a sigh of relief, turn my back once and for all on the possibility of ever again having to go through such an awful time.' And in May, writing to his business partner, John Gibson, he said again: 'I am very heartily sick of the whole war business. Its horror, its ghastly inefficiency, its unspeakable cruelty and misery has always appalled me, but there is nothing to do but set one's teeth and stick it out as long as one can.'

The Division went on from Messines to distinguish itself in the Third Battle of Ypres and at Passchendaele. Monash, always an art-lover, wrote sadly: 'The town of Ypres, once a marvel of medieval architectural beauty, lies all around us a stark, pitiable ruin.' But he was elated by the outcome of the battle, cabling Melbourne, 'All well division again brilliantly victorious in "greatest battle of war".' Passchendaele, however, he described, in a notable under-statement, as a 'hare-brained venture'.

Monash went on leave in March, 1918, sightseeing in Paris and on the Riviera. Then he was summoned back to the front on receipt of news of a German spring offensive that threatened to break through to Amiens. He achieved a miracle of organization, moving his battalions twenty miles by every form of transport, including trains and buses, and finally

Below: Lieutenant-General John Monash receives his knighthood from King George V at Australian Corps Headquarters, Bertangles Château, on 12 August, 1918. *Left:* Sir John Monash resumed a distinguished career in engineering after the 1914–18 war, in which he and his Australian troops achieved outstanding successes.

Bernard Baruch, adviser to Presidents, taking part in the opening session of the United Nations Atomic Energy Committee at Hunter College, Bronx, in June, 1946.

plugging the vital gap between the Ancre and the Somme to halt the enemy advance.

In May came a reorganization at the top and the long-awaited appointment to the command of the Australian Army Corps with its five Divisions totalling 166,000 men. Proudly he wrote: 'My command is more than two and a half times the size of the British Army under the Duke of Wellington, or of the French Army under Napoleon Bonaparte, at the Battle of Waterloo.' In fact, during the next six months, he was also to assume command of British, Canadian and American units, and at the end of the war had over 200,000 men serving under him.

In *The Australian Victories in France in 1918* Monash described in precise detail the part played by the Australian troops in launching the mighty offensive which was the prelude to Germany's surrender. The capture, early in July, of the village of Hamel and its surroundings, was a copybook example of cool and resourceful planning, in which Monash employed infantry and tanks in an unprecedented manner, as a unified instrument of offensive warfare. He had firm faith in the tank as an offensive weapon but had to overcome the distrust and suspicion of his colleagues. This he achieved by devoting a short training period to joint manœuvres, during which men and officers mingled freely in order to build up mutual respect and confidence. He likened his battle plan to 'a score for an orchestral composition, where the various arms and units are the instruments, and the tasks they perform are their respective musical phrases. Every individual unit must make its entry precisely at the proper moment, and play its phrase in the general harmony.' Success was in this instance complete. 'No battle within my previous experience,' Monash wrote, 'passed off so smoothly, so exactly to time-table, or was so free from any kind of hitch. It was all over in ninety-three minutes. It was the perfection of team work. It attained all its objectives; and it yielded great results.'

The same methods were used in the great attack of 8 August. In a surprise offensive, spearheaded by Monash's Australian and Canadian Corps, a huge twelve-mile gap was ripped through the German defence lines, inflicting tremendous casualties. The German Chief of Staff, Ludendorff, described it as 'the black day of the German army'.

On 12 August George V personally bestowed on John Monash the Order of Knight Commander of the Bath at his headquarters at Bertangles Château. This was the first time for almost two centuries that a British monarch had knighted a commander in the field.

From then on it was a record of unbroken success as the enemy was driven back over the Somme to the Hindenburg Line. Then the Line itself was broken and penetrated to a depth of over ten miles. After the capture of Montbrehain on 6 October the Corps was rested and Monash went on leave to London. Next day Germany sued for peace. On 11 November the armistice was signed and the march into Germany began. Sir John was recalled to London a week later to supervise the demobilization programme.

As Director General of Repatriation and Demobilization he applied himself diligently and vigorously to the problems of the transition period from war to peace, his most inventive contribution being the scheme he initiated whereby the Australian government paid for the training of soldiers awaiting demobilization in a variety of subjects likely to be of value to them in their civilian careers. He led the Anzacs in triumphant procession through London and was entertained at Buckingham Palace. Then, his job done, he returned home and resumed the civilian career he had always promised himself.

His years as General Manager and Chairman of the Victoria State Electricity Commission were distinguished by his customary combination of tireless effort and far-ranging vision. Under his inspired guidance the power-resources of the state of Victoria were developed to the point of self-sufficiency. The power station built at Yallourn, in the face of determined opposition, began to supply Melbourne with electricity in 1924; and it was thanks to Monash's experiments with the brown-coal deposits in the area that a thriving new industry for this new type of fuel was developed.

Monash was accorded many honours in the post-war

decade. From 1923 onwards he was Honorary Vice-Chancellor of Melbourne University. In 1931, he and Sir Harry Chauvel were made full generals – the first Australians ever to receive this rank. He regularly attended the annual Anzac Day marches through Melbourne and was one of the men responsible for accepting the design of the Shrine of Remembrance, Victoria's National War Memorial. His last official function was to represent Australia in 1931 at the celebrations in New Delhi when that city became India's capital.

Sir John Monash died on 8 October, 1931. He was mourned by an entire nation and given a state funeral, his body lying in state in Parliament House. In 1950 a fine equestrian statue of him was unveiled in the Domain Gardens, facing towards the city he loved. In 1958 the University bearing his name was opened in the Clayton suburb of the city – Australia's last and fitting tribute to a great scholar, engineer and soldier.

Bernard Baruch
1870–1965

Bernard Mannes Baruch was born on 19 August, 1870 in Camden, South Carolina. His father, Simon Baruch, was an immigrant from East Prussia, a doctor who had come to America to avoid conscription at home and had ended up serving as a Confederate surgeon in the Civil War. His mother, Isabelle Wolfe, was of New York stock and descended from Isaac Rodriguez Marques, a shipowner and trader, contemporary of the celebrated Captain Kidd, who had come to America shortly before 1700.

Bernard was, according to his own account, a shy, sensitive boy, rather chubby – his nickname was 'Bunch'. With his three brothers, he led a carefree life in a warm family atmosphere. He attended a typical one-room village school and spent the long summer days fishing, hunting and swimming. Yet it was a war-shattered area in which they lived, and although young, the boy retained vivid and poignant memories of devastation (his grandfather's mansion had been burned to the ground by Sherman's troops), of poverty and hunger, of cotton crops going to waste, of the misery of poor whites and Negroes alike.

Though his early heroes were Robert E. Lee and the Confederate generals, he had seen the aftermath of war at first hand, and the corruption and violence that it bred. The injustices of carpet-bagger rule in that Reconstruction period remained etched on his mind. The welfare of the South, dependent almost wholly on the cotton industry, was to be one of his main concerns throughout his life. Though he lived and worked in New York and Washington, it was to the South he returned to find relaxation, on his estate at Hobcaw, among the familiar sights and sounds of his childhood.

Dr Baruch moved to New York when Bernard was eleven and the family soon adapted themselves to the brash glitter of a great city already famed for its contrasts of extreme wealth and deprivation. At Public School 59, Bernie Baruch, now growing into a tall, handsome lad, received his first award – a copy of *Oliver Twist* for 'Gentlemanly Deportment and General Excellence'. He learned Hebrew and went to synagogue with his mother, for his father was not observant though adhering firmly to the ethical principles of the Jewish faith. It was in the streets of New York that members of rival gangs first hurled the epithet 'Sheenie' at the Baruch brothers. Hartwig, the eldest boy, was well able to cope with this sort of trouble and later Bernie himself took boxing lessons, recalling with pleasure the time he was congratulated on his prowess by champion Bob Fitzsimmons himself.

At City College Bernard was a good though not brilliant student, his favourite subject being economics. His mother had hoped he would follow his father into medicine but he could summon up little enthusiasm for it. His own hopes of entering the military academy at West Point were dashed when it was discovered he was deaf in one ear as a result of an early baseball accident. A phrenologist suggested he was best suited to a career in finance or politics.

He was now a strapping youth, standing six feet three inches, still shy in the company of girls, but eager to take advantage of all the city could offer, especially vaudeville and the theatre. His brother Hartie who should have been a rabbi chose a career on the stage, but Bernie had no such clear ideas of his calling.

What did fascinate him, however, was money – not only the excitement of gambling but also the application of those inexorable laws of supply and demand which Professor Newcomb had first outlined in his college lectures. On a personal level he was intrigued by the idea of making money – cards, horses, the stock market, all had their attractions – but the sources of a nation's wealth were far more absorbing and rewarding fields of study.

The structure of the economy, the principles of business, the workings of high finance, the exploitation of natural resources in farming and industry, the development of communications across a vast continent, the fluctuating patterns of trade, the relations of capital and labour, the phenomena of booms and slumps – these were the problems which soon obsessed him.

All his reading, his conversation, his observation, revolved around the basic laws and facts governing his country's very existence. The knowledge which he stored up in those formative years was to lay the foundation of his own fortune and to serve the nation in times of need.

His first job, as office boy for a firm of wholesale glass dealers at three dollars a week, was sheer misery. More instructive, though not more lucrative, was his apprenticeship with Julius Kohn, a former clothing-merchant who had gone into Wall Street. Here Bernie gained experience in arbitrage – trading in currency and securities on an international scale – mastering the principles of foreign exchange and market speculation, which stood him in good stead when he landed his first real job as office boy and runner for the brokerage firm of A. A. Housman & Co. in 1891.

Here he quickly blossomed out, studying book-keeping and contract law at night. It was appropriate that with his lifelong love and knowledge of railways his first sale should be for a single bond in Oregon and Transcontinental. Soon he was bringing in a steady flow of orders, on commission. He began to speculate on his own account too, and after a few initial mistakes found that he had a natural flair for it, applying common sense and specialized knowledge rather than trusting to chance and tipsters. It was not long before he was given an eighth share in the company, earning $6,000 in his first year. But an investment in the stock of the American Sugar Refining Company netted him ten times this figure and enabled him to marry his sweetheart, the tall and beautiful Annie Griffin, daughter of an Episcopalian glass merchant. They lived first in a modest house on West End Avenue and Dr Baruch delivered their first child, a girl, in the summer of 1899.

Naturally Bernard had his share of luck in his early deals. One occasion was reminiscent of Rothschild's coup after Waterloo. He and Arthur Housman received inside information of the end of the Spanish–American War. It was on 3 July, 1898. Next day the New York Stock Exchange was on holiday – but London was open for business. The telephone was ringing all day in Housman's New York office as customers were persuaded to place huge orders. When the news broke and the Exchange opened after the holiday weekend, prices rocketed. So did the prestige of A. A. Housman – and the fortunes of Bernard Baruch.

From then on nearly everything he touched turned to gold. Rubbing shoulders with the most renowned financiers, speculators and industrialists of the age, Baruch and his colleagues brought off a series of shrewd and daring deals. The Liggett and Myers tobacco deal brought him in $50,000; the Louisville and Nashville Railway negotiations more than a million dollars; the Amalgamated Copper transaction $700,000.

He was rich and he was respected. He bought two seats on the Stock Exchange, one for Hartie, the other for himself. He could afford the luxuries of life and he could be independent. In 1903 he opened his own office at 111 Broadway, at the foot of Wall Street.

In five years he amassed a fortune of over three million dollars. Known as 'The Lone Eagle' he held his own with the wealthiest and toughest financiers of the age – Edward Harriman, the Rockefellers, the Guggenheims, the legendary

J. P. Morgan the elder. He mingled with men like Diamond Jim Brady, the great speculator James R. Keene, and the famous gambler John Gates, whom he once watched place half a million dollars on a single card.

In the decade prior to the war his interests embraced the whole field of American production and industry – iron and steel, copper, gold, rubber, chemicals. In natural and syn-thetic rubber he became an acknowledged expert, helping to form the Intercontinental Rubber Company to explore new sources of supply for this vital raw material in Mexico, South America, the Congo and Borneo. His only disappoint-ment was his failure, on two occasions, to control and operate a railway.

His money was put to constructive use in many directions, but few things gave him greater pleasure than to be able to retire his father from general practice to set him free for research in his special fields of hydro-therapy and the surgery of appendectomy. And his dream of returning to his native South Carolina was fulfilled in 1905 when he purchased the beautiful 17,000-acre estate known as Hobcaw Barony where he and his family spent most of their leisure time. To Hob-caw, until it was devastated by a hurricane in 1954, came many of the world's most distinguished men, to hunt and fish, to converse and to relax in what was, to Bernard Baruch, the most beautiful spot on earth.

Sometimes, though, life on Wall Street seemed sterile and unproductive and he longed to be of service, as was his father, to the community. The opportunity came when he met a fellow trustee of City College, William McCoombs. McCoombs introduced him to the Democratic candidate for the 1912 presidential election, Woodrow Wilson. The two men, both of them Southerners, met in New York's Plaza Hotel and at once struck up a friendship that lasted till Wilson's death in 1924. As Baruch said in *My Own Story*, the first part of the autobiography which he wrote when he was almost ninety: 'Looking back to that first meeting, I know that I came away profoundly impressed. Although I did not then realize it, I had met a man I would soon regard as one of the greatest in the world.'

Bernard Baruch

Wilson was duly elected and immediately embarked on an
unprecedented programme of reform known as the New
Freedom – precursor of Roosevelt's New Deal. It was a programme which Baruch whole-heartedly endorsed, the first
time an American government had stepped in to direct the
economy. There was new legislation affecting tariffs and
trade, agriculture and industry, monopolies and child labour,
banking and taxation. Baruch applauded Wilson's practical
grasp of realities and his idealism. Both qualities were to be
sorely needed as America slowly but inevitably became involved in the European war which soon shattered the nation's
complacency and signalled her emergence as an international
power.

Baruch became increasingly wrapped up in affairs of state,
giving generously of his time and fortune. He travelled
widely, assessing means for mobilizing all the nation's resources in preparation for the war that was surely coming.
The co-ordination of the nation's financial, business, industrial
and agricultural interests, the harnessing and distribution of
raw materials, the most economic use of manpower, and
governmental control over prices and profits, were problems
on which he reported to the President. In September, 1915,
he visited Wilson at the White House and urged him to
place American industry on a wartime footing. The nation
was, in his view, tragically unprepared for the coming
challenge.

Wilson heeded Baruch's advice, though it was more than a
year before America declared war and longer still before her
vast resources were organized and centrally directed as
Baruch had recommended.

Baruch himself had, in December, 1916, been forced to
defend himself before a Congressional investigation against
allegations of profiteering as a result of a 'Peace Leak'. He
was able to convince his detractors that the money he had
made had been the result of shrewdness rather than confidential information, but he was never completely to dispel
hostile accusations of being little more than a clever Wall
Street speculator – and Jewish to boot. Baruch was sensitive
to such attacks throughout his life. At City College he had

resented bitterly being barred, for religious reasons, from the Greek-letter fraternities. The attacks which came during the twenties, spearheaded by Henry Ford's vindictive *Dearborn Independent*, were far more damaging and may have been the main reason why he decided not to seek high public office. He had deliberately refrained from associating himself with any single sector of industry, and when appointed to the War Industries Board he sold his Stock Exchange seat and disposed of all bonds and shares in enterprises which might have profited from government contracts.

Wilson first made official use of Baruch's talents on the Raw Materials Committee of the Advisory Commission of the Council of National Defence. Out of this stemmed the War Industries Board, of which he was made Chairman in March, 1918. No other American apart from the President had ever wielded comparable power and responsibility. Baruch discharged this immense task with distinction and modesty, winning the support and friendship of the leaders of American business, industry, banking and labour, as well as the armed forces. With the aid of a talented and enthusiastic staff, he was responsible for mobilizing the huge material, financial and human resources of the nation on a strict priority basis. Throughout 1918 the Board forged ahead, keying America's war potential to its maximum effort, purchasing and allocating materials, enforcing price controls, increasing production, curbing competition and profiteering, placating capital and labour, recruiting women for factory work, conserving fuel, rationing consumer goods and coordinating activities with the allied war effort. It was a gigantic achievement and played no small part in bringing the war to an early and successful conclusion.

The work of the WIB ended with victory in Europe and the organization was disbanded. It was typical of Baruch that he paid the fares home of hundreds of secretaries stranded in New York. It cost him $45,000 from his own purse and it was the kind of gesture that endeared him to countless friends and colleagues in private and public life during his long career.

Wilson and Baruch were in agreement that the lessons

learned in wartime had to be applied to peacetime reconstruction. Government had to play a judicious part in keeping the economy stable. Private enterprise could not be allowed to flourish unchecked and uncontrolled. Yet government intervention could not be permitted to go too far. Baruch, essentially a conservative, recoiled from communist or socialist doctrinaire solutions, and for all his later support of Roosevelt he was disturbed by some of the more extreme measures of the New Deal.

In Paris, as one of Wilson's advisers to the Peace Conference, Baruch did not underestimate the task which faced America, unscarred by war. He was aware of the threat of a revived Germany but convinced that the security of the world depended on a sound, flourishing Europe in which Germany had to be a partner. But as he stood with Wilson on the battlefield of Ypres, he could understand the revengeful sentiments of Clemenceau's France and the bitterness of Lloyd George who had promised his countrymen to 'squeeze Germany until the pips squeak'.

Baruch helped to frame the economic clauses of the Peace Treaty which unwittingly sowed the seeds for a later and more catastrophic conflict. The shortcomings of the Treaty and the dashing of Wilson's high hopes for an effective League of Nations, dashed by his own countrymen who refused to support it – these events belong to history. Baruch was disillusioned and saddened by the developments during the five years following the war, when Wilson lay half-paralyzed and the nation drifted into isolationism.

There were personal shocks too, the death of both his parents preceding by three years that of his hero Woodrow Wilson. With the Republicans – Harding, Coolidge and Hoover – he never forged the same close links, nor, despite his studies and reports on the economic situation, was his advice so frequently sought. He still had his Stock Market successes – the Alaska Juneau gold mine venture was one such – but he was disgusted by the unregulated scramble for wealth, gloomy about the economy, and hardly surprised by the Crash when it finally came at the end of a superficial and unproductive decade.

1932 brought Franklin Delano Roosevelt to the White House and Baruch, though not initially a supporter, soon came to believe in the amazing ability of this handicapped man to boost the nation's morale, and to admire the determination with which he took swift, revolutionary action to tackle the post-Depression situation. Baruch was not directly involved in the New Deal and the measures which during those famous Hundred Days gradually restored the nation to an even keel. But throughout Roosevelt's presidency he was a valued friend and adviser and particularly devoted to the President's remarkable wife Eleanor. The two New Deal experiments with which he was closely associated were the Agricultural Adjustments Act and the National Industrial Recovery Act. Yet again, as in the twenties, he shrank from real, personal power. He was the trusted presidential adviser, soon to become the revered Elder Statesman.

As another war drew closer Baruch warned America to prepare again in good time, keeping in close touch with his old friend Winston Churchill who also had no illusions about Hitler's intentions. At home, with unemployment still hovering around the ten million mark, he became increasingly critical of Roosevelt who, in his view, had failed to get to the roots of the recovery problem. He suffered a grievous blow in 1937 with the death of his wife but found comfort in the company of his three children, his loyal secretary and a host of intimate friends. Over everything loomed the growing international crisis. In 1938 Roosevelt sent him on an unofficial mission to Europe to report on the defence situations abroad, promising to appoint him on his return to the chairmanship of a Defence Co-ordination Board. But a few months later the idea had been abandoned. Nor was his name among the members of the War Resources Board formed a month before war broke out. In May, 1940, when F.D.R. formed a National Defence Advisory Commission, Baruch's name was still missing.

Yet Baruch's expert advice was continually sought and unstintingly given. He still urged that a one-man overseer for the defence effort was essential, that the lessons of the First

World War had to be applied, on an immeasurably larger and more complex scale, to the Second. Such an appointment was made a month after Pearl Harbor, when Donald Nelson was made Chairman of the War Production Board. Baruch worked closely with Nelson and with his successors, but again turned down the offer to become Economic Stabilizer in the autumn of 1942, a post which went to James F. Byrnes. He was content to work behind the scenes, to advise and report on ordnance, synthetic rubber, aircraft, manpower and inflation controls. And when victory approached he immediately turned his mind to the problems of post-war reconstruction. In February 1944 came his brilliant report on *War and Post-war Adjustment Policies*, in which he analysed the measures required to effect a smooth transference from wartime to peacetime economy. Though he had a Washington office he spent much of his time planning and discussing matters of the day from a park bench in Lafayette Square, not far from the White House, literally within hailing distance.

A further mission to London in April, 1945, was cut short by the sudden news of Roosevelt's death. Baruch placed himself at the service of his successor Harry Truman who astutely appointed him as U.S. representative on the United Nations Atomic Energy Commission. Venturing into a completely unfamiliar field, he now devoted all his time to resolving this most urgent and potentially dangerous of post-war problems. His skill and tact won him the co-operation of scientists, politicians and defence chiefs alike.

On 14 June, 1946, his four-point plan for the control of atomic energy was put before the Atomic Energy Commission. It called for the creation of an International Atomic Development Authority responsible for developing the use of atomic energy, with full powers to control, license and inspect atomic activities, whether for peaceful or warlike purposes; to share knowledge, promote research and to punish nations infringing the regulations. Once a system of effective controls had been introduced America would cease production of her bombs and destroy her stockpiles. If successful the work of the Authority might be extended to other weapons of mass destruction as a step towards outlawing war itself.

Tragically, this sensible plan was torpedoed when it came before the Security Council, not least by an intransigent Russia bent on developing her own stock of atomic weapons. The opportunity once missed, both Powers raced full speed ahead in a seemingly endless arms-race.

Baruch considered his work done and resigned in January 1947. In the critical period of the Korean War and the Cold War, which showed no signs of thawing until the death of Stalin, Baruch, now past eighty, was still called upon by Truman and his Republican successor Eisenhower to advise on defence and economic matters. Even when he had passed his ninetieth birthday he was still devoting his acute powers of logic and analysis to the many pressing world problems of the atomic age.

On 10 May, 1964, Baruch presented to Princeton University a collection of 1,200 letters from nine Presidents, spanning half a century of history, as well as 700 letters from his friend Churchill. They were to form the nucleus of a new study-centre in twentieth-century American statecraft and public policy. On his 94th birthday he confessed to reporters that he felt his age – 'I could shoot quail at 92 and keep up with the dogs,' he remarked. 'Now I can't keep up with the dogs or with people.' He died in New York on 20 June, 1965.

His position as elder statesman and adviser to Presidents was unique. Yet important as his influence was, it could surely have been even greater had he accepted or fought for a cabinet post. The reasons for his reluctance to accept the challenge of high office will remain matters for conjecture. But in terms of prestige and public service Bernard Baruch will long retain an honoured place in the hearts and minds of his countrymen. America came of age during his long career and few men can have been more concerned to see her play a responsible and constructive role in a changing world.

Chaim Weizmann
1874–1952

In the winter of 1946 I motored with my parents through northern Europe down to the Swiss frontier city of Basle. The contrast between this bright, bustling town and the dingy, war-torn villages of the Ardennes and northern France was breathtaking. One felt a sense of relief yet also a faint twinge of shame.

Our destination was the 22nd Zionist Congress where the representatives of world Jewry were assembling for the first time in seven years. Victory and peace had been achieved but at frightful cost. The delegates mourned the loss of six million Jews, but their brief was to plan for the future. It was the survivors who needed help now, and urgently.

We sat at the back of the crowded conference hall. Suddenly a tall, slightly stooped figure walked from the wings on to the platform and the delegates rose in a body to applaud. There was no mistaking that great domed head, the small, trimmed beard. Peering with difficulty through his spectacles – his eyesight failing now with age – waiting for the applause to subside, Chaim Weizmann, the greatest figure in the Jewish world since Herzl, began his opening address.

He spoke in Yiddish, the language of his childhood, the language in which he had always expressed himself most vividly, and I understood not a word. Yet as the quiet, firm voice rang through the hushed hall, the sense of the words were intelligible even to me. With only an occasional touch of emotion he spoke of the horror and tragedy of the Nazi holocaust, the bitter loss of valued friends, the need to re-group and rebuild, to concentrate all efforts on the goal which was now, after fifty years, almost within reach – a national home in Palestine. And though this proved to be Weizmann's last Congress, and though many had come to criticize and oppose him publicly, there could be no doubt that here was a man of heroic stature, a man of honour and integrity, who even now, frail with ill-health and a grievous sense of personal and national loss, commanded love, loyalty and deep respect.

Looking back I feel privileged to have seen Weizmann if only from the back of a stuffy conference hall – it was a brief brush with history. For he was one of the two chief architects of the Zionist movement and the Jewish State, influencing the lives and fortunes of his people during the first half of the twentieth century as only Theodor Herzl had done in his decade of Zionist work.

Herzl conceived the grand idea, made the plans, laid the foundations. Weizmann continued the work, added the bricks and mortar, and lived to see the dream fulfilled.

Much has been written about Weizmann, and much penetrating comment and analysis has come from the pens of colleagues, friends, journalists, scientists and statesmen who knew him at some stage of his long career. But our main source of information is his autobiography *Trial and Error*, published in 1949. It has its shortcomings, as does every autobiography; no man can see himself with a clear, objective gaze. But Weizmann's narrative, as cool, precise and unimpassioned as his oratory, remains a classic account of a vital period of history. His recollections of men and public affairs, sometimes disarmingly naïve, but distinguished throughout by characteristic qualities of human insight, un-compromising candour, humour and compassion, tell us more about Weizmann the man than all the learned articles rolled into one.

Weizmann's account of his childhood and early years as a student is tantalizingly brief but full of fascination; and the story of these formative years, his orthodox background in a small Eastern European *Shtetl*, is essential for a full under-standing of his outlook on the Jewish problem – a viewpoint which no Jew raised in the comparative comfort and security of Western Europe could ever hope to appreciate.

Motol, where the Weizmann family lived, was a tiny, un-distinguished village in Russia, one of many similar com-munities in the area known as the Pale of Settlement, where Jews were permitted under the Czarist régime. Here his life followed the traditional ghetto pattern. He received his formal Jewish instruction in the typical dirty, one-roomed school. The home was simply furnished, crowded (there were twelve children), steeped in Jewish tradition; Sabbaths and festivals were scrupulously and joyfully observed. Ezer Weiz-mann was a 'transportierer', or timber-merchant, a sober, practical and respected member of this tightly-knit com-munity which was united in its defence of Jewish standards and values. It was fortunate to escape the harsh and brutally oppressive measures familiar to other villages, but it was isolated, enjoying only the most superficial contacts with the local peasantry and the outside world.

At the age of eleven Chaim was sent to a Russian school in the nearby town of Pinsk. Here his horizons broadened. He mixed with non-Jews. He was involved in the busy life of a city whose population of 30,000 comprised about 20,000 Jews. It was a traditional centre of Jewish learning and at that time a hotbed of Zionist thought and discussion; no young man of Chaim's abilities and vision could fail to be stimulated by all this intellectual and political foment. These young Zionists, keenly aware of the sufferings of the mass of Russian Jewry, were not content to remain a submerged and submissive minority. They were already working, though in a very amateurish and disorganized fashion, towards the realization of a Messianic dream – a home for the Jewish people in a free land.

It was in Pinsk that Chaim met a talented science teacher named Kornienko who taught him the rudiments of chemistry and launched him on a career which was to bring him distinction and fame. Weizmann wrote: 'It was here that I grew from boyhood into early manhood, here that I had my social and intellectual contacts, and here that I was inducted into the Zionist movement. Pinsk . . . set the double pattern of my life; it gave me my first bent towards science, and it provided me with my first experience in Zionism.'

Yet even Pinsk was parochial compared with Berlin where the young Weizmann went to continue his scientific studies. Here, in the midst of a vibrant Russian-Jewish student colony, exposed to intellectual currents from East and West, revelling in the cosmopolitan atmosphere, working, going to concerts, arguing with friends into the small hours, he grew into 'something like maturity'. It was in Berlin that he became fully aware of his life's dual directions. 'When I left Berlin for Switzerland, in 1898, at the age of twenty-four, the adult pattern of my life was set. . . . My political outlook, my Zionist ideology, my scientific bent, my life's purposes, had crystallized.' That he now saw the way ahead so clearly was in large measure due to the double influence under which he and so many of his contemporaries fell during the closing years of the century – the influence of Asher Ginsburg, the celebrated Zionist thinker and writer known by his pen-name of Achad Ha-am ('One of the People'), and of a Viennese journalist named Theodor Herzl.

Achad Ha-am had won international fame with an article entitled *Truth from Palestine* and had identified himself with Zionist work in many practical ways. He saw Palestine as the only answer to the Jewish question, but he was severely critical of the methods thus far attempted – small, random groups of colonizers under the philanthropic umbrella of Baron Edmond de Rothschild, no matter how worthy his intentions. He pleaded for a Jewish Renaissance, a complete re-education of the people. Those who went to Palestine had to be steeped in Jewish tradition and culture; the physical process of colonization was not enough. This message appealed instinctively to Weizmann and his friends who regarded Zionism as a burning spiritual issue as well as a political and economic necessity.

It was from the West, however, that the moving spirit of World Zionism finally emerged. The Hungarian-born Herzl, whose background as a virtually 'assimilated' Jew could not have been more at variance with Weizmann's, was the man who gave the call to action. He linked together the disparate strands of Zionism and convened the first Zionist Congress which created the World Zionist Organization. He formulated the policy which was to result, exactly fifty years later, in the proclamation of a Jewish State.

Weizmann was inspired by Herzl's ideals, entranced by the courage and clear purpose of this handsome, almost prophetic figure with his imposing black beard, his aristocratic manner and dynamic personality. But Weizmann and his friends were critical of his approach and tactics. Herzl pinned his faith on the goodwill and charitable instincts of wealthy philanthropists and powerful rulers. He was prepared to negotiate with the Sultan of Turkey, the hated Russian Cabinet Minister Plehve, the Kaiser, the Pope, the British Government – anyone who could help to bring about a quick, miraculous solution to the Jewish question. Weizmann had no faith in this course of action. Many years after his Congress clashes with Herzl, he wrote: 'To me Zionism was something organic, which had to grow like a plant, had to be watched, watered and nursed, if it was to reach maturity. . . . Herzl was an organizer; he was also an inspiring personality; but he was not of the people, and did not grasp the nature of the forces which it harboured.'

Without Herzl's guidance and administrative brilliance the Zionist Organization would not have come into being, but as time passed it became obvious that the movement was splitting into two factions – the 'political' and the 'practical' Zionists. Weizmann moved to Geneva in 1898 where he continued his research work. Here he met the young medical student Vera Chatzman, his future wife, and plunged ever more enthusiastically into Zionist propaganda work. Here was founded the first Zionist publishing house, and among his friends were two young men destined to make their marks in very different fields: the fiery revolutionary Vladimir Jabotinsky, and a wealthy aesthete named Martin Buber. In Geneva too he came into closer contact with Menachem Ussishkin, described by Weizmann as the practical leader of Russian Zionism as Achad Ha-am was its spiritual leader. Weizmann and Ussishkin were to lead the opposition to Herzl in the bitter Congress debates of those early years.

Matters came to a head in 1903. A trip by Weizmann to Russia, collecting funds and enlisting support, almost coincided with the news of the terrible Kishinev pogrom organized by the Czarist Minister of the Interior, Plehve. The entire Jewish population of this Russian city were left to the mercies of the bloodthirsty mob – forty-five were killed and over a thousand wounded. The sixth Zionist Congress met in the shadow of this massacre where the crucial issue under debate was the British government's offer of Uganda as a national home (described in an earlier chapter). The 'practical' Zionists won the day. Herzl's policy was discredited and he died shortly after, an exhausted and disappointed man. It was clear that there could be no compromise now. It had to be Palestine or nothing.

After the official rejection of the Uganda proposal, in 1905, Weizmann took a decisive step. He moved to England. There was a double motivation. Not only did he feel that here he could continue his scientific work undisturbed, but he sensed that Britain, with her traditions of fairness, compromise and practical good sense would, of all the Great Powers, be the most sympathetic and receptive to Zionist ideals. The link which Weizmann was now to forge with Britain became the central feature of his life. It was Weizmann's work before and during the First World War that paved the way for the Balfour Declaration, it was Britain on whom he placed his reliance during the 1920s, Britain who failed to live up to the promises of the Mandate and reneged on her pre-war pledge to reverse the inflexible terms of the 1939 White Paper. It was for his persistently pro-British policy that he was later attacked and overruled by those who placed little trust in the promises of great nations. But this came much later.

Weizmann was thirty and it was in Manchester that he spent the next ten years, establishing himself on the one hand as a research scientist of unusual calibre and on the other as spokesman, albeit unofficial, of the world Zionist movement. He hired a laboratory in the dingy basement of the university, mastered the English language, then moved on to a lecturer's post. He was unhappy at the start: 'My greatest difficulty was with the fogs, which depressed me terribly. . . . I was home-sick for my European surroundings; I was cut off from Zionist work; and I had seen my fiancée only once since my departure from Geneva.'

The period of depression soon passed. After a year he became involved with the Manchester Zionist Society where he met Harry Sacher, Simon Marks and Israel Sieff, three young men who were destined to play an important role in Zionist history. Achad Ha-am also moved to London and Weizmann's friendship with him ripened over the years.

In January, 1906, came the famous meeting with Arthur James Balfour in the Queen's Hotel, Manchester. The con-versation, often recorded, is worth repeating. Balfour men-tioned Dr Herzl and the Uganda offer. Then, in Weizmann's own words:

'I said: "Mr Balfour, supposing I were to offer you Paris instead of London, would you take it?"

'He sat up, looked at me, and answered: "But Dr Weiz-mann, we have London."

' "That is true," I said. "But we had Jerusalem when London was a marsh."

'He leaned back, continued to stare at me . . . and said: "Are there many Jews who think like you?"

'I answered: "I believe I speak the mind of millions of Jews whom you will never see and who cannot think for themselves, but with whom I could pave the streets of the country I come from."

'To this he said: "If that is so, you will one day be a force."

'Shortly before I withdrew, Balfour said: "It is curious. The Jews I meet are quite different."

'I answered: "Mr Balfour, you meet the wrong kind of Jews." '

Balfour remembered this talk when he met Weizmann later during the war. It illustrates vividly Weizmann's preference for direct, forthright speaking and equally clearly reveals Balfour's unformulated attitude towards a problem of which he had, at that time, no real understanding. Weizmann resolved to make the politicians understand. He intensified his Zionist work both in Jewish and non-Jewish circles.

In 1906 Chaim and Vera Chatzman married in Sopot, near Gdansk. After braving the rigours of a Manchester winter in a decrepit boarding-house they managed to afford a small house of their own. Vera, a brilliant medical student, adapted herself rapidly to her strange new life. During their long and happy life together she was to give her husband invaluable support and encouragement for his work, both in the scientific and political fields. Their first son Benjamin was born the following year. Shortly afterwards Weizmann paid his first visit to Palestine.

He was both elated and depressed – thrilled to set foot on the soil of the Promised Land, to travel round the country and visit legendary Biblical sites, to meet young settlers from Eastern Europe, to discuss future development with Zionist workers; but shocked at the incredibly difficult conditions which the Jewish population had to face in this forgotten outpost of the Turkish Empire.

Of the 80,000 Jews living in Palestine, the great majority lived in the six main cities and their life was painfully reminiscent of the ghetto-like existence of Eastern European Jewry. The colonies, of which there were twenty-five, were 'more in the nature of businesses than agricultural enterprises'. Living standards were low, funds were inadequate, Arab marauders were a continual menace, disease was still taking a heavy toll of lives, and there was a dispiriting lack of organization and purpose.

Yet the picture was not as dismal as it sometimes appeared. The new wave of settlement known as the Second *Aliya* which brought in 20,000 new immigrants between 1906 and 1914, set the pattern for the future. They were to establish the new type of communal settlement known as the *kibbutz* on land bought by the Jewish National Fund. They were to build up the trade-union movement, revive Hebrew as a living spoken and written language, make the deserts and swamps fertile and give the motto 'return to the land' a real meaning.

There were men, too, who believed that agriculture, vital though it was, could not provide all the answers – that industry, commerce, higher education, communications, administration, were all crucial to the future development of a stable and prosperous economy. Urban life also needed a fresh stimulus. One such man was the sociologist Arthur Ruppin, a German Jew with a conservative, commercial background, and director of the Palestine Department of the Zionist Organization. Weizmann could have hoped for no more able and far-sighted collaborator.

One day he took a stroll with Ruppin across the sand dunes north of Jaffa. Suddenly Ruppin stopped, gazed out over the empty stretches of sand and the dazzlingly blue Mediterranean, and announced, 'Here we shall create a Jewish city!' Excitedly he outlined his plans to Weizmann who was immediately captivated by the boldness of the scheme.

It proved to be no dream. Two years later residents of Jaffa founded Tel Aviv (*The Hill of Spring*), a great city built literally on the sands. And it was Ruppin who also bought the land on Mount Scopus which later provided the site for another of Weizmann's life-long dreams, the Hebrew University.

By the time war came in 1914 Weizmann was an internationally respected figure, recognized by Zionist colleagues and statesmen as the leading representative of world Jewry. But the war was a grievous blow to Zionist hopes. When Turkey eventually joined the Central Powers, life for the Jews of Palestine became almost unendurable. Many of the Jewish leaders, sympathetic to the Allied cause, were expelled and active Zionist work came to a halt.

Back in England, however, Weizmann was busier than ever with his research work and his Zionist responsibilities.

In December, 1914, thanks to the intervention of his friend C. P. Scott, editor of the *Manchester Guardian*, he was granted an interview by David Lloyd George, then Chancellor of the Exchequer. Lloyd George expressed sympathy for the idea of a Jewish homeland and suggested a meeting with Balfour at the Admiralty. This was a longer and far more fruitful discussion than the earlier one and Balfour urged Weizmann to visit him again and elaborate on his proposals.

Even more significant was the news that Herbert Samuel, a prominent Jew, but not known to have Zionist sympathies, had prepared a memorandum on *The Future of Palestine*, which, in his capacity as a member of the government, he submitted to the Prime Minister, Asquith. The Palestine issue was at last transmitted from drawing-room and conference hall to government office level.

These unofficial meetings proved to be important to the Zionist cause and the Press also joined in the debate. C. P. Scott was an invaluable ally, but other newspapers reflected the violent opposition which was now looming from many quarters, not least among non-Zionist Jews, who argued that Jews were merely members of a religious community owing allegiance to the countries in which they were born. Orthodox and assimilated Jews alike voiced their strong disapproval of Zionist plans.

Science and politics merged again in another vital interview in March 1916, this with Balfour's successor at the Admiralty, the brilliant young Winston Churchill. Britain was desperately short of acetone, an essential ingredient of high explosive for naval guns. The government had been informed of Weizmann's work in this field and he was greeted by Churchill with the blunt demand: 'Well, Dr Weizmann, we need 30,000 tons of acetone. Can you make it?'

So official recognition had come at last. The next two years were to be devoted to the war effort, with full government backing. He severed his links with Manchester and moved to London. Auspices were favourable. Lloyd George was now Prime Minister with Balfour at the Foreign Office. He met influential people in the banking world, in business, in journalism and – 'one of our greatest finds' – Sir Mark Sykes, Chief Secretary to the War Cabinet with special responsibility for Middle Eastern affairs. It was to Sykes that a memorandum was handed in January, 1917, entitled *Outline for a Programme for the Jewish Resettlement of Palestine*; and it was during the next ten months that the numerous discussions, debates and high-level negotiations took place culminating in the Balfour Declaration of 2 November, 1917.

These negotiations, dramatic as they were, must be covered briefly here. Weizmann, as President of the English Zionist Federation, had to steer a hazardous diplomatic course amid the cross-currents of power politics, military strategy and communal dissension. Across the Atlantic Judge Louis Brandeis rallied official American support while Weizmann, Nahum Sokolow, Herbert Samuel and Lord Rothschild exerted pressure on the British government. Hopes were temporarily dashed by the revelation of the secret Sykes-Picot agreement to divide Palestine after the war into French and British spheres of influence, but this was eventually shelved. When the United States entered the war and the tide turned again in the Allied favour, Zionist expectations once more ran high, though they still had to fend off attacks from representatives of British Jewry and from the Secretary of State for India, Edwin Montagu, himself a Jew but a confirmed anti-Zionist.

On 18 July, Lord Rothschild handed to Balfour the draft form for a declaration of policy following the successful outcome of the war. There ensued another three tense and hectic months of bargaining. Finally it was debated by the War Cabinet, of which Jan Smuts was a particularly sympathetic member. Brandeis kept up the pressure on President Wilson, and it was largely America's acceptance of the Declaration which turned the tables. On 2 November, the famous letter known as the Balfour Declaration was sent to Rothschild. The crucial section read:

'His Majesty's Government views with favour the establishment in Palestine of a national home for the Jewish people, and will use their best endeavours to facilitate the achievement of this object, it being clearly understood that nothing shall be done which may prejudice the civil rights of existing non-Jewish communities in Palestine, or the rights and political status enjoyed by Jews in any other country.'

Weizmann wrote in *Trial and Error*:

'While the Cabinet was in session, approving the final text . . . Sykes brought the document out to me, with the exclamation: "Dr Weizmann, it's a boy!"

'Well – I did not like the boy at first. He was not the one I expected. But I knew that this was a great event. . . . A new chapter had opened for us.'

It was indeed the end of an era and the dawn of a new and very difficult period. By the end of the war the Turks had been driven out of Palestine by General Allenby. Prospects were bright, but Weizmann knew this was no time to relax effort. The battle to translate words into deeds was only now beginning.

Weizmann headed a Zionist Commission to Palestine in 1918, established friendly contact with Allenby and met the Emir Feisal in his camp outside Akaba, together with the legendary Colonel T. E. Lawrence. The reception was extremely cordial and an agreement was drawn up, drafted by Lawrence himself, outlining future policy. Feisal saw no reason why Jews and Arabs should not live together harmoniously and promised to gain the support of his father, the Sherif Hussein. In a letter to Felix Frankfurter, quoted by Weizmann in his autobiography, Feisal wrote:

'We feel that the Arabs and Jews are cousins in race, suffering similar oppressions at the hands of powers stronger than themselves, and by a happy coincidence have been able to take the first step towards the attainment of their national ideals together.

'We Arabs . . . look with the deepest sympathy on the Zionist movement. . . . We are working together for a reformed and revived Near East, and our two movements complete one another.'

Brave words but, alas, destined to be dashed to dust with the subsequent rise of Ibn Saud and the destruction of the Hashemite dynasty. Arab–Jewish co-operation on a national level still remains a distant dream.

July, 1918, saw the laying of the foundation stones of the Hebrew University on Mount Scopus by Balfour, a proud moment for Weizmann. Then came the Peace Conference at San Remo and here, on 23 February, 1919, Weizmann eloquently put the case for the Jewish home. After an agonizing wait the Conference confirmed the Balfour Declaration and gave Britain the Mandate for Palestine. Now indeed Weizmann's faith in Britain seemed vindicated and when Herbert Samuel was appointed first High Commissioner all seemed set fair.

In 1920 Weizmann's work for the movement was officially recognized as he was elected President of the World Zionist Organization. For the next decade he travelled widely, to Europe, to Palestine, to America, speaking to public gatherings, raising funds, negotiating with statesmen and successive High Commissioners, supervising the ever-increasing activities of the Zionist Organization, and having the satisfaction in 1929 of seeing the formation of an enlarged Jewish Agency. This was a major achievement since, for the first time, non-Zionist leaders agreed to join the executive, thus creating a fully representative body of Jewish opinion, authorized to treat with the government on all matters relating to Palestine.

The preamble to the Mandate, which included the words 'recognizing the historical connection of the Jews with Palestine', was ratified by the League of Nations in July, 1922. A month previously the so-called Churchill White Paper had detached Transjordan from the Jewish sphere of influence but it reaffirmed that 'A Jewish National Home will be founded in Palestine. . . . The Jewish people will be in Palestine as of right and not on sufferance. . . . Immigration will not exceed the economic capacity of the country to absorb new arrivals.' Again the loose wording of the document was to cause trouble. What was to constitute Palestine? What was the country's absorptive capacity?

Undeterred by the ambiguities of government declarations, Jewish immigration continued at an increasing rate during the 1920s until by 1928 the Jewish population was around 170,000. But the constructive work both in the newly founded communal settlements and in the growing cities had to contend with a background atmosphere of increasing tension. Arab unrest, fanned by Haj Amin al-Husseini, Mufti of Jerusalem, broke out spasmodically in riots and attacks on border setlements. The Arab upper classes, the *effendis* whose prosperity depended on the perpetuation of a feudal system based on cheap peasant labour, were alarmed at the signs of Arab–Jewish co-operation, the employment of Arabs on Jewish land and the rise in Arab standards of living. Moreover, Arab protests carried considerable weight with British officialdom; both civil and military authorities made it quite obvious that they viewed Jewish aspirations with little enthusiasm, while Whitehall's sympathies cooled visibly as the years passed.

In Zionist circles disillusion set in fast and Weizmann came in for heated criticism and attack at the Congresses, particularly from those who now urged stronger action to assert Jewish rights and protect Jewish lives and property. The stockade and water tower were the symbols of the new settlements and as it was clear that the Jews could not rely on outside assistance the foundations were laid for a Jewish defence force, *Haganah*, later to form the nucleus of the Israeli army, but now condemned by Britain as illegal. It also harboured a minority extremist element which by countering terrorism with terrorism was later to damage the Jewish cause in the eyes of world opinion. Weizmann condemned extremist action throughout his life, but realized too well that soft words alone were unlikely to achieve stability and security.

There were ominous signs of danger too from Europe. Hitler's *Mein Kampf* was published in 1924 and anti-semitism was on the increase in Poland, Rumania and Hungary. Those who read the signs correctly knew that time was not on their side.

1929 was a black year. Against a world background of economic depression riots erupted with a ferocity never previously experienced. The British government, alarmed, sent out a Commission and in November, 1930, issued the Passfield White Paper, restricting immigration and cutting back Zionist operations in an attempt to placate the Arabs. Although the government was forced to relent in the face of violent opposition, the White Paper was a blow to Weizmann's prestige. At the 17th Congress at Basle he was voted out of office. Dejected, feeling a keen sense of betrayal, he returned to the world of science, though continuing to work actively at home and abroad for the cause nearest his heart. Although he had had the satisfaction of seeing his cherished Hebrew University opened in 1925, he now felt that the control of events in Palestine had slipped from his grasp.

Weizmann was recalled as President of the World Zionist Organization in 1935, but he never again enjoyed the undivided respect and support of his colleagues. A new generation of leaders had come to the fore, convinced, in view of the rapidly blackening picture in Europe, that more urgent, forceful methods were necessary to save persecuted Jewry. In 1936 came further riots and another inquiry, the Peel Commission. Weizmann spoke with force and dignity of the plight of the Jews in Central Europe:

'There are in this part of the world six million people doomed to be pent up in places where they are not wanted, and for whom the world is divided into places where they cannot live, and places into which they cannot enter.

'The task of the Royal Commission is complex, and it has come at a time when the Jewish position is darker than ever before, even in our history.'

It was then that the idea of partition was first formally advanced as a possible solution of the problem. It was hotly debated by the Zionist Congress and reluctantly agreed in principle. Yet the ensuing White Paper, curtailing immigration still further, was regarded as a betrayal, a confession that the Mandate was unworkable. A second team, the Woodhead Commission, was sent out amid renewed violence in which many Arab, Jewish and British lives were lost. Then, as international tension rose, a futile Tripartite Conference was convened where the terms of the fatal 1939 White Paper were worked out. This slammed the doors of Palestine in the face of the victims of Nazi Germany at a time when all the other Great Powers were turning their backs. At Westminster the Socialist Opposition bound itself to repeal the White Paper if and when returned to power, and the last pre-war Congress in Geneva condemned it as illegal. Here Weizmann bade farewell to the delegates, most of them he was never to see again:

'It is with a heavy heart that I take my leave,' he said. 'Perhaps a new light will shine upon us from the thick black gloom. . . . We shall meet again. We shall meet again in common labour for our land and people. Our people is deathless, our land eternal. . . . May we meet again in peace.'

Weizmann was spared to meet in peace, but meantime six million Jews perished. During the war he had continued his researches in London, lost a son in the R.A.F., rallied support for the allied cause, and agitated for the formation of a Jewish Brigade. In 1945 a Labour Government was returned to power, but Zionist hopes were again dashed as political expediency once more shaped events. The assassination in Cairo of Lord Moyne had created a wave of anti-Jewish feeling and the government, paralyzed by Arab propaganda, set up yet one more Commission of Inquiry. A thin trickle of refugees, 1,500 monthly, was to be permitted. There followed a desperate sequence of illegal immigration attempts, many ending tragically within sight of the Palestine coast. There was more violence, there was terrorist activity on all sides, a depressing, sinister atmosphere of mutual hate and resentment.

It was President Truman who seemed most fully aware of the urgency of the problem, recommending an immediate influx of 100,000 Jews. An Anglo-American Commission heard evidence from both sides and again Weizmann testified. He made a deep impression on the Commission members. They advocated a higher rate of immigration than the British government would accept and a stalemate was reached.

Weizmann welcomed the post-war delegates to the Basle Congress of 1946. Though still a respected figure many felt he was out of touch with events and the initiative passed to the new leaders from Palestine. Success for them came when Britain renounced the Mandate and referred the issue to the United Nations. In the summer of 1947 the United Nations

Commission of Inquiry on Palestine recommended partition and the matter now rested with the General Assembly in New York. Weizmann himself was convinced that partition was the only solution combining 'finality, equality and justice'

Although Weizmann was no longer entrusted with the negotiations and others pleaded the Jewish case in the General Assembly, he was largely responsible for persuading Truman to include the Negev region, with its outlet to the Red Sea, in the territory allotted to the Jewish State. It was his last diplomatic activity on behalf of his people and it paved the way for the vote on 29 November, 1947.

After the requisite two-thirds majority which gave United Nations approval to partition and the setting up of independent Jewish and Arab States, Britain formally relinquished her Mandate and pulled out her troops and civil administration. On the same day, 14 May, 1948, the State of Israel was proclaimed as Arab armies massed on the frontiers. The two giant powers, the United States and the Soviet Union, both recognized the new State and on 17 May Chaim Weizmann was elected first President. David Ben-Gurion, who differed with him on many occasions, but always held him in the highest esteem and affection, wrote: 'I doubt whether the Presidency is necessary to Dr Weizmann, but the Presidency of Dr Weizmann is a moral necessity for the State of Israel.' No man had worked harder, over a longer period, for this moment – the fitting fulfilment of a lifetime's toil.

Weizmann returned to his home in Rehovoth and spent his last years there, his health failing, surrounded by his friends and fellow scientists who now journeyed from all parts of the world to work at the fine Science Institute which bears his name. He died on 9 November, 1952, and was buried in the grounds of his home. On the Memorial Plaza in the Institute gardens are inscribed some words from the speech he made when the foundation stone was laid: 'I believe that science will bring to this country both peace and renewal of its youth.' This short sentence aptly conveys the essence of Chaim Weizmann's philosophy and life's work.

Postscript

During my recent visit to Israel a moving ceremony took place on Mount Scopus to commemorate the fiftieth anniversary of the laying of the foundation stone of the Hebrew University. Plans are now under way to reopen and expand the University which for twenty years had been closed and inaccessible as a result of the 1948 war. A new University on a site in the Jewish section of Jerusalem has in the meantime gone far towards fulfilling Weizmann's dream of a Hebrew University of international stature. A special supplement in the *Jerusalem Post* was devoted entirely to articles and photographs recalling that historic occasion, and quoted in full Weizmann's address, which concluded with these words: 'Here the wandering soul of Israel shall reach its haven, its strength no longer consumed in restless and vain wanderings. Israel shall at last remain at peace within itself and with the world. There is a Talmudic legend that tells of the Jewish soul deprived of its body, hovering between heaven and earth. Such is our soul today; tomorrow it shall come to rest, in this our sanctuary. That is our faith.'

Left: Chaim Weizmann, chemist and Zionist statesman, was the leading Jewish negotiator in the talks with the British government which culminated in the Balfour Declaration of November, 1917. *Centre:* Weizmann, seated next to David Ben-Gurion, at the St James's Conference in 1939, which resulted in the White Paper curtailing the entry of persecuted European Jewry into Palestine. *Bottom:* Chaim Weizmann takes the oath of office in 1948 as first President of the State of Israel.

Below left: This bronze head of Einstein by Sir Jacob Epstein was made in 1933 (*by kind permission of the Trustees of the Tate Gallery*). *Below right:* Albert Einstein, physicist who formulated *The Theory of Relativity*. This photograph was taken in 1932, shortly before he was forced to leave Germany for America. *Bottom:* Einstein on one of his visits to the Mount Wilson Observatory, California.

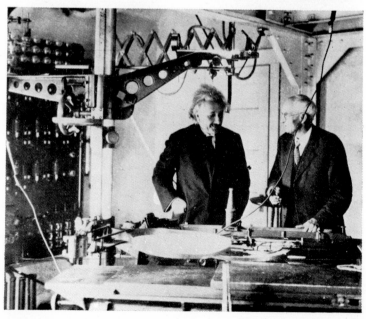

Mendel Beilis
1874–1934

Of all the famous personalities in this book probably the least familiar or memorable, even among Jewish readers, is Menachem Mendel Beilis, overseer of a brick factory in a suburb of Kiev in 1911.

Few men could have been more inoffensive and nondescript. The father of five children, almost forty years old, he was of medium height and stocky in build. Looking at his photograph, you might guess that this bearded, bespectacled man was a doctor, a lawyer, a scholar. In fact, he had few intellectual pretensions. He was not even an orthodox Jew. He was simply a decent family man, a devoted husband and father, an honest, hard-working, responsible employee, seeking for himself no more than modest comfort and security. Neither physically nor mentally was he in the least equipped for the cruel role that destiny chose for him – the central figure in a notorious trial for ritual murder.

The Blood Libel which alleged that Jews traditionally killed Christians, particularly children, to obtain blood for ritual purposes goes back to classical times. It made its first appearance in the Christian world in 1144 with the death of the Norwich skinner's apprentice. Although almost every pope in history denounced it as a monstrous absurdity, the allegation cropped up again and again, often coinciding with the familiar features of religious persecution – mob-violence, tortures and executions. In the nineteenth century there were more than forty recorded cases in Eastern Europe and the Near East.

Russia, in the opening years of the twentieth century, was ripe for such incidents. During the reign of Czar Alexander II the Jews had benefited from a programme of social reform; then, under his son Alexander III and his grandson Nicholas II, the climate of opinion was more hostile than ever. It suited the authorities to see Jewish inspiration in every eruption of revolutionary zeal. The terrible massacres of 1903 and 1905, if not government-organized, were without doubt government-condoned. An anti-semitic, ineffectual Czar, a corrupt, conscienceless Minister of Justice, an army of downtrodden civil servants and minor police officials, and the leaders of the extreme right-wing political groups – they were all responsible for the shocking events in Kiev in 1911. The administration was desperate, the empire on its last legs. Whoever were the real instigators, whatever the basic motive, a new ritual murder case might be expected to divert attention from the incompetence of the administration both at home and abroad. In fact, it had the opposite effect, revealing to the citizens of Russia and the world the depths of decadence and corruption which spread downwards from the royal court through every corridor of public life. This was not to be another Dreyfus case. It was a conspiracy which failed miserably.

So much for the background. Now for the facts. The body of thirteen-year-old Andryusha Yushchinsky was discovered in a cave about half a mile from the brick factory where Mendel Beilis worked, eight days after the date on which he was murdered, on 12 March, 1911. The body was half-clothed and covered with terrible stab-wounds, forty-seven to be precise. Two autopsies were performed and the funeral took place a week later. At the graveside leaflets were handed

out which accused the Jews, in hysterical terms, of torturing
and killing the boy for ritual purposes. The body had
allegedly been drained of blood for use in the manufacture
of Passover *matzohs*. The accusation was echoed in local
newspapers and the mother of the dead boy received anonymous letters to the same effect, all giving surprisingly accurate and detailed information about the state of the body and
the nature of the wounds. It was clearly the work of the
notorious Black Hundreds and two other anti-semitic organizations, the Union of the Russian People and the Double-
Headed Eagle. A mentally unbalanced young student from
Kiev University, Golubev, was instrumental in whipping up
frenzy at local level and persuading the authorities to take
action.

There was absolutely nothing to connect Mendel Beilis
with the crime, apart from one crucial coincidence. By
special dispensation – for the factory was outside the Pale of
Settlement to which Jews were legally restricted – Beilis and
his family were permitted to live on the premises in an ordinary single-storey, working-class house. Out of a population
of some 10,000, his was the only Jewish family; he himself
was the only Jew among five hundred factory employees.
The body had been found within a short distance of his home.
The Jews had murdered Andryusha. Hence Mendel Beilis
was the murderer. Once the administration had decided, no
matter how powerful the contrary evidence, that a ritual
murder charge was to be concocted, Beilis was doomed.

At first Andryusha's own family came under suspicion. He
had been an illegitimate child, and it was remarked that his
mother showed few conventional signs of grief when the
news broke. But the boy, who was described as quiet, studi-
ous and well-behaved, had not been ill-treated at home, either
by his mother or step-father. They were simple, illiterate, but
fundamentally honest folk, and there was no possible motive
or opportunity for such a crime. Nor did they ever subscribe
to the ritual murder accusation, despite strenuous police
efforts to prise damaging admissions from them.

Suspicion fastened much more strongly on Vera Tchebiriak, the mother of Andryusha's school friend Zhenya,

whose home was also a conveniently short distance from the cave where the body lay. She had a notorious local reputation. Married, with three children, her apartment was known to be the habitual meeting-place of every type of scoundrel and criminal, and very possibly a brothel as well. That the police discovered clues linking her with the crime was proved when she and three associates were arrested shortly after the murder and held for questioning. The trio consisted of Vera's half-brother Singayevsky, and two men with criminal records, Latishev and Rudzinsky. Vera was held for five weeks before being released, and the men produced an alibi. They claimed they had been breaking into an optical goods store in the city on the night the murder was committed. Unfortunately somebody at police headquarters had misinformed them. The murder had taken place in the morning.

The detective assigned to the case, Mishchuk, was in little doubt as to where the guilt lay. Intuition, plus available evidence, convinced him that Vera Tchebiriak and her gang had killed the boy in her house, probably because he had seen or heard something unwelcome, and dragged his body to the cave. If the wounds pointed to ritual murder, as seemed unlikely, it must have been simulated. Mishchuk's mistake, however, was to insist on investigating the murder as if it were an ordinary crime, despite warnings from his superiors that truth was a secondary consideration. Soon he was removed from the case. His successor, however, one Krasovsky, proved to be an even more assiduous searcher for truth, to the embarrassment of the authorities. It was he who arrested Vera after hearing a well-circulated story – never confirmed – that the two school friends had quarrelled, that Andryusha had threatened to reveal the presence of stolen goods in Vera's house, that Zhenya had dutifully reported back to his mother and that the gang had announced their intention of getting rid of Andryusha. Under pressure, Vera admitted Andryusha had been in her flat that morning, but disclaimed all further knowledge.

The gathering weight of evidence was not at all to the liking of those who were now committed to the fabrication of a ritual murder charge. By now the Czar himself was involved, and his rabidly anti-semitic Minister of Justice, Scheglovitov, issued instructons that evidence must be found linking the unfortunate Mendel Beilis with the murder. Already Mendel had been visited at the factory on numerous occasions and asked meaningless questions about owning a cow, going to synagogue, observing Jewish laws and so forth. And although he had heard the far-fetched rumours which were circulating, it came as a bolt from the blue when one morning, while still asleep, a force of policemen under Colonel Kubianko, chief of the *Okhrana* (Secret Police), hammered on his door and arrested him. His eldest son was dragged away as well, but released after two days. Beilis himself was questioned at length and confined to the city gaol. There he was to remain for twenty-six months while the case against him was being painfully and laboriously constructed.

In charge of investigations by now was Magistrate Fenenko, an honest official who made it clear both by the form of his questions to Beilis and his attitude throughout the case that he was acting on superior instructions and did not believe in Beilis' guilt. The 'evidence' at this stage consisted mainly of statements made by an illiterate lamp-lighter and his wife, who claimed to have seen Andryusha and Zhenya on the fateful morning. After further questioning – and, as it later appeared, a mixture of threats and glasses of vodka – the lamp-lighter introduced the figure of a man with a black beard who, according to Zhenya, had chased the boys out of the brickyard one day. His wife delighted the authorities even more by adding her touch of fantasy. Her husband, she swore, had actually seen Beilis dragging young Andryusha towards the kilns. The fact that the imaginative couple later retracted the entire story made little difference. The eye-witness account of a black-bearded abductor remained the central pivot of their case.

The unhappy Beilis, lying in his filthy, verminous cell, was not to know all the sinister machinations designed to reveal him as the symbol of Jewish barbarity and wickedness. But he knew what he was accused of, realized he was the helpless victim of a vast conspiracy, and waited, distraught and without hope, for the formal indictment and trial. Autumn and winter passed, and still he was held prisoner, endlessly questioned, brutally treated by the guards, occasionally consoled by a sympathetic fellow-prisoner who had read about his case and believed in his innocence. Sometimes he had to be wary of excessive friendliness, for police informers were placed in his cell. One of these, Kozatchenko, persuaded him to dictate a letter to his wife, which he promptly showed to the authorities, concocting, at the same time, a wild story of a conversation he had had with Beilis in which the latter had asked him to poison two witnesses.

His spirits were raised, however, that winter by visits from his lawyers, who assured him that some of the finest brains in the country were being assembled in his defence. The authorities were getting really desperate. The Czar himself had visited Kiev and been assured that the case was proceeding according to plan; and the murder of Prime Minister Stolypin by a Jew named Bogrov, whilst unconnected with the Beilis case, added to the already tense atmosphere. Things had gone too far now to retract. The investigations continued. 'Experts' were called in to prove that this was a genuine ritual murder. The original autopsies had failed to establish this, the first refuting it completely, the second failing to prove that the wounds had been inflicted prior to death, as would have been necessary in order to collect the blood in sufficiently large quantities. Now the second team were encouraged to add a statement to the effect that the child had indeed died from loss of blood and that this was consistent with the circumstances of a ritual killing.

These findings were much publicized, as were the opinions of a psychiatric 'expert' named Sikorsky who confirmed that the murder bore all the signs of a religious crime of vengeance. The selection of a young victim and the bloodletting were in keeping with traditional precepts, according to the theologian Father Pranaitis, who, having browsed through the anti-semitic literature of past centuries, produced a string of extraordinary facts in support of his claim that the Jewish religion, the Talmud itself, enjoined its adherents to practise ritual murder.

All this mumbo-jumbo of pseudo-religion and science was immediately ridiculed by theologians and scientists of standing, both in Russia and abroad. The prosecution was undeterred. Meanwhile Mendel Beilis spent more than another year in prison before being placed in the dock.

Happily, other investigations were going on behind the scenes. A journalist named Brazul-Brushkovsky and Krasovsky, the detective who had already uncovered strong circumstantial evidence against Vera Tchebiriak and her friends, were following up new clues in private. Of the three male suspects, Latishev was now dead. It was rumoured he had committed suicide by jumping out of a window. Zhenya, Vera's son, had also died, apparently from dysentery. A detective who had been at his death-bed revealed how his mother had tried to prevent him answering police questions. She had actually begged him to tell them that she had had nothing to do with the murder, to which the boy had replied, 'Leave me alone, mother.' He was also reported to have cried out in his delirium, 'Don't scream, Andryusha. Don't scream!' And there was supporting evidence by neighbours which, when produced at the trial, pointed the finger of guilt even more implacably in her direction.

With the aid of a young revolutionary, Makhalin, and his underworld friend, Karayev, the two private investigators managed to corner Singayevsky in a Kharkov hotel room. There he confessed to having committed the crime in conjunction with the dead Latishev and the degenerate Rudzinsky, now serving a prison sentence in Siberia. They had no alibi for the morning of 12 March. The robbery confession was invented, based on false information. Brazul-Brushkovsky gave the confession full newspaper coverage and accused the culprits openly. Dismayed, the authorities saw their case crumbling. They had already dropped one indictment. Now they clutched at anything to bolster the case against Beilis. They came up with new 'evidence'.

Vera Tchebiriak herself, though having been questioned five times, suddenly remembered that Zhenya had told her that Beilis had dragged Andryusha away to the kilns that March morning. Then, even more remarkably, Lyudmilla,

Vera's nine-year-old and only surviving child, questioned more than a year after the murder, solemnly testified that she, Zhenya, Andryusha and several other children, had been playing in the brickyard when Beilis, with two other Jews, had dragged Andryusha away. A saddle-maker's awl was also produced as the probable murder instrument. With such 'evidence' the prosecution felt secure enough to proceed. A second indictment, running to some thirty pages, was presented to the prisoner, and the trial was fixed for 25 September, 1913.

After two years in prison, Beilis was ceremonially dressed on that cloudy autumn morning, escorted to a waiting coach, and driven in procession through the streets of Kiev. Crowds were held back by Cossacks as they made their way to the court.

The inflammatory feeling which the government had hoped to arouse was not in evidence. The whole plot had misfired badly. World opinion had rallied unanimously behind him in condemning the case as a tragic mockery of justice. From America came an open letter in *The Independent*, addressed to the Czar. Responsible papers everywhere denounced the trial as degrading and deplorable. Within Russia itself anti-government feeling was equally intense. In December, 1911, leading intellectuals, scientists and politicians had signed a manifesto, and there were nation-wide strikes and protests, not activated exclusively by revolutionaries, and embracing every section of the people, from professional men to factory workers and peasants.

The terms of the indictment only underlined the flimsiness of the prosecution's case, which was comprised of the contradictory statements of two or three uneducated eyewitnesses, the unlikely recollections of a small girl, the testimony of a woman desperately struggling to disentangle herself from a web of incriminating facts, and the expert evidence of witnesses who had been bribed and cajoled to venture opinions which flew in the face of every known fact and vestige of common sense. Added to this was a conglomeration of rumour and invention about Beilis' association with pious Jews, the fact that he was known to distribute *matzohs* at Passover, that a man with the same surname as an eminent Rabbi had visited Andryusha's home, and similar far-fetched and utterly irrelevant snippets of information. The prosecution itself knew it was pretty hopeless. The real truth was known, documented and suppressed.

Yet it was far from being a foregone conclusion. The jury was patently rigged, including seven peasants and two government clerks among the twelve impartial men summoned to sift evidence of considerable complexity and detail. Moreover seven members of the jury belonged to the anti-semitic Union of the Russian People. As for the judge, he was to show, throughout the case, by his handling of witnesses and his summing up, where his sympathies lay.

The reading of the indictment took an hour and a half. Significantly, the section devoted to the whitewashing of Vera Tchebiriak and her confederates took up three times as much space as the arraignment of the prisoner. The prosecution witnesses were a grave disappointment from the very start. The carters and drivers from the factory testified to Beilis' good character and refuted the lamp-lighter's statement that Beilis had been alone on the crucial Saturday morning. According to the records, work had gone on normally throughout the day and Beilis could have had neither the time nor the opportunity to entice his victim away without being noticed. The lamp-lighter and his wife completely disowned their earlier statements, admitting that their depositions had been obtained under pressure. Another eye-witness, a pathetic old woman who had previously testified to seeing Beilis carrying his victim off on his shoulders, denied everything on the stand and was unable to identify Beilis.

Zhenya's father, who had told a vague story about the boys being chased off by Beilis and two other Jews, was clearly unreliable. Little Lyudmilla told her tale off pat, word for word, but dissolved in tears when confronted by a friend who denied the whole story. Another witness proclaimed boldly that the whole case was a tissue of lies, and that she had information from a neighbour, Adele Ravich, who had actually seen the boy's body in the bathtub in Vera's house. But Mrs Ravich was not in court. She had emigrated with her husband to Canada, and the court refused to hear her deposition.

The trial, which continued for thirty-four days, was dramatically transformed as one witness after another pointed the accusing finger at Vera Tchebiriak and her colleagues. Mendel Beilis faded completely into the background. Two sisters appeared on the stand, one confirming Adele Ravich's account of having seen the body, this time wrapped in a rug under a table, the other having visited the house in the morning, to be confronted by Vera and the three men in a state of great excitement and confusion, and prevented from entering the living-room. Another neighbour, living below Vera's flat, had heard doors slamming, sounds of scuffling and a child screaming. And so it went on, with the prosecution desperately fighting a rear-guard action, trying to show that all these unfavourable witnesses had been bribed with Jewish gold. They even produced two *Tsadikim* – ultra-pious Jews – who were alleged to have been seen at Beilis' house. They could hardly speak Hebrew, and were laughed out of court.

Vera Tchebiriak proved to be her own worst enemy when she appeared as a prosecution witness. So confused and contradictory were her statements under gruelling and relentless cross-examination that even the sympathetic judge had to warn her to stick to the truth. And one of the prosecutors, the virulently anti-semitic Smakov, jotted down in his notebook the revealing fact that only at the sixth of her interrogations had she recalled that Zhenya had told her he had seen Andryusha's abduction. He himself labelled her a 'lying bitch'.

On the twentieth day of the trial Father Pranaitis publicly repeated the theological evidence he had so diligently unearthed. He was utterly demolished by the defence who produced a genuine scholar. A few succinct inquiries established the fact that Father Pranaitis was neither a Hebrew nor a Talmudic authority. Sikorsky's elaborate explanations of

Jewish ritual customs were equally decisively refuted by five theologians, four of them Christians.

In summing up, the prosecution spent the entire day in a vain attempt to piece together the fragments of their case. The defence reviewed the facts as they had emerged at the trial. Yet although it was an unanswerable case the judge, in his two-hour address, posed two questions to the jury, both of them most provocatively worded. Paraphrased, they were as follows: firstly, 'Has it been proved that on 12 March, 1911 . . . Andrei Yushchinsky was gagged, and wounds inflicted . . . totalling forty-seven, causing agonizing pain and leading to almost total loss of blood and death?' Secondly, 'If the above is proved, is the accused guilty, in conjunction with other deeds still undiscovered and inspired by religious fanaticism, of planning to murder Andrei Yushchinsky, and did he seize him and carry him off to a building in the brick factory and there . . . kill him?' In a tense courtroom the foreman of the jury answered 'Yes, it has been proved', to the first part of the charge – then, a determined 'No, not guilty', to the second question.

It was over. Mendel Beilis was a free man. The courtroom erupted in a spontaneous demonstration of hysterical rejoicing. Beilis had to be taken back to his cell to protect him from the spectators outside. It was not until late that night that he was allowed home to rejoin his family.

The liberal Press and the world at large hailed it as a triumph for justice. The prosecution, no longer interested in Beilis as an individual, were satisfied that the ritual murder charge had not been rebutted. Not until after the Revolution were the unsavoury facts of the entire conspiracy revealed. Vera Tchebiriak and her half-brother were shot in 1918. As for Mendel Beilis, he emigrated to Palestine with his family, failed to make a living there, later settled in America, where he wrote his memoirs of the case, and died in 1934. Within a few years of the trial, he was almost forgotten.

It was his fate to be used as a pawn in a sinister game which adhered to no rules or coherent pattern. Even his memoirs leave us with little impression save of an ordinary man, enduring the agonizing physical and mental strain of a long prison sentence with patience and fortitude. In retrospect the case appears as an incredibly amateurish, bungled affair, handled throughout in such a clumsy and inept fashion, that one wonders how it ever came to court. Clearly, those who were responsible miscalculated badly. They insulted the intelligence of their own people, they underestimated the international repercussions, and they were completely outmanœuvred by an experienced and highly professional team of defence lawyers.

One fervently hopes that it was the last of the ritual murder trials, although it is depressing to note that the hoary old blood libel story was revived in the 1920s and 1930s, and played an essential part in Nazi propaganda. What is more, the totalitarian régimes of our own time have shown themselves far more efficient and ingenious in concocting evidence and in staging show-trials than their half-hearted predecessors in the Russia of 1912. The circumstances are very different, but the motives and the techniques are the same. But perhaps there is some consolation in the fact that on that occasion decent, intelligent people rose up in protest and won the day.

Albert Einstein
1879–1955

$E = MC^2$. A neat little mathematical equation. Yet this harmless-looking formula was to project twentieth-century man headlong into the atomic age, heralding a scientific revolution so immense and startling that even today, more than sixty years later, its implications for the future of humanity are incalculable.

Einstein used to joke that there were perhaps only a dozen people who really understood the meaning of his Theory of Relativity. He was amused, but also rather bewildered by the tremendous publicity it was given in non-scientific circles. He was not taken in by the screaming headlines, the champagne and the confetti, the mountains of letters, telegrams and presents. The public was obviously interested in the man who had proved Newton wrong, who had 'abolished time and space'. So he smiled and gestured helplessly when reporters asked him to explain Relativity in simple, comprehensible terms. Yet the attempts were made, with varying degrees of success, and in order to begin to understand the scope of his achievement we have to come to grips – very briefly – with the intractable problem in this introductory section.

Scientists in the latter part of the nineteenth century – physicists, mathematicians, philosophers – had already begun to challenge the seemingly unshakeable laws of Newton, and Einstein grew up among a generation which was making astounding discoveries about light and heat, electricity and magnetism, stars and atoms. Einstein's genius lay in his ability to build upon the theoretical and experimental work of past and contemporary science by mathematical means alone. He freely admitted that his theories stemmed from imagination and intuition, but the proof lay in his remarkable mathematical inventiveness. His facility in using mathematics in an entirely new way enabled him to break through the barriers of traditional thinking and teaching, and opened the eyes of science to the realities of a world governed by laws very different from those formulated by centuries of philosophical speculation and mathematical inquiry.

Einstein upset all the fundamental ideas about the universe, about time and space, about matter and energy, about gravitation. Newton had spoken of 'absolute space, similar and immovable', and of 'absolute, true and mathematical time, flowing equally without relation to anything external'. Einstein proved him wrong by showing that nothing in the universe is fixed and at rest, that all motion is relative, that moving objects shrink in size in relation to the observer's position, that time itself, under certain conditions, could contract or expand. Time and space themselves were neither separate nor measurable, but were inextricably linked in what he termed a 'space-time continuum'. Time could be viewed as a fourth dimension, and in applying mathematical methods to investigate the physical laws of the universe, traditional geometry as formulated by Euclid could not supply the answers. Only his special four-dimensional system of geometry could unlock the cosmic mysteries.

Matter and energy, proclaimed Einstein, were fundamentally alike. The experiments of Michelson and Morley had proved the unvarying speed of light. Einstein used this as a springboard to his world-shaking discovery about the relationship of light and motion, expressed in the deceptively simple equation $E = MC^2$ – Energy is equal to Mass multiplied by the square of the velocity of light. This applied even to the particles thrown out by radio-active substances, and from this stemmed the statement that matter could be converted into energy, a theory conclusively and diabolically proved forty years later by the explosion of the atomic bomb.

These findings were published by Einstein in 1905 in what came to be known as the Special Theory of Relativity. By 1915, when he published his General Theory of Relativity, he had challenged Newton's theories of gravity, and found them similarly at fault. Einstein held that gravitation was not a force, that its effects could be reproduced by acceleration, that objects took a curved line of least resistance. Space itself, Einstein deduced, was curved. Light rays were also affected by gravitation – they too were bent – and the proof of this was to be triumphantly demonstrated. In simplest terms, owing to the curvature of space, parallel lines, if extended far enough, might, indeed *would*, eventually meet.

Einstein received a Nobel Prize for physics, surprisingly not for his Theory of Relativity, but for his 'photo-electric law and his work in the field of theoretical physics'. This referred to his work on the Quantum Theory, discovered by the German physicist Max Planck and as revolutionary in its way as Relativity in shattering the classical concepts of mechanics. Einstein extended Planck's theories in the field of radiation. The Quantum Theory opened the gates to twentieth-century atomic physics, but Einstein never accepted it as providing the final answer to the behaviour of the individual atom. For the greater part of his life he struggled with this problem and laboured on a highly complex Unified Field theory – a synthesis of gravitation and electro-magnetism – the theory which might unravel the ultimate secret of the universe. But this proved to be beyond even his capacities.

Albert Einstein was born in Ulm, at the foot of the Swabian Alps, on 14 March, 1879, to Hermann and Pauline

Einstein. Shortly afterwards, the family moved to nearby Munich. He was an easy-going, none too successful businessman, she a cultured, artistic woman, who played the piano and encouraged her son's aptitude for music. Like many budding geniuses Albert was an outwardly unremarkable boy, given to day-dreaming, late in learning to speak (he always found difficulty in expressing himself without hesitation and deliberation), disinclined towards sports and games, bored by the apparent pointlessness of school routine. Except in mathematics, that fascinated him from an early age, his school work was poor, due in large measure to the rigid military-type discipline which held sway. His hatred and contempt for all brands of constraint and compulsion was deep-rooted, an ineradicable trait of personality which revealed itself in later years in his allegiance to pacifism and other liberal causes.

It soon became evident that his main interests were reading, mathematics and music. He started violin lessons at the age of six and derived much joy throughout his life from what he called 'an inner necessity'. Music and mathematics often go hand in hand and he understood the identity of his scientific and artistic impulses, writing, towards the end of his life: 'There is such a thing as a passionate desire to understand, just as there is a passionate love for music. . . . Without it, there would be no natural science, and no mathematics.'

Two early incidents impressed themselves on his memory. Once, when he was ill as a small boy, he was given a pocket compass and was engrossed for days by the mystery of the invisible force which swung its needle to the north; and when he was twelve he was given an elementary textbook on geometry, which stimulated his interest in an entirely new subject. It was his uncle who recognized and fostered his love for algebra and popular science. School work was neglected as he sat up at nights poring over mathematics, physics, poetry, philosophy and natural history.

A turning-point came when he was fifteen. His father went bankrupt and went off to Italy with his mother and his sister Maja, leaving Albert to fend for himself in Munich. After

six miserable months he obtained a doctor's certificate testi-
fying to a nervous breakdown, left his 'Gymnasium' with a
letter from the mathematics teacher to the effect that he was
qualified to enter university, and joined his family. He spent
a glorious year in Italy revelling in the simple outdoor life,
soaking in art and music, and rebelliously announcing that
he proposed abandoning both his German citizenship and
orthodox Judaism. But he had to go back to school. So he
took a train for Zürich where he sat for the entrance examination for the famous technical school, the Polytechnic. He
failed, but sufficiently impressed the director with his results
in mathematics that he was promised a place once he had obtained a Swiss school diploma.

So he joined a small school at Aarau where he was pleasantly surprised by the free and liberal atmosphere, and where
he lived happily with one of the teachers, Jost Winterler, and
his large family. One of the sons, Paul, was later to marry
Albert's sister Maja. His second attempt to enter the Polytechnic was successful, and he embarked on an intensive
four-year study of physics. He had definitely decided to make
physics his life's work. This meant abandoning mathematics,
a decision he later came to regret. He often attributed his
failure to make progress in his Unified Field theory to his
inadequate knowledge of higher mathematics.

At the Polytechnic he made a number of friends – Friedrich Adler, a socialist and staunch pacifist who gave direction to the young Einstein's political opinions; Marcel Grossmann, who tried to keep his lackadaisical colleague up to
the mark in the set curriculum and hammered facts into him
at week-ends; and Mileva Maric, an attractive girl from
Hungary, though of Serbian origin. They shared a common
interest in physics and she tried to bring some order into
Albert's life, even if it only meant regular meals. Though
opposites in ability and temperament they were, perhaps
predictably, attracted to each other. They decided to get
married after Albert had graduated and begun earning a
living.

This proved to be unexpectedly difficult. He failed to get
a teaching job at the Polytechnic and after months of misery

and deprivation – he never ate enough at the best of times and at this stage could not afford to – he took a temporary teaching post at a school in Winterthur, then a job at a boarding-school in Schaffhausen as tutor to two backward boys. He was rescued by his friend Grossmann, who managed to get him a job in Berne at the Patent Office. For the first time in his life he had security and a reasonable salary. He married Mileva and within a few years was the father of two boys, Alfred and Edward.

Although he once described it as a 'cobbler's job', life as a civil servant was far from unendurable. Inventions passed through his hands, some of them novel and interesting, and he had plenty of time to work on his own scientific problems. He would discuss physics, philosophy and music with his friends and work feverishly into the early hours. His mind wrestled incessantly with the laws of physics, until gradually a pattern evolved. The Relativity solution did not burst on him suddenly like a lightning flash, but the slow, patient research and study of those three years in Berne led inevitably and unerringly towards it.

Since 1901 he had published an article each year in the *Annalen der Physik* (*The Physics' Year Book*). In 1905 he published five articles on different subjects. One of them, entitled 'A New Determination of Molecular Dimensions', won him a Doctor of Philosophy degree from Zürich University. A second one called 'The Photo-electrical Effect' helped to win him the Nobel Prize and paved the way for television.

It was the fourth in the series, however, which earned him enduring, though not immediate, fame. Entitled 'On the Electrodynamics of Bodies in Movement' and occupying thirty pages in the *Year Book*, containing no footnotes or references, it formulated revolutionary new concepts of light, motion, time and space – all neatly proved by algebra. Later it became known as the Special Theory of Relativity. A fifth article dealt with mass and energy, summed up his findings in terms of an equation which galvanized the scientific world, and posed, in print for the first time, the possibility of harnessing atomic energy.

For Einstein the experience had been so emotionally and

physically exhausting that he was in a state of near-collapse for a fortnight. Yet he was profoundly contented to know that at last he had added something of real and permanent value to the sum of human knowledge. Fame was beyond his dreams or desires, but recognition, he told himself, must surely follow.

Amazingly, there was silence after the articles appeared – evidently no widespread scientific interest, and no prospect of shedding the obscure role of Patent Office examiner. It took two years for the significance of the Special Theory to be recognized. But outside Switzerland men such as Max Planck needed no convincing. He and others trumpeted the importance of Einstein's work until eventually Professor Kleiner of Zürich University took the first step towards launching him on the road to fame.

Einstein himself was not by any means wedded to the idea of an academic career, but consented to become a *Privatdozent*, or unsalaried lecturer, at Berne University. Kleiner dropped in on one of these lectures to discover, to his consternation, that there were only two pupils, both personal friends, and that Einstein did not seem to be teaching anything, just chatting about Relativity. Kleiner told him bluntly that this was hardly satisfactory, to which Einstein retorted that he hadn't asked to be a university teacher in the first place. Nevertheless, he got his university post – Professor Extraordinary of Theoretical Physics at Zürich University, followed a year later by an appointment at the German university in Prague as Professor of Experimental Physics.

He enjoyed his new life, together with the international recognition which was now his. But he still refused to make any concessions to formality and ceremony. He still had the reputation of eccentricity both in manner and dress and was happiest in an open-necked shirt, shabby trousers and faded slippers, puffing at his indispensable pipe, playing with his children, performing string quartets or discussing scientific matters with his friends. Though he appeared brusque and unsociable to some, his close friends knew him for a man of great warmth, humour and generosity.

In Prague, however, he became deeply aware of religious and political problems – of the insidious nature of anti-semitism and the stultifying effect of nationalist rivalries, German and Czech. He met Jewish writers such as Franz Kafka and Max Brod and the young Zionist Hugo Berg-mann. Yet at this stage Zionism seemed petty and parochial compared with the vast cosmic problems ever on his mind.

A welcome break came in 1911 when he was invited to represent Austria at a physics congress in Brussels. Here he met distinguished colleagues – Paul Langevin, Marie Curie and Henry Poincaré from France, Sir Ernest Rutherford from Britain, Max Planck and Walter Nernst from Germany, Paul Ehrenfest from Russia. Among this galaxy of world science Einstein found himself enthusiastically accepted at last.

Meanwhile he continued to tussle with the problem of gravity. Was it a force or a field? The seeds of his General Theory of 1915 were sown in this period in Prague. And would it not be possible to put his bending of light theory to the practical test? An eclipse of the sun was scheduled for the autumn of 1914. It would be visible in Russia. If photographs could be taken of stars, during the eclipse, and compared with their known positions, the theory could be proved. Such an expedition was in fact planned, but the outbreak of war prevented further action. Planck was convinced the theory was valid and predicted that Einstein would be regarded as 'the Copernicus of the twentieth century'. But five years were to elapse before it could be tested and triumphantly proved correct.

From Prague he travelled back to Zürich, as newly appointed Professor at the same Polytechnic where he had graduated. Mileva was happy to return to Switzerland. The last few years had imposed strains on the marriage which proved irreparable. But Zürich was a short-lived episode. Germany's leading physicists, Planck and Nernst, determined to acquire him as a colleague, offered him an appointment in Berlin which was to decide the course of his entire life. He would have a chair at the University, with as little lecturing as he wished, coupled with a handsome salary and membership of the Royal Prussian Academy of Sciences – a remarkable academic distinction. He would have as much time as he needed for research and would eventually head the physics department of the projected *Kaiser-Wilhelm-Institut*. After much heart-searching and careful thought Einstein accepted, on one condition – that he should be allowed to retain his Swiss nationality. His terms were accepted. But Mileva and the family remained in Zürich. The separation was final, though even after the formal divorce, Einstein watched over their welfare and kept closely in touch with them. They parted without bitterness, and the war set the seal on it.

War brought a harrowing conflict of loyalties. His instinctive hatred of Prussian militarism increased with every new communiqué. Einstein was appalled by the narrow, unswerving patriotism of his fellow scientists. and his refusal to sign a Manifesto of German Intellectuals, equating German militarism with German culture, branded him as a renegade. Happily, as a Swiss citizen, he was beyond the authority of the government. He became a fearless and outspoken pacifist, founded a pacifist society, joined anti-war organizations, and journeyed to Switzerland to meet another ardent pacifist, the writer Romain Rolland.

During these terrible years he brought to perfection his General Theory of Relativity. The *Physics' Year Book* devoted sixty-four pages to it in 1916. Here was his entirely new theory of gravitation, describing the curvature of space, yet another direct challenge to Newtonian principles. The time could not have been more inauspicious, with the war at its peak, but Einstein knew that he had reached another milestone in his life's work. To Arnold Sommerfeld, a physicist friend, he wrote: 'This last month I have lived through the most exciting and exacting period of my life: and also the most fruitful.'

But wartime privations had taken their toll. His stomach ailment was serious. His broken marriage disturbed him deeply. And then, in Berlin, he met again his cousin Elsa, divorced, with two daughters. She helped to nurse him through his illness and it seemed only natural for them to marry when the divorce was settled. Elsa could not share in the excitement of his scientific work, but she provided the calm, serene, secure background which he badly needed. Her tolerance, humour, patience and understanding were to be of immeasurable value in the harsh and difficult years ahead.

When the war ended, in the bleak and chaotic atmosphere of a defeated Berlin, fame finally arrived. Sir Arthur Eddington, the British astronomer, had persuaded the Royal Society to send out two expeditions to test Einstein's starlight theory. A total eclipse of the sun was due on 29 May, 1919. Eddington led one team to the island of Principe in Portuguese West Africa, the second group went to Sobral, in northern Brazil. The Brazilian pictures proved useless. So did fifteen of the photographs from Principe. The sixteenth showed clearly a cluster of stars against the black rim of the sun. The plate was minutely examined and compared with the known positions in the night skies of the stars concerned. Then at a Royal Society meeting on 6 November the Astronomer Royal announced their findings. The photograph bore out Einstein's mathematical calculations. 'It is concluded,' he told the members, 'that the sun's gravitational field gives the deflection predicted by Einstein's generalized theory of relativity.' The President of the Royal Society hailed it as 'one of the greatest achievements in the history of human thought'.

Einstein was famous, and, to his consternation, a hero. The letters and telegrams flowed in, and reporters hammered at the door for interviews. The scientists weighed the theory's implications, came down for and against, while German feelings were partly pride that a German scientist should have made the discovery, partly embarrassment that he should also be a Jew. Einstein was well aware of their dilemma. To a *Times* reporter asking for a simple explanation of his theory, Einstein replied jocularly: 'Today I am described in Germany as a German scientist and in England as a Swiss Jew. Should I ever come to be regarded as a *bête noire*, I should, on the contrary, become a Swiss Jew for the Germans and a German scientist for the English.' An offhand statement, but one which was to ring ominously accurate in the decade to come.

The blaze of publicity caused Einstein wry amusement, but the reaction in scientific circles was far more important.

Outside Germany his work was seriously discussed and favourably received. At home things were different. Post-war depression and growing political violence nurtured an ugly atmosphere which disturbed him profoundly. He could no longer hide away in an ivory tower of intellectualism. Now he was to become increasingly and passionately involved in causes which had always been important, but now seemed indispensable. War and all its horrors must be abolished. To Einstein, as to most men of goodwill, the League of Nations held out a glimmer of hope for a future based on international concord and co-operation. He was to devote much time and energy to the Committee for Intellectual Co-operation, sponsored by the League, but this was only one of many similar organizations which failed to live up to its original glowing ideals.

Zionism was a different matter. Einstein was now made unpleasantly aware of the fact that the Jewish problem was his problem as well. The undisguised anti-semitism which seeped into political debates and newspaper comments was also invading academic discussion. Many of the 'scientific' attacks on Einstein's theories were inspired by no other motive. There could be no evading the issue. Now he identified himself formally with the Jewish people, convinced that only in a Jewish state in Palestine would they find refuge and fulfilment. He accepted an invitation from Chaim Weizmann to join him on a fund-raising visit to America. It was an irresistible combination – Weizmann, the chemist of international renown and instigator of the Balfour Declaration, and Einstein, the world-famous physicist and public idol, rallying support for the Zionist cause and for the project dearest to them personally, the Hebrew University in Jerusalem.

As he stepped off the *Rotterdam*, in the spring of 1921, Einstein, in his shabby overcoat and floppy felt hat, looked like a street-corner musician. He clutched his briar pipe in one hand, his violin case in the other. He gracefully explained the meaning of Relativity to the eager reporters and then endured a traditional New York ticker-tape welcome. At the head of the motor parade to City Hall a giant poster bearing his photograph proclaimed, 'This is the Famous Professor

Einstein'. Yet, despite the ballyhoo, the trip was rewarding, both from the financial point of view and for his contacts with American scientists. Particularly enjoyable was a three-day visit to Princeton where he received an honorary degree. In Washington he was honoured at a special meeting of the Academy of Sciences. Through it all he maintained complete composure, underplaying his own achievements, refuting accusations of being anti-religious, puzzled yet flattered by the warmth and friendliness of his welcome.

He travelled next to London where he lectured at King's College, meeting such eminent personalities as Lord Haldane, Lloyd George, A. N. Whitehead, Shaw and the Archbishop of Canterbury; then to Paris, at the invitation of his friend Paul Langevin, to lecture and to discuss science and pacifism with Marie Curie; then back home. Here reaction to his work was mixed. Although an astronomical laboratory was built in Potsdam and labelled the Einstein Tower, this could not conceal a dangerous undercurrent of opposition and hatred, led by the scientist Philipp Lenard, a rabid nationalist who, by tortuous reasoning, proved that Einstein's theory was the work of a patriotic Austrian physicist who had died in the war, named Hasenohol. The mob murder of Walter Rathenau, Germany's Jewish Minister of Foreign Affairs and a personal friend of Einstein, gave unmistakable warning of the horrors still to come. Einstein himself was a marked man and Elsa, without his knowledge, arranged for police protection.

They both enjoyed a much needed respite at the end of 1922 when they left for a trip to the Far East, travelling via Ceylon, Singapore and Shanghai to Japan where they stayed for two months. Einstein lectured throughout the country, was received by the Emperor and received the news of his Nobel Prize award – for work he had done seventeen years previously. On his way home he visited Palestine, writing enthusiastic letters about the pioneering work of the post-war wave of settlers. He was greatly impressed by the vitality of the new city of Tel-Aviv; and although it was not officially open, he gave the first lecture ever at the Hebrew University.

In science he was now moving into more rarified spheres and absorbed by his research into the Unified Field theory.

He published a first version of this in 1929, but felt he was on the wrong lines and set about modifying it. The mental and physical strain, however, had resulted in serious illness – enlargement of the heart – needing months of recuperation. Happily he made a complete recovery.

The publication of a new Einstein theory delighted the public, although this one was completely beyond the comprehension of any non-scientist. But it coincided with his fiftieth birthday, which was celebrated, to his dismay, with great pomp and ceremony. Typically, he avoided the showers of greetings and presents by taking refuge in the country, though he took great pleasure in one gift – a new sailing boat. And he had an opportunity to indulge in this his favourite sport on the lake adjoining the summer villa which they acquired that year at Caputh, about an hour's journey from Berlin. This villa was to have been presented to them by the Berlin City Council but Nazi pressure blocked the scheme.

In the winter of 1930 he paid the first of three successive winter visits to California as lecturer at the Institute of Technology in Pasadena. It gave him the chance to see the great Mount Wilson Observatory and to renew many American friendships. But the delights of a Californian winter could not blind him to the sinister trend of events in Europe. Though he spoke as passionately as ever in public about peace and international understanding, he knew in his heart that ringing phrases and lofty resolutions were powerless to stem the tide which was already engulfing freedom of speech and action in Germany. The Nazi onslaught on Jews in the professions, in schools and universities, in public life, was gathering momentum. Each time he returned to Berlin it was to find the Nazis in ever tighter control, until, in January 1933, Hitler was appointed Chancellor. He had had a presentiment of catastrophe the previous winter as they left Caputh, telling Elsa they would never see the place again. While in America he received news that storm-troopers had ransacked it.

Clearly his own life was in jeopardy now. He was bewildered and desperate. The world was going mad. The Geneva Disarmament Conference, in which he had still pinned some hopes, proved a fiasco. As a gesture he renounced his German citizenship and resigned from the Prussian Academy of Sciences. Offers of teaching posts came from many famous universities. After a few last, indecisive months in Belgium he decided to accept an offer from Abraham Flexner to take a position at the projected Institute for Advanced Studies at Princeton. In October, 1933, he and Elsa took up residence at 112 Mercer Street. America was now his permanent home.

Although he had security and unlimited facilities for research he became increasingly despondent and withdrawn as the thirties wore on. Locally he was loved and respected, still refusing to bow to convention, still sloppily dressed in a loose shirt or jacket, ill-fitting trousers, and soft shoes or sandals. He still identified himself with liberal causes, now running the risk of being labelled a Communist. He never refused assistance or advice to a fellow refugee. But disillusionment was setting in fast.

Abandoning his lifelong pacifist stand, he warned of the dangers ahead. As the shadows of war deepened over Europe, there came news of Otto Hahn's sensational experiment with atomic fission at the *Kaiser-Wilhelm-Institut* in Berlin. Lise Meitner, Hahn's Jewish ex-assistant, now in exile in Copenhagen, flashed a warning to American scientists that Hahn would be heading a team of German physicists dedicated to producing a weapon of unprecedented power and destructiveness. Hahn's experiments were reproduced at Columbia University, New York, by the Italian physicist Enrico Fermi. It was he, together with the expatriate Hungarians Leo Szilard and Paul Wigner, who persuaded Einstein himself to write to President Roosevelt, urging him to give priority to nuclear research and to make sure that America had access to supplies of uranium should the necessity arise. The letter began:

'Some recent work by E. Fermi and L. Szilard leads me to expect that the element uranium may be turned into a new and important source of energy in the immediate future. Certain aspects of the situation seem to call for watchfulness and, if necessary, quick action on the part of the Administration. . . . It may become possible to set up a nuclear chain reaction in a large mass of uranium by which vast amounts of power and large quantities of radium-like elements would be generated. . . . This new phenomenon could also lead to the construction of bombs, and it is conceivable – though much less certain – that extremely powerful bombs of a new type may thus be constructed.'

The name of Einstein, America's most eminent scientist, carried the intended weight. Roosevelt ordered work to begin on the Manhattan Project, which culminated in the fateful explosion of the atomic bomb five years later.

When Einstein was told of the dropping of the first atomic bomb on Hiroshima, he could find no other words but 'Oi, weh!' – an untranslatable expression of grief and horrified shock.

His life was more than ever secluded after the war. He was cared for by his devoted secretary Helen Dukas and had as companion his ailing sister Maja, who died in 1948. That same year he received news of Mileva's death in Zürich. He himself was desperately ill the following year, but he battled on in a world which seemed increasingly desolate and devoid of hope. He called for an end to the suicidal arms race, wrote an open letter to the United Nations, appealed on television to America not to proceed with the hydrogen bomb project. But it was too late. His warnings went unheeded now. He was over seventy, unable any longer to play the violin, friendless and isolated. Yet in 1952, to his deep gratification, he was offered the Presidency of Israel in succession to Weizmann. He pleaded his unsuitability, his need for time to complete his work.

On 18 April, 1955 he died. By his own severe standards, his work was incomplete. 'God does not play dice with the world,' he frequently said, but even he failed to discover the answer to the universal riddle. The atom still retained its secret. Yet, towards the end, he was heard to remark, 'Here on earth I have done my job.' As a scientist he had opened up new vistas of knowledge and experience. As a 'citizen of the world' he had fought for the highest principles of peace and truth. The 'job' was well done.

Sir Jacob Epstein
1880–1959

Jacob Epstein, protesting against 'racialism' in art, wrote in his autobiography: 'I am most often rather annoyed than flattered to be told that I am the best or foremost Jewish artist. Surely to be an artist is enough.' One hopes he would have raised no more than a token protest at his inclusion in this book. Tough and unsentimental though he appeared to be in public, there was a touch of nostalgia in his recollections of his childhood and adolescence, and his Jewish background may have had more influence on his thought and work than he cared to admit. He admitted, however: 'I saw a great deal of Jewish orthodox life, traditional and narrow. As my thoughts were elsewhere, this did not greatly influence me, but I imagine that the feeling I have for expressing a human point of view, giving human rather than abstract implications to my work, comes from those early formation years. I saw so much that called for expression that I can draw upon it now if I wish to.'

It would be irrelevant even to try to trace a specifically Jewish theme in Epstein's art. For he was the most universal of artists, and would never consent to be bound by any rules and conventions. In fact he broke all the set rules, all accepted canons of taste and style. He was a 'shocker' in the literal sense and hardly a major work of his appeared without a predictable eruption of furious criticism from the self-appointed arbiters of good taste and guardians of moral values. This continuous flow of anger and abuse, which did not die down until the twilight of his life, brought him the sort of publicity which he loathed. For his contribution to art was serious and profound, and accusations of blatancy and sensationalism wounded him deeply.

It was his originality and willingness to experiment that won him the reputation of being an *enfant terrible*. He could easily have confined himself to portrait commissions – far more profitable and less controversial. The large carvings which stirred up all the furore were mostly done for his own pleasure and never brought him much financial reward. In fact, he admitted he could have made more money out of paintings rather than sculpture, as he proved with his drawings of Epping Forest and his flower studies. But to judge him by his portraits alone, superb though they are, is to ignore the essential Epstein. He himself demanded to be judged for his work as a whole, summing up his methods thus:

'I have . . . gone my own way and have never truckled to the demands of popularity or pot-boiled. I have enjoyed myself at work. Sculpture, drawing and painting I have felt a natural call to do, and I have had the opportunity to create a body of work which, taking all in all, I am not ashamed of.'

Epstein's autobiography provides us with the main information about his life, work and philosophy. There are places where he cannot conceal the bitterness he felt towards those who had vilified him throughout his life – not so much anger for not having been more widely acclaimed, as resentment that his aims should have been so misunderstood, that so few appreciated his concern to express truth rather than portray mere surface beauty. Time and time again they accused him of brutality, primitivism, insensitivity, blasphemy and every rude word in the book; and for every ten attacks there would be only one who would leap to his defence, who recognized his importance, the reverence and profound love of humanity which inspired his art, the uncompromising honesty of purpose which he displayed in everything he did. Even in his portrait busts he never flattered the sitter, and many of them were shocked and disappointed at the result. His attempt to convey the essential spirit of his subject was a world removed from the mainstream of traditional portraiture. The hundreds of portraits which he made during his long career are vibrant with life. The famous and the unknown, babies, children, models, film stars, musicians, artists, soldiers, tycoons, statesmen, aristocrats and kings – they are all intensely individual, unmistakably 'Epstein', never idealized.

So it is best to skip lightly over those passages in his book which return to the fray again and again, raking over the cold embers of attack and counter-attack; and one must discount those parts which are clearly engendered by personal spite and which betray the writer into one-sided and exaggerated statements of opinion. There still remains a wealth of fascinating material, particularly the accounts of his childhood and student years, his working methods and his views on the artist's role in society.

The descriptions of his family and life on New York's East Side in the 1880s are full of affection, colour and gusto. The Jewish quarter, the Bowery, Chinatown, the Hudson river, the Battery, Coney Island – the teeming, restless city, with its variety of nationalities and occupations, was endlessly fascinating to this imaginative boy as he wandered at will, notebook in hand, sketching whatever caught his eye. His parents, immigrants from Eastern Europe, were not orthodox, but there were the automatic visits to Synagogue, the celebration of Jewish festivals, the Barmitzvah. They were unable to understand or approve his decision to be an artist, but there was never any doubt in his mind. He read, visited museums and art galleries, listened to music, went to the opera, drew sketches of actors in their dressing-rooms and was commissioned to illustrate a book. Finally he switched his interest to sculpture, worked in a bronze-casting foundry and studied modelling at night under a teacher he much admired, George Grey Barnard. He soon realized that it was only in Europe that he could really gain the experience he needed, and in 1902, using the money he had earned for his book illustrations, he boarded a ship for France.

In pre-war Paris he found the inspiration he had hoped for. Though temperamentally unsuited to a wild, Bohemian style of life, he found the city stimulating. He worked like a slave, utterly absorbed, first at the École des Beaux Arts, then at the Julian Academy. His energy was prodigious and his fellow students warned him that he would exhaust himself. They were happy years but he was still restless, unsure how best to develop his ideas. London was his next port of call in 1905 and there he decided to stay.

He worked first in Camden Town, then in Fulham, modelling, carving and drawing – it was two years of intense and not very remunerative work. He met Muirhead Bone, Augustus John and other contemporary artists. He paid many visits to the British Museum, admired the Elgin Marbles (years later he protested vigorously at their cleaning and renovation), and was deeply impressed by the Polynesian and African collections which so influenced his own work.

In 1907 came his first important commission, a group of eighteen large figures to adorn the new British Medical Building in the Strand. Here was his chance to express himself freely on a grand scale, and he worked enthusiastically on the project for over a year. The Strand Statues were a foretaste of what was to come. Art critics and eminent public figures expressed their horror after the unveiling of Epstein's powerful, symbolic carvings – so undecorative and so undraped. The tone of the attacks is amusingly reminiscent of what is still heard today in pornography cases. The *Evening Standard* thundered: 'To have art of the kind indicated, laid bare to the gaze of all classes, young and old, in perhaps the busiest thoroughfare of the Metropolis of the world . . . is another matter.' (It would have been acceptable decently hidden away from public view, by some strange application of double standards.) 'We are concerned most of all with the effect the figures will produce on the minds of the young people.' (Shades of *Lady Chatterley*!) There were letters to *The Times*, questions in the House and a determined attempt made to remove them. But there was plenty of support as well, including a petition by Kenneth Clark and other art-lovers. The President of the Royal Academy, however, refused to add his signature, upon which the celebrated painter Sickert resigned. By this time Epstein, like it or not, was news. The statues were saved, but demolished thirty years later on the grounds that the stone had dissolved. Their fragmentary remains can be seen on the façade of the former Rhodesia House.

The next four years were spent mainly on portrait work. He was married now to a Scotswoman, Margaret Dunlop, and earning a living was naturally his prime concern. The work flowed in with pleasing regularity as he became known. Then came another public commission, a memorial tomb to Oscar Wilde. Epstein transported a twenty-ton block of Derbyshire stone to his studio and worked on it for nine months. When he showed it to the Press – a winged male figure with the face of a 'demon-angel', even the *Evening Standard* called it a 'dignified sculpture'. 'The first thing that strikes one,' it said, 'is Mr Epstein's regard for his material and its purpose. . . . It is not executed but conceived in stone.' The monument was erected in the Père Lachaise cemetery in Paris where Wilde had been buried. Then the trouble started. The tomb was banned, the site solemnly guarded by a gendarme. There was a storm of controversy, letters of support from leading French artists and writers, and finally a crowning concession – a plaque, applied fig-leaf fashion, to rebut the charge of indecency!

In Paris he met influential people. He was particularly impressed by Modigliani and Brancusi, and on returning home took a small cottage near Hastings where he continued to work during the early part of the war. Now he exhibited his first religious subject, a bronze statue of Christ, at the Leicester Galleries. 'Immediately,' wrote Epstein, 'a most hellish row broke out. The statue was reviled, attacked by the Press, the Clergy, R.A.s, Artistic Associations, and Social

Sir Jacob Epstein in his studio
(a portrait study by Karsh of
Ottawa).

Right: David Ben-Gurion as a young man during his stay in Turkey before the outbreak of the 1914–18 war. *Below:* David Ben-Gurion, Israel's first Prime Minister.

bodies.' Epstein intended it as an expression of disgust and anger at the tragedy of war, and his Christ was an attempt to portray 'the dignity of man, his feebleness, his strength, his humility, and the wrath and pity of the Son of Man'. This was not evident to all, and one Father Vaughan wrote in *The Graphic*: 'I have studied the unshapely head, the receding brow, the thick lips, the untipped nose, the uncanny eyes, the poorly built body, with its ugly feet and uglier hands, till I felt ready to cry out with indignation that in this Christian England there should be exhibited the figure of a Christ which suggested to me some degraded Chaldean or African. . . . Save us,' he exclaimed, 'from the reproach of utter Pagan profligacy in our mammoth metropolis.' Vaughan was a well-known eccentric, a hell-fire preacher, but critics renowned for restraint, felt impelled to use equally extravagant language. True, there were voices raised in Epstein's defence, including that of George Bernard Shaw, but the man in the street (who always knows what he likes) was especially incensed, to Epstein's evident bewilderment.

It was not for another six years, until 1924, that Epstein received another important public commission, for by now the authorities were wary of his reputation and felt it would be courting disaster. The W. H. Hudson Memorial – Rima – so called after the heroine of *Green Mansions*, was unveiled in Kensington Gardens in the spring of 1925, and as usual the accusations flowed in fast and furious. Clearly it was the depiction of nudity, publicly displayed, which offended. Attempts were made to have it removed, but unsuccessfully. A life-sized figure entitled *The Visitation*, now in the Tate Gallery, was better received. Intended as part of a group, it showed a draped female figure with folded hands, and to avoid controversy Epstein called it simply *A Study*.

Meanwhile he continued with his portrait work, which included many famous sitters – the elderly, ailing novelist Joseph Conrad, the Ninth Duke of Marlborough, the Indian poet Rabindranath Tagore – and a series of busts called *Kathleen*, these of Kathleen Garman who became his second wife in 1947. His comments on his working methods are interesting:

'In my portraits it is assumed that I start out with a definite conception of my sitter's character. On the contrary, I have no such conception whatever in the beginning. The sitter arrives in the studio, mounts the stand, and I begin my study. My aim, to start with, is entirely constructive. With scientific precision I make a quite coldly thought out construction of the form, giving the body formations around the eyes, the ridge of the nose, mouth, and cheek-bones, and defining the relation of the different parts of the skull to each other. As the work proceeds, I note the expression, and the character of the model begins to impress itself on me. In the end, by a natural process of observation, the mental and physiological characteristics of the sitter impose themselves upon the clay. This process is natural and not preconceived.'

Later portraits included Chaim Weizmann, Paul Robeson, Emperor Haile Selassie, Lords Rothermere and Beaverbrook, Augustus John, Nehru, Bevin, Churchill, T. S. Eliot, Shaw, Bertrand Russell, Princess Margaret, and a host of others. No other sculptor has boasted such a varied and distinguished array of subjects.

In 1927 came his first *Madonna and Child* – a large-scale bronze, showing the Madonna seated and depicting Christ, as in the later study of the same subject, as a six- or seven-year-old boy. That year he visited the United States and his childhood haunts with his wife and daughter, and attended an exhibition of his works in New York, where fifty of his bronzes were shown. On his return to England he bought a house in Hyde Park Gate, where he lived for the rest of his life.

Two years later came another public commission – two statues entitled *Night* and *Day* for the London Underground Headquarters Building at St James' Park Station. The carvings were made directly on stone and were in his massive 'primitive' style. As usual the groups were attacked in sections of the Press, but R. H. Wilenski, the art historian, praised them as 'the grandest stone carvings in London . . . certainly the best things Epstein has done.'

Genesis, his great, brooding mother-figure, carved out of marble, appeared in 1931. The customary cries went up from the critics and pseudo-critics – 'obscenity', 'insult to womanhood' and so forth. In fact, it was a carving which, despite its outward semblance of ugliness, was fashioned with great feeling and tenderness. There was nothing sensuous and erotic about this figure which symbolized the eternal female principle, the dignity and agony of motherhood. Admitting that Epstein still provided the unexpected, Wilenski again leapt to the defence, calling him 'far and away the most skilful modeller in this country – perhaps in Europe'.

An interlude from sculpture came in the early thirties when he produced a charming series of some hundred watercolours of Epping Forest, followed by a large portfolio of flower paintings and Old Testament drawings. To his ironic amusement, but also his gratification, they sold better than his sculpture, and provided him with the leisure to concentrate on his more ambitious carvings, the next one being the remarkable *Ecce Homo*, of 1935.

Carved from a block of Subiaco marble, he again envisaged this Christ figure as a symbol of man gazing with profound pity at a tragic world. Again spokesmen for the Church used the familiar epithets – 'debased', 'insulting', 'grotesque', 'sacrilegious'. Perceptive critics, however, were unanimous in their praise of this great square figure, eleven feet high, with its massive head crowned with thorns, the hands shackled with ropes.

Adam, dating from 1938–9, was the male counterpart of *Genesis*, a squat, exaggeratedly muscular figure in the primitive style, straining upwards, head flung back, eyes fixed heavenward. It was exhibited with other bronzes at the Leicester Galleries and criticism was, for once, muted. Evidently he was at last becoming 'accepted', part of the British cultural scene, even in danger of being labelled 'traditionalist'!

During the forties he continued to work steadily without any abatement of energy, doing portraits of famous people and of children, the latter especially delightful. Among the larger works were *Lucifer* (1944), a splendid winged bronze, and a foreboding, bound *Lazarus*, reviled at first and returned unsold to the studio, but later placed in New College Chapel, Oxford.

It was not until 1949, however, at the age of 69, that Epstein was deemed 'respectable' and public commissions came in steadily, making the last decade of his life one of the busiest and most satisfying. Now there was no doubt of his pre-eminent place in British sculpture. There was *Youth Advancing*, a rather rigid figure of a boy for the Festival of Britain, and then the magnificent *Madonna and Child*, considered by many to be his finest work. This may be seen on the wall of the Convent of the Holy Child Jesus in Cavendish Square and was undertaken for the modest fee of £1,000. As Epstein remarked, 'No work of mine has brought so many tributes from so many diverse quarters.' The Madonna, with her calm, bland expression, stands behind the boy-Christ, arms outstretched in the form of a cross, beautifully simple and absolutely right in its setting.

Even larger works were to follow: *Social Consciousness*, a group for Fairmont Park, Philadelphia; *Christ in Majesty*, simple and austere, now in Llandaff Cathedral and dedicated in 1957; and the uncompromising Trades Union Council War Memorial – a mother with a dead child in her arms. Despite his failing health he still managed to complete a superb *St Michael and the Devil* for the new Coventry Cathedral – the saint standing in triumph over a shackled devil at his feet; and the fine group of figures for Bowater House, which cost £10,000 to cast. This stands at the Duke of Edinburgh's Gate in Hyde Park and shows a satyr behind a family group – man, woman, child and dog. It conveys a marvellous sense of excitement and motion, quite unlike anything attempted before. Epstein remained unpredictable and original to the last.

In 1961, two years after his death, the Edinburgh Festival held an exhibition of his work which astonished many visitors by its huge range and versatility. Blunt, fearless and rugged in manner and appearance, Epstein's work reveals the same qualities. He belonged to no school, nor did he found one. He was a great individualist and his contribution to the history of sculpture was revolutionary and, one hopes, enduring.

David Ben-Gurion
1886 –

On 14 May, 1948, under a huge photograph of Theodor Herzl in the Tel-Aviv Museum, a stocky, white-haired man, his voice full of emotion, announced to the world the birth of a new State – Israel. David Ben-Gurion had reached a milestone in a journey that had begun more than half a century ago, when for him, as for thousands of other Zionists, a Jewish homeland was a distant dream. Now, as he accepted the office of Prime Minister, he realized that, at the age of sixty, he was embarking on a new, dangerous and challenging phase of that same journey.

He had been born David Green, on 10 October, 1887, the sixth child of Avigdor and Sheindal Green. His birthplace, Plonsk was a typical small town in the Russian Pale of Settlement. Chaim Weizmann, who had just reached Barmitzvah age, was brought up in a similar environment and was subjected to similar pressures and influences. David Green grew up in the centre of the same fierce debates about Zionism, came under the spell of the same writers and thinkers – Pinsker, Achad Ha'am, Herzl – and was imbued with the same deep sense of identification with the Jewish people, their history, their language, their culture and their destiny. Yet although their goals were identical they were to take divergent paths. David Green was essentially a man of impulse and action. He was to give practical expression to the well-worn motto – return to the land – and the socialist principles which were to guide him throughout his life stemmed from the realities of toil, deprivation and bloodshed, during his pioneering days in Palestine.

His father, Avigdor, was a lawyer with a reputation of being a rebel. Instead of the traditional *kaftan* and fur hat he preferred a frock coat and striped trousers. He numbered Gentiles among his clients, read books on secular subjects, spoke and wrote Russian as well as Yiddish and was an ardent member of the Lovers of Zion movement. David went to a religious school and learned to speak Hebrew fluently. Unlike Weizmann he was not destined to go on to university. After school, he was entirely self-taught, an exercise that came easily to a boy inclined to be serious, solitary and introspective.

When he was twelve his mother died. She had always predicted that he would be a great man and, although his memories of her must have been dim, he described her as 'the embodiment of purity, love, human nobility and devotion'. So, at an early age, David learned to become independent in thought and action. At fourteen, he and some friends founded a Zionist youth group which they named the Ezra Society. They had no doubts about their objectives; it was to be part of the return to the Promised Land, the only answer to anti-semitism and pogroms.

By the time he announced to his father his firm intention to go to Palestine, he was already a skilful and impassioned public speaker. In Warsaw, which he regarded merely as a stopping-point, he continued his studies and his Zionist work of propaganda and recruitment. He lived on an allowance from his father and modest fees for teaching Hebrew. Once he was arrested, on no other grounds than that of looking like an intellectual and hence an agitator. Avigdor had to rush to the rescue, aided by the coincidence of the police officer's name also being Green.

David and his Ezra friends had decided that neither charity-spcnsored colonialism nor diplomatic wrangling was the answer to the 'Jewish problem'. Only literally by a return to the land, by personal labour and sacrifice, by the political organization of the working classes, could the Jews in Palestine find their salvation. The *Poalei Zion* – Workers of Zion – movement to which they now pledged their allegiance was the instrument which would, by stages, achieve these basic aims. There were to be no circuitous methods for David Green. Direct political action was his guiding principle.

It was his friend Shlomo Zemach who set the example by going out to Palestine with the second wave of settlers and returned with glowing and excited reports of life there. David Green needed no further prompting. In 1906 he sailed from Odessa with Zemach in a Russian cargo ship bound for Jaffa. The great adventure had begun, although Jaffa itself depressed him. 'The air smelt of charity and *bakshish*,' he wrote to his father. Then he set out on foot to Petach Tikvah, the oldest colony in the country. Here he found a completely different and refreshing atmosphere. He wrote: 'That night, my first night on homeland soil, is forever engraved on my heart. . . . I lay awake. Who could sleep through his first night in the homeland? The spirit of my childhood and dreams had triumphed, and I was joyful. I was in the Land of Israel, in a Jewish village, and its name was Petach Tikvah – Gateway of Hope!'

For the first time he had escaped from the constricting environment of the ghetto, the material pursuits of city life. This was an uplifting experience: 'I smelt the rich smell of corn, I heard the braying of donkeys and the rustle of leaves in the orchards. Above were clusters of stars, shining clear and bright against the deep blue of the heavens. My heart overflowed with happiness, as if I had entered a legendary kingdom. But now my dream had become a reality.'

For a year he worked on the land in a number of settlements around Petach Tikvah. It was a tough life and, like most of his colleagues, he was ill and lost weight. 'I sweated in the Judaean colonies,' he wrote good-humouredly, 'though for me there was more malaria and hunger than work. But all three – malaria, hunger and work – were new and full of interest.' For a time he worked in the vineyards of Rishon-le-Zion. He attended *Poalei Zion* meetings and conferences. One of his new acquaintances was a young Ukrainian, Isaac Ben-Zvi, a future President of Israel.

Still he yearned for the wide open spaces, the dangerous but rewarding frontier life he had read about. So he went north, walking sixty miles with Zemach and other friends to an all-Jewish agricultural settlement in Galilee – Sejera – one of the first colonies run on communal lines, precursor of the *kibbutz*. Here he was entirely, unreservedly content. 'No shopkeepers or speculators, no non-Jewish hirelings or idlers living on the labour of others. The men ploughed and harrowed the fields and planted their seeds; the women weeded the gardens and milked the cows; the children herded the geese and rode on horseback to meet their fathers in the fields. These were villagers, smelling wholesomely of midden and ripening wheat, and burnt by the sun.' Here, ploughing in the shadow of the encircling mountains, under a clear blue sky, he felt as if he were 'a partner in the act of creation'.

There were dangers too at Sejera. It was an isolated outpost in an alien land surrounded by hostile neighbours. Local Circassians were traditionally employed as watchmen, but they were a drunken, unreliable lot, and David felt it was essential for the settlers to be responsible for their own defence. It was here that he and his colleagues founded the *Hashomer* (Watchman) organization, soon to spread to other settlements and later to burgeon into the *Haganah*. Thus was inaugurated the so familiar pattern of work by day and watch by night – the ploughman with a rifle across his back. The necessity for it was grimly brought home by frequent incidents and the deaths of two close friends.

It was Ben-Zvi who called him away from Galilee to Jerusalem, inviting him to write for the new journal *Achdut* (Unity), the mouthpiece of the *Poalei Zion* movement. First he had to make a hurried trip back to Plonsk for a brief period of military service – one week to be exact. Then he donned civilian clothes, slipped across the Hungarian border, and made his way back to Palestine. He took up residence in the new city of Jerusalem in 1910, and threw himself whole-heartedly into journalism, signing his first article with the pseudonym Ben-Gurion – son of the young lion. He wrote vigorously and uncompromisingly on the themes of Jewish solidarity, the unity of the working class, the need for con-certed political action. The name of Ben-Gurion began to make its impact.

Then followed yet another change of career and environ-ment. He and his colleagues decided to go to Turkey, to learn the language and study the rudiments of Turkish law. They felt that only by acquiring such knowledge and experience would they be able to deal with the occupying power on even terms. It seemed to them a necessary step towards political independence. Sailing for Salonika, Ben-Gurion wrote to his father: 'In future I shall have to make up my mind whether to become a land-worker or a lawyer. I feel I can do both. . . . But whether a land-worker or a lawyer, I have only one aim: to labour on behalf of the Jewish worker in the Land of Israel.'

The exercise proved, in retrospect, to be partially a waste of effort, but nobody could have dreamed that within five years the Turks would be driven out of Palestine, to be re-placed by another occupying power. But in Constantinople, where he shared a room with Ben-Zvi, he met a young man from Tel-Aviv, Moshe Shertok (later Sharett), who was to be associated with him throughout his life; and Joseph Trumpel-dor, a Jewish officer in the Russian army, who had lost an arm at the siege of Port Arthur, and was now living in Degania, Palestine's oldest communal settlement. There is a photograph of the law student in Constantinople. Sporting a neat black moustache, Ben-Gurion is an unfamiliar figure with his fez, wing collar, frock coat and pocket watch. Except on diplomatic occasions in later life, he was a devotee of in-formality in dress and behaviour.

When war broke out in August, 1914, Ben-Gurion and Ben-Zvi returned home. To their consternation Jews were coming out rather than going in. The Turks, on the side of the Central Powers, were arresting or expelling Jews in their thousands. In Jerusalem there was famine among the pious Jews who relied on foreign food shipments for their very existence. Trumpeldor disappeared, later to head the Jewish mule-corps at Gallipoli. Shertok became an officer in the Turkish army. The *Achdut* offices were raided, and Ben-Gurion and Ben-Zvi arrested as subversives. They were thrown into gaol, questioned and informed that they would have to leave the country. When they reached Alexandria they were re-arrested as enemy aliens. Eventually they were allowed to leave for America, with 'never to return' stamped on their documents. A new chapter had begun.

America was a revelation – a rich, bustling, noisy world, still at peace, haven for tens of thousands of refugees from Europe. It boasted an active and well-endowed Zionist organization, but the Jewish community at large was disjointed and uninformed. The two friends lost no time in trying to bring a semblance of purpose and unity to Zionist efforts. Ben-Gurion taught himself English – his seventh language – wrote articles in Yiddish and Hebrew, toured up and down the country, lecturing and holding conferences, arguing not only for Zionism but also for the allied cause. Support for the allies was far from being a foregone conclusion, for many of the Russian refugees were sympathetic to the Germans. Together they wrote a book on the history and geography of Palestine, entitled *Eretz Israel* (The Land of Israel). And when America entered the war they agitated, together with their counterparts in Britain and Palestine, for the formation of a Jewish Legion to fight on the allied side in the Middle East.

In 1915 Ben-Gurion met and married a young nurse from Minsk, Paula Munweis. They shared a common background, although few common interests. She was not an intellectual, spoke no Hebrew, had no Zionist sympathies. But they were in love and she came to believe passionately in her husband's work and destiny. She was to devote her life to his care and comfort for the next fifty years.

Recruits flowed in rapidly to the office in New York for

the projected Jewish Legion. In London, the fiery Vladimir Jabotinsky was doing the same. Gradually the fortunes of war turned in the allies' favour. There were exciting developments as well on the diplomatic front. November 1917 brought the Balfour Declaration with its equivocal promise of a Jewish State. December saw Jerusalem captured by the British under Allenby.

In April 1918, Ben-Gurion volunteered for the British Army and was sent to Egypt, a corporal in the all-Jewish 39th Royal Fusiliers. It was an anti-climax, a dreary life of drilling and heel-kicking. Whilst down with a bout of dysentery he learned of the birth in Brooklyn of his daughter Geula; and he relieved the monotony of camp life by taking French leave to call on Chaim Weizmann, then in Jerusalem at the head of a Zionist Commission. It was the first time the two men had met and the discussion was amicable. It cost him his stripes and thirty days' confinement to barracks.

With the end of the war and with British occupation, Palestine entered upon a hopeful new era. The British were an unknown quantity, yet surely an improvement on the Turks, and the first High Commissioner, Sir Herbert Samuel, was himself a Jew. But the Arabs were likely to prove implacably hostile to the terms of the Mandate. Ben-Gurion's own attitude was one of cautious optimism. He was still convinced of the urgent need for a unified socialist programme. Now he was to plunge into politics in earnest.

Ben-Gurion's vision of a political union of workers took shape, first with the formation of *Achdut Ha'avodah* – Socialist Union of Workers – then in the great *Histadrut* – General Federation of Labour – of which he was to be General Secretary for fourteen years. From its modest beginnings the *Histadrut* was to grow into the largest and most powerful organization in the country, controlling not only the nation's labour force, but itself the nation's largest employer. It was to become a paramount force in the fields of industry, commerce, transport, building, banking, insurance, education, publishing, journalism and the arts. Ben-Gurion was largely responsible for the emergence of this mammoth organization which played such a vital part in the country's development and prosperity, often controversial but an undeniable, omnipresent feature of national life.

Without plunging into the complicated details of the internal politics of the next four decades, it is relevant to mention that Ben-Gurion was to occupy three posts of supreme importance – General Secretary of the *Histadrut* till 1935, then Chairman of the Zionist Executive and of the Jewish Agency, and finally Prime Minister of Israel. He was thus the dominant personality in politics for over thirty years, a single-minded, aggressive, courageous leader, boasting few close friends but multitudes of supporters, yet also arousing much enmity and opposition. But to the majority of the Jews in Palestine he was simply the symbol of a nation reborn. As time went on, and the impossible terms of the British Mandate fostered an increasingly ugly atmosphere of brutality and hatred, it was he who had to steer the precarious course between diplomacy and moderation on one side and extreme terrorist methods on the other. He succeeded in imposing his will on both sides, not without tragic cost, and shaped the destiny of a nation whose attitudes and policies today bear the stamp of his remarkable personality.

But this was far in the future. The twenties began and ended in violence. Two settlements in northern Galilee were attacked by Bedouin bandits; Trumpeldor was killed in the defence of Tel Hai. Later there was a Russian-style pogrom in the old city of Jerusalem with killings, rape, looting and burning of synagogues. It was a bitter beginning to the Mandate.

At a Zionist meeting at the Albert Hall in London a new voice was heard, the authentic voice of the young pioneer. On the same platform Weizmann advocated caution and limited immigration. Ben-Gurion would have none of this, demanding dynamic leadership, more funds, more immigrants.

Ironically, it was during their short visit to London that Amos, the Ben-Gurions' only son, was born. Only Renana, their second daughter, was to be born a *Sabra*. Later they went on a trip to Europe, revisiting Plonsk where Avigdor Green, now remarried, still lived. But it was a brief break and soon they were back in a troubled Palestine.

Yet the twenties were also exciting and constructive years. The third large wave of immigration from Eastern Europe was under way, more than doubling the Jewish population in five years. Swamps were drained. settlements founded, schools, universities and factories built. Towns grew in size, with modern roads and communications to link them. To pay for it all money and yet more money had to be raised. Despite the impatience of Ben-Gurion and his lieutenants, voiced at every Zionist Congress, the fund-raising agencies of the Zionist Organization gave invaluable support to the practical task of strengthening the country's economy, while Zionist workers all over the world, in their tens of thousands, each played their small, unpublicized but crucial part in the unfolding drama.

By the late twenties it was clear that Britain was bent on checking the growing influence of the Jews and appeasing the Arabs. The Arab riots of 1929 took an appalling toll of lives and property in Jerusalem, Hebron and Safad. We have seen how the White Paper of 1930 and the British government's equivocal attitude to immigration and land-purchase led to the crisis at the 17th Congress at Basle in 1931 and to Weizmann's resignation. Here Ben-Gurion, leading his newly formed *Mapai* party – named from the Hebrew initials of its full title 'Party of the Workers of the Land of Israel' – made a rousing speech criticizing Weizmann for accepting Britain's pledges, pleading for more funds and immigrants, warning against Arab antagonism, but dismissing the concept of unrestrained nationalism preached by the formidable Jabotinsky and his Revisionists. For Jabotinsky was now his chief rival, having won a large following within Congress as well as in American and European Zionist circles with his impassioned advocation of a Jewish State on both sides of the Jordan. Ben-Gurion realized that Jabotinsky's extremism was more of a threat than Weizmann's caution; and it was Jabotinsky's renunciation of moderate methods that led to the later activities of the *Irgun Zvai Leumi* – the National Military Organization – and its offshoots.

So the thirties progressed, under the terrible threat of

Hitler's persecution. A fourth wave of immigrants, mostly professional and businessmen from Germany, brought badly needed skills to the expanding economy. Ben-Gurion's tour of Europe in 1933, undertaken with a view to countering the propaganda of the Revisionists, bore fruit at the Zionist Congress of the same year. He had the satisfaction of winning almost half of the 320 seats and was now firmly in control. Against a background of growing violence at home he tried desperately to reach agreement with Jabotinsky, but failed. The Revisionists seceded from the Zionist Organization. Jabotinsky died in 1940, but he had many able and willing followers.

Ben-Gurion had always hoped for an amicable agreement with the Arabs and now entered into secret negotiations with an influential Arab friend, Musa Alami, who had the ear of the Mufti himself; but whatever slender hopes there might have been of reaching an understanding were dashed by the 1936 riots. The Arabs launched a full-scale strike, paralyzing the country and bringing in its train and the all-too-familiar pattern of murder, arson and looting. The Peel Commission sent out by the government recommended partition into separate Arab and Jewish states. After heated debate Ben-Gurion persuaded his colleagues to consider it, despite the fact that the Arabs had rejected it out of hand. 'This is the beginning of the redemption for which we have waited 2,000 years,' he declared. But it was not yet to be. The British government itself disclaimed the plan.

Two more years of increasing violence ensued. Although Britain imposed restrictions on immigration, boatloads of refugees from Europe continued to arrive. Ben-Gurion knew that the Jews might have to take their fate in their hands. Illegal immigration, under the aegis of *Haganah*, he was prepared to authorize, but violence was not to be met by violence, and he continued to condemn such methods with all the power at his command.

Nevertheless, *Haganah* itself was undergoing transformation. Under the guidance of the eccentric and brilliant English captain Orde Wingate it was discarding its purely defensive role. Arms were already being smuggled in from abroad and future generals such as Yadin, Allon, Dayan and Dori were gaining the tactical experience which would be desperately needed ten years later. *Haganah* night squads fought back against infiltrators and protected vital stretches of oil pipelines. Wingate himself said: 'We are assembling here the foundations for the Army of Zion.'

Then, as time ran out for the Jews in Europe, the fateful White Paper, Command 6019, dashed the hopes of world Jewry, Zionists and non-Zionists alike. Millions who might have been saved were destined for the death camps. Yet even now, with war imminent, in the bitterest moment of Zionist history, Ben-Gurion announced, on behalf of the Jewish people, a dual aim. 'We shall fight side by side with Britain in our war against Hitler as if there were no White Paper, and we shall fight the White Paper as if there were no war.'

More than 100,000 young Jewish men and women volunteers from Palestine signed on to fight with the allies immediately when war broke out. They were accepted somewhat reluctantly, and it was not until late in 1944, after years of negotiation, that Churchill finally agreed to the formation of a Jewish Brigade.

Ben-Gurion spent a year in London during the Blitz, indulging in his favourite pastime of bookshop-browsing, teaching himself Greek, and delving enthusiastically into Greek military strategy and philosophy. Then he visited America, realizing that, particularly after Pearl Harbour, it would be America, not Britain, who would have the decisive voice in Middle East affairs after the war. He called an emergency conference at the Biltmore Hotel in New York and announced, for the first time, his intention of proclaiming a Jewish 'Commonwealth' after the allied victory. The Biltmore Programme was adopted by Zionist organizations throughout the world and committed Ben-Gurion unambiguously to his post-war policy of national independence.

The terrorists interpreted this as a call for action. The *Irgun*, under Menachem Beigin, and the even more fanatical Stern Gang were responsible for a series of horrifying crimes which in turn provoked equally brutal and indefensible reprisals by the British. The tragic pattern of violence and counter-violence continued in the years immediately following the war, particularly after the Labour government's broken pledge to repeal the 1939 White Paper. Given Ernest Bevin's uncompromising hostility towards the idea of a Jewish national home, there was an even greater determination to resist tooth and nail. Illegal immigrants were put ashore by night, others, less fortunate, were turned back in sight of shore to be detained in Cyprus; arms still found their way in, terrorist incidents multiplied bringing the inevitable counter-measures, and the atmosphere of mistrust and hatred built up to boiling-point. It is hardly necessary to recall in detail these unhappy events, which all parties concerned, none of them guiltless, would probably prefer to forget. In the midst of it all Ben-Gurion remained consistent in condemning extremist methods, whilst forcefully arguing the Jewish case.

We have already covered the events leading up to the historic vote in the General Assembly of the United Nations on 29 November, 1947. By thirty votes to thirteen, with ten abstentions, including Britain, the United Nations resolved to set up two independent States and called on Britain to relinquish her Mandate by 1 August, 1948. Ben-Gurion watched the singing and dancing in the streets of Jerusalem and rejoiced that Herzl's dream had at last been fulfilled. But the stern realist in him knew equally well that there still remained a grim struggle ahead. The Arabs had already announced their intention of resisting the Assembly's decision. Five armies, including the British-trained Arab Legion, stood poised to attack. The War of Independence was about to begin.

The vulnerable border settlements were among the first targets of Arab guerillas. The *Palmach* – the crack, independent assault force – and *Haganah* fought off these early attacks, but four villages in the Hebron region were lost to the Arab Legion. The most serious situation, however, developed in Jerusalem which the Arabs cut off from the rest of the country by gaining control of the road to Tel-Aviv. Convoys bringing food, water and medical supplies were ambushed, but many fought their way through. In one of these, the largest ever assembled, Ben-Gurion himself insisted on travelling. Whatever happened, Jerusalem, with its mystical and historic significance, would not be abandoned.

Two terrible incidents took place during this 'unofficial' war period. The *Irgun* massacred the population of the village of Deir Yassin, a crime instantly condemned by Ben-Gurion, who sent a message of sympathy to King Abdullah of Transjordan. Then a non-military convoy of scientists, doctors and nurses, bound for the Hebrew University and Hadassah Hospital on Mount Scopus, was ambushed. All were brutally murdered. One of the victims had been engaged to Ben-Gurion's younger daughter.

Ben-Gurion showed his abilities as a military commander during this critical period. The qualities he habitually displayed at the conference table, toughness, resolution and imagination, stood him in good stead for the trying times to come and they rallied the people behind him. Morale was unbelievably high.

The British Mandate petered out on 14 May. The machinery of government was completely dismantled. But now Ben-Gurion had a free hand. Against international advice, he was determined to proclaim the Jewish State without delay. On that Friday afternoon, in a moving but simple ceremony at the Tel-Aviv Museum, David Ben-Gurion announced the foundation of the State of Israel. The new national anthem, *Hatikvah* (Hope), was played. Ben-Gurion would be Prime Minister and Minister of Defence in the provisional government, and although his name was missing from the thirty-seven signatories of the Declaration – and he unfortunately ill, in New York – Chaim Weizmann was to be rightly honoured by becoming Israel's first President. Within a year, but only after proving her capacity to survive by force of arms, Israel was admitted to the United Nations.

The Declaration of the State was the signal for the Arab armies to attack. A highly sophisticated fighting force, vastly superior in numbers, supplied wtih the most up-to-date weapons, was pitted against a small, hastily-mustered 'civilian' army possessing only a handful of tanks, scarcely any artillery and the merest skeleton of an air force and navy. Yet the experience and training of twenty years, and the morale of a people fighting for its life, proved to be the deciding factors. For the first time in the modern world the Jews demonstrated to an astonished world their fighting abilities.

In Galilee, Jewish forces captured the Crusader city of Acre and cleared the coastal strip to the Lebanese border. Soon the eastern half of Galilee was also in Jewish hands. In the south, the powerful Egyptian army advanced to within twenty-five miles of Tel-Aviv and was there halted. Jerusalem, however, was in dire straits. The Arab Legion overran the Old City and tightened the ring around the new section. During a brief truce period Ben-Gurion gave orders for an alternative road to be constructed in order to lift the siege. Working by night, under the noses of the Arab Legion, young men and women built a six-mile stretch of road from what had been little more than a donkey track. It was called the Burma Road and it was to save Jerusalem.

The United Nations' mediator, Count Bernadotte, had brought about a temporary stop to hostilities and it was during this time that Ben-Gurion had to make another momentous and courageous decision. The *Irgun* had chartered a ship, the *Altalena*, to bring in volunteers and more than 500 tons of arms, ammunition and military equipment. Its arrival had been well publicized. 750 men and women, volunteers and refugees, slipped ashore at Kfar Vitkin, north of Tel-Aviv, but an attempt to unload arms was resisted by *Haganah*. The *Irgun* was a private army refusing to recognize the government. Moreover, this was a clear breach of the truce. Ben-Gurion made it a test case. The *Altalena* moved down the coast and became grounded within a few hundred yards of the Tel-Aviv waterfront. Thousands of people watched the last act of the drama as *Haganah* guns fired two salvoes, set it on fire and sank it with all its precious cargo. There was some loss of life, inevitably, but Ben-Gurion was unrepentant. It broke the back of the *Irgun*, and Ben-Gurion further strengthened his hand by absorbing the independent *Palmach* into the defence forces shortly afterwards. Both actions gave rise to bitter controversy, but Ben-Gurion was determined on unity at all costs.

The truce was not renewed. During the second phase of the war Israeli forces captured Nazareth, Ramle and the airfield and town of Lydda. Jewish planes bombed Damascus and Cairo, and the tiny Jewish navy went into action off the Lebanese coast. The siege of Jerusalem was lifted. During a second truce period Bernadotte was murdered by members of the Stern Gang. Ben-Gurion outlawed the gang, but despite an intensive hunt the murderers were never caught.

The second truce was broken when Egyptian forces attacked a food convoy in the Negev. Israeli forces swept southwards and in a ten-day campaign captured Beersheba and the northern part of the Negev, encircling a large Egyptian force at Faluja. Among the captured officers was one named Gamel Abdel Nasser. Then the Israeli army drove on to Sinai. The new frontiers were larger than those originally awarded by the United Nations, and there had to be modifications. There was still only a narrow corridor between Jerusalem and the western part of the country, but in Eilat, on the Red Sea, Israel possessed a port of great potential, vital to her future trade with the East. Armistice agreements were signed in the spring of 1949, followed by elections in which Ben-Gurion was formally confirmed in his post of Prime Minister.

He now faced the challenge of an uneasy peace and the test of his powers as a world statesman. The first task was the 'ingathering of the exiles'. Ben-Gurion insisted that every Jew had the right to become a citizen of Israel, and unlimited immigration – no matter what the resultant problems – was from the start a basic policy decision. Now Jews flocked in, often in entire communities, from the displaced persons' camps, from Eastern Europe, from Iraq, from Yemen, from North Africa. The difficulties facing the new nation were colossal – hundreds of thousands of new immigrants to be housed, fed, educated, found jobs. A large proportion of them were too old to work, many others were illiterate. One of the first tasks was to teach them to speak Hebrew. Education was free to all, and the army was to play a prominent part in teaching and training the new citizens so that they should take their place as soon as possible in the work of reconstruction.

With all these new immigrants, with new settlements to be founded, new towns to be built, new industries to be developed, money and foreign investment were desperately needed. Israel could not hope to be self-sufficient for many years to come. Ben-Gurion himself visited America once more, receiving a hero's welcome, calling for more Jewish immigration from the West as well as its financial assistance. For in addition to building up a healthy economy, Israel still had to look to her borders, to keep her civilian army permanently on call, to devote a crippling proportion of her budget to defence.

One of the most important decisions taken during his first term of office was to make a reparations agreement with Germany. Germany's admission of guilt and responsibility for the victims of the concentration camps could not be repaid in terms of money and goods, but the agreement did much to bolster the tottering economy. It was a statesman-like move, in the teeth of those who wished to have nothing to do with murderers. Ben-Gurion knew that nothing could be forgotten, but it was fully in keeping with his principles of peace and justice that a fresh start should have been made. That he himself would never forget was attested by his taking full responsibility some years later for the tracking down and bringing to trial of Adolf Eichmann, not as an act of cold vengeance, but as a reminder, particularly to the younger generation, of the suffering which men like Eichmann had inflicted on their parents and grandparents.

After five years in office Ben-Gurion made a personal decision which stunned the nation. He resigned in order to go to live in a small *kibbutz* in the centre of the Negev – Sde Boker. In a farewell broadcast he paraphrased the prophet Habakkuk, trying to explain his reasons for returning to the simple communal life of his early days in Palestine. 'The righteous man shall live by his faith.' It was not enough to exhort, it was for him personally to set an example.

It proved not to be a final farewell. Two years later, at the request of Prime Minister Sharett and his cabinet, he returned, at a time of crisis, to resume his duties as Minister of Defence, and then, following an election, Prime Minister once more. This term of office was punctuated by a series of raids by Egyptian *fedayin* bands in the south and frequent breaches of the armistice by Syria in the east. With the nationalization of the Suez Canal by Nasser and the conclusion of a military pact between Egypt, Jordan and Syria, Ben-Gurion took the last of his important military decisions – to strike against Egypt rather than wait tamely for a much-publicized and inevitable attack.

The result was the brilliantly executed Sinai campaign of 1956, when, in five days' fighting, Israeli forces routed the Egyptian army and occupied the entire Sinai peninsula. The aim, as Ben-Gurion repeatedly explained to world leaders, was not expansion but the securing of Israel's borders and her continued existence as a free nation. The subsequent British and French intervention did not substantially affect the outcome, although the political repercussions were great. Ben-Gurion's decision to withdraw Israel's army, under strong pressure from the United Nations, was perhaps wrong in military terms, right in diplomatic terms. Whilst raising Israel's reputation in the eyes of world opinion, it led to the emergence of an even more serious situation eleven years later as the Arab armies grouped for a third round.

Ben-Gurion's final years in office saw the continued expansion and improvement of the national economy and his tireless efforts to see Israel firmly established as a nation with much to offer to other emergent countries, especially in Africa. He had to contend with much bitter political strife in his own government. In the controversial Lavon spy case he was as hard-hitting and stubborn as ever. The rumblings from this affair linger on. And as Middle East tension showed no sign of slackening, he continued to use every weapon in his diplomatic armoury to prevent Israel becoming a pawn in the East–West power game. He was to bow out for good in 1963, the State now fifteen years old, well and truly launched towards maturity.

Today, past his eightieth year, his wife Paula having died a few years ago, David Ben-Gurion lives peacefully at Sde Boker as a *kibbutznik*. In the summer of 1967 he saw yet another triumph of Israeli arms, although this time others directed the strategy. He is attentive to all that goes on in the world but he takes no part in the affairs of state. He has his indispensable books and is surrounded by green fields and orchards – fruits and crops miraculously growing in the middle of a parched and empty expanse of desert. He has his memories and the knowledge that he has fought well for his people. Beyond the rage of political controversy, he lives out his last years, loved and respected, a truly great man. And the message he gave to the nation when he made his decision to leave public life and return to the land on which Israel's future basically depends, can be read as a guide to the young people on whom he relies to continue his work – 'Do not weep: follow me.'

Marc Chagall
1887–

Astride a yellow roof a red and white animal – part cow, part donkey, part goat – suckles a green lamb and a green child. Above the blue dome of a church, topped by a greenish-yellow cross, a headless torso floats in a blue-black expanse of sky. One hand grasps a green bucket, while the severed head of a woman gazes into the void. The picture, painted by Marc Chagall at the age of twenty-four, is enigmatically entitled *To Russia, Asses and Others*. It sounds like a nightmare, a fairy-tale, a psycho-analyst's treasure trove. Perhaps. But it is also a stunning and unique work of art, the sort of painting which has made Marc Chagall one of the most original, unclassifiable artists of modern times.

The young Chagall was as dexterous with words as he was with paints. He could equally well have been a poet. His autobiography, *My Life*, completed after the First World War when his international career had barely begun, is a vivid and lyrical impression of his childhood in the Russian town of Vitebsk, but infuriating for anyone who insists on a smooth chronological sequence of events. Childhood memories, dreams, hopes, fears and sensations are fused imaginatively into a remarkable word-portrait of life in a *Chassidic* community – a community which the mature artist was to evoke nostalgically throughout his career.

The story unfolds bit by bit, in short and tantalizing peep-show episodes. He was born in 1887 and on the night of his birth the Jewish quarter of Vitebsk, as on many other occasions, was on fire. We are told that the father carted barrels in a herring plant, plodded to synagogue every morning at six, and sat up over the samovar in the evenings making himself endless cups of tea. We see his mother, plump, cheerful and talkative, managing the large household, encouraging her son to draw but cherishing the hope that he will be a clerk, an accountant or a photographer. One grandfather was a teacher of religion, the other a butcher who spent much time lying on top of the stove and who was one day discovered sitting on the chimney-pot eating a bowl of carrots. And there were numerous uncles – an indistinct group of black-bearded, round-bellied individuals – including Uncle Neuch who played the violin like a cobbler; and eight brothers and sisters, though what their names were we are not told, except for a younger brother David, who was to die of tuberculosis.

They make their entrances and exits like figures in a shadow play. What happened where or when does not matter. Sights, sounds, smells are brilliantly evoked – the crowded parlour with the samovar, the huge black stove, the pendulum clock, white cloth and Sabbath candles, herring, pickled cucumbers and black bread. Above, the young Marc gazes dreamily out of the attic window at the shifting cloud-scapes, the swelling crescent of the moon, the twinkling stars. He watches the busy flow of humanity in the street below, the peasants on their way to market, the elders bound for synagogue, the children tumbling in the gutters. Sometimes, like his grandfather, he scrambles out on the roof to get a better view of a fire. He spends endless hours in synagogue, accompanying the cantor in his childish treble, day-dreaming of girls, longing to be outside, swimming in the river. Babies are born, young people get married, old men die. He stores up the memories, scribbling, sketching, revelling in his childhood, longing for new experiences, bursting with ideas, confident of his destiny.

It is a marvellous account of the mental development of a precocious and talented boy, told with wit, charm and nostalgia – and a pointer to his later development as an artist. For neither in words nor in paint was he interested in depicting things as they were. True, he was capable of painting 'conventional' pictures – portraits of his parents, his sister, his fiancée, his daughter, a praying Jew – though these possessed an individuality of form and colour which made them more than ordinary portraits. But the typical Chagall painting is of the universe which he alone inhabited, compact of dreams, experiences, memories and myths. Certain themes and motifs were to recur throughout his work – the curious horned animal, the topsy-turvy buildings, the cocks and fishes, the candles and samovars of childhood, the clock, the fiddler, the beggar with the sack, the roofs and spires of Vitebsk, the flaming angels, the floating lovers, the floral bouquets, the crucified figures, the clowns and acrobats.

To say this and to note their recurrence is no aid to understanding the essential Chagall. His art, though rooted in experience, is of no set time or place; nor, except when his life was touched by the traumatic experience of war or revolution, can one unerringly place a picture in a particular period. He experimented with, and was to some extent influenced by, the fashionable techniques of the day – Fauvism, Cubism, Expressionism. The Surrealist school hailed him as a pioneer. But he never belonged to a single school or movement, for he could never be bound by rules or conventions. Without any hint of arrogance, he knew he was different and that he would be false to himself if he expressed himself in any other way. Like his other great contemporaries, Matisse and Picasso he is simply himself.

Vitebsk was his life, but Vitebsk was too narrow and provincial for a boy with such unusual gifts and such lofty ambitions. Once determined to paint, nothing could hold him back. His room was filled with his sketches, teeming with colour and movement, but he needed instruction in technique, contact with other artists. The local art teacher, Yehuda Pen, could teach him only the rudiments – two months were enough – and touching up photographs was monotonous and unproductive work. So off he went to St Petersburg, with twenty-seven roubles from his father in his pocket, moving from one dingy, rat-infested room to another, unable to afford to eat properly, unauthorized, being a Jew, to live in the city itself, and wasting two years at an art school which could contribute little to the development of his wayward talent.

St Petersburg was at that time a flourishing centre of literature, theatre and music. Although Russian art was flat and unimaginative compared with painting in western Europe, there were many art lovers and patrons in society who were ready with advice, and one or two who were prepared to assist and even subsidize him. He met the celebrated designer Léon Bakst, one of the shining lights of the Diaghilev ballet, and was admitted to his school. At the next easel, in Bakst's studio, was the dancer Nijinsky. After two unsuccessful attempts, one of Chagall's sketches won the approval of the master himself, but Bakst lost interest when he admitted an inability to paint scenery. Soon Bakst left St Petersburg for ever. But Chagall's horizon had broadened. He was already painting with more boldness and freedom, inspired by the memories of Vitebsk, which he frequently revisited. He painted familiar childhood scenes like *The Sabbath* and *The Wedding*, and a remarkable picture in sombre greens and browns, called *The Dead Man*, in which a corpse lies in the street, surrounded by candles, a road-sweeper hunches over his broom, a grief-stricken woman raises her hands in supplication, and a man sits astride a roof, playing his fiddle. But Vitebsk had happy associations as well, for here lived Bella Rosenfeld, the girl he was to marry. He painted the first of many portraits of her, in a white dress and frilled lace collar, wearing black gloves.

But St Petersburg was too restricting. The image of Paris beckoned from afar, and thanks to a generous patron who bought two of his pictures, installed him in a flat near his own house and then provided him with a monthly subsidy, he was able to realize his ambition in 1910. The artistic capital of the world provided him with the intellectual and cultural stimulation he so desperately needed. He was still poor, but he could wander at will through the galleries and museums, seeing for the first time the collected works of the Impressionists and Post-Impressionists, familiarizing himself with the wealth of European art over the centuries, and savouring the atmosphere of a cosmopolitan city bursting with revolutionary ideas. He took a studio in the artists' colony La Ruche (The Beehive).

He met fellow-painters, poets, musicians, intellectuals. In his cramped studio he covered canvases, sheets, napkins, nightshirts with paint, revelling in what he called the *lumière liberté* of this wonderful city. His colours were richer than the earlier browns and greens and yellows of Vitebsk, the patterns bolder and more experimental. Bakst came to visit him and simply remarked, 'Now your colours sing.' These Paris years produced a splendid harvest of pictures – oils, gouaches and drawings – many of them shocking to conventional tastes. There was a self-portrait of the artist with seven fingers, the remarkable *I and the Village* (complete with fabulous animal, Vitebsk skyline, upside-down figures and houses, the canvas divided into colour segments), views of Paris, a geometric *Homage to Apollinaire* (one of his closest friends), and his first overtly religious painting *Calvary*. This picture, glowing with greens, reds, yellows and blues, depicted a crucified Christ, with his own parents weeping at the foot of the Cross, and mysterious figures in the background, a boatman and a peasant with a ladder – a typical composition, eloquent and moving.

It was poets such as Blaise Cendrars and Guillaume Apollinaire who encouraged Chagall to follow his own stylistic inclinations, regardless of fashion and popular taste. Cendrars persuaded an art dealer to commission Chagall to paint seven paintings a month, while Apollinaire induced Herwarth Walden, editor and founder of German Expressionist painting, to mount a one-man exhibition of Chagall's work in Berlin. This was the real breakthrough, but not destined to bear fruit until after the war. Now, a few months before war broke out, Chagall journeyed back to Vitebsk, leaving over two hundred of his works in Berlin.

The return to Vitebsk ushered in a wonderful new series of paintings devoted to everyday life and celebrating his marriage to Bella. He painted Jews at prayer, he depicted himself confidently standing in front of his parents' house and reclining in a field, and he embarked on a lyrical series of paintings of lovers – himself and Bella – sailing weightlessly over the rooftops, or balanced one above the other in joyful, ecstatic praise of young love.

This was one aspect of his return home. War brought another – the harsh, bitter reality of suffering, bloodshed and useless heroism, reflected in a series of poignant studies of wounded soldiers. He was posted to a desk job in St Petersburg and saw Czarist society crumbling about him. There was little time for painting, but he was acquiring a reputation. There were exhibitions of his work in Moscow, one almost coinciding with his marriage, the other with the birth of his daughter Ida.

His private drama of happiness was, however, played out against a background of terror and tragedy. The Russian army reeled back in defeat. Jews were made scapegoats. There were pogroms in the towns. Once he was cornered on a dark night by an armed gang of looters.

'The moment they catch sight of me they ask: "Jew, or not?"

'For a second, I hesitate. It is dark.

'My pockets are empty, my fingers sensitive, my legs weak, and they are thirsty for blood. My death will be of no use. I wanted so much to live.

' "All right! Get along!" they shout.

'Without a moment's hesitation I run towards the centre of the town where the pogrom started.

'Gunshots. Bodies falling into the water.

'I run home.'

Then came the Revolution. New hope for the Jews, new hope for Russia. Although he had never been active in politics, he stood firmly behind the new government. To his amazement he was given an important administrative post,

Commissar for Fine Arts in the Vitebsk district and Director of the Vitebsk Academy of Art. Organizing and staffing schools, academies and museums was an enormous responsibility, and Bella was quick to realize that it would block his creative growth. Yet he threw himself into the work with enthusiasm. On the anniversary of the Revolution he set all the local decorators and painters to work copying his animal pictures to display on banners and posters. It was a gay and festive occasion. Only the local bigwigs were angry. They saw little connection between Chagall's flying green cows and pink horses and the doctrines of Marx and Lenin. Earnestness and austerity were the order of the day. Though Chagall had seen the Revolution initially as a liberating force, he soon discovered that art in post-war Russia remained as academic and constricted as ever. His heart was still in Russia, but Russia had little to offer a freely developing spirit such as his. He was often away in St Petersburg and Moscow collecting art materials, even food, for his colleagues and pupils. One day he returned home to find himself ousted from the Academy. It was a blessing in disguise. They moved to Moscow, never to return.

In a corner of a demolished apartment house they lived, almost penniless. Then came a stroke of good fortune. Alexis Granowsky, manager of the newly established State Jewish Theatre, invited him to paint a series of murals for the Moscow opening, and to design sets and costumes for the theatre's repertoire. This commission afforded him free scope for his talents. The long wall of the theatre was transformed into a gay processional mural entitled *Introduction to the New Theatre*, in which Chagall depicted actors, musicians and dancers, with the young Jewish actor Mikhoels as Hamlet, Chagall himself with his palette, and an array of animals and nature motifs. Four other murals showed typical scenes of Jewish life and ritual, painted in Chagall's inimitable style, bursting with energy and humour. His stage designs and costumes were equally revolutionary, departing completely from traditional naturalism. He was particularly happy in capturing the essence of the writer with whom he shared a special affinity – Shalom Aleichem. Audiences were attracted to the theatre as much by Chagall's designs as by the plays themselves. It was a fruitful period and brought other commissions in its wake. One such was for the Theatre of Revolutionary Satire – to design sets and costumes for Gogol's *The Government Inspector*, another comic masterpiece which instinctively appealed to a man of Chagall's temperament.

Chagall's work in Moscow initiated a life-long association with the theatre, which was to be vividly recalled in his later ballet designs and circus paintings. But half of his heart was still in the west. And now Europe called him, in the person of a poet named Rubiner, writing from Berlin. Rubiner asked him whether he was still alive, assuring him that his paintings were now very much in demand. He was famous as the high priest of Expressionism. Chagall got permission to leave Russia – this time for ever.

Back in Berlin he found his pictures distributed among galleries and private collections. Though famous, he was unable to recover more than three of his major works, and, thanks to inflation, he was ill-rewarded for his earlier pictures. He had completed his autobiography in Moscow, together with illustrative etchings, but found that Berlin was not conducive to serious work. A letter from Ambroise Vollard, the Paris publisher, proved another turning-point. He returned to the city he loved, only to find his former studio ransacked, his sketches and paintings gone. Patiently he set to work reconstructing them from photographs and launching out on new pictures. And this time he could afford to travel – down to the Pyrenees, the Riviera, Savoy – visits which brought to his work a new, natural, open-air feeling. Blue skies, rural landscapes, flowers, fruit and trees featured prominently in his paintings; and now, happy and secure once more, the old themes recurred – the lovers, floating freely among the clouds, embracing by moonlight, lying in trees and under clusters of flowers. Once again the canvases pulsated with colour.

As a regular source of income, Vollard commissioned him to illustrate Gogol's *Dead Souls* and then the *Fables* of La Fontaine. Both assignments were brilliantly carried out. The Gogol etchings showed his mastery in a new black and white medium. The engravings were varied in style and technique and Chagall's native wit and humour responded intuitively to Gogol's satirical characters and situations. The *Fables* were equally inspired, one hundred colour engravings, witty and inventive, giving full rein to the artist's affection for animals, and providing a triumphant answer to those critics who cried out in horror at the thought of a Russian artist defiling a hallowed French text.

In France Chagall painted once more with complete abandon. He painted Ida sitting at an open window with a bowl of flowers, an almost traditional portrait in green and blue; a double portrait of himself and Bella in profile, she in white with a bouquet of roses, he with palette and easel; another window picture of an embracing bride and groom with the Eiffel Tower in the background. Vitebsk was recalled again in a group of Jews returning from synagogue. There were paintings of Paris, of southern France, circus impressions of clowns, acrobats and animals. Finally there was a new commission, after the completion of the *Fables* in 1931, for a series of illustrations to the Bible.

In order to gain first-hand experience of the places where the biblical happenings occurred, Chagall visited Palestine for the first time. He felt immediately at home, encountering, in Jerusalem and the ancient Jewish town of Safad, characters and scenes from his childhood, and recording his impressions in oils and water colours. Palestine provided the spiritual background to the sixty-six biblical etchings which occupied him for the next eight years. They were beautiful compositions in terms of form and colour, and to each Chagall brought a quality of simplicity and rapt devotion, a feeling of near-innocence, which conveyed both the humanity of the characters and the immense, profound grandeur of the drama which they enacted.

As with any great and sensitive artist living in the troubled thirties, and not only because he happened to be Jewish, Chagall was deeply concerned and influenced by the events in neighbouring Germany and fully aware of the gathering storm clouds. His art in the latter years of the decade reflect his obsession with these terrible events and the horrors yet to come. The *White Crucifixion* of 1938 returns to the *Calvary* theme, and although the central figure is that of Christ, the enveloping scenes and characters leave one in no doubt that the subject is the catastrophe of world Jewry. Christ is a Jewish figure, loins wrapped in a prayer shawl; a synagogue is in flames, holy scrolls, prayer books and candlesticks are scattered in the street. A howling mob, armed with sticks and banners, sweep down on the town whose inhabitants lie dead or flee across a river. An elderly man with a scroll, a blind beggar, a grieving woman and the familiar Jew with a sack stumble in different directions. Above the illuminated Cross a group of traditional Jewish figures float in lamentation. It is a magnificent, moving and humane expression of the artist's sense of outrage and compassion.

In many other pictures dealing with the war and crucifixion the same qualities are apparent. Sometimes the overtly Jewish reference is absent. The spirit of these paintings is religious in the truest sense, transcending both Judaism and Christianity. It is human suffering which is portrayed in these harrowing works.

When France was invaded and the Vichy government installed, it was no longer safe for Chagall and his family to stay. After eighteen years he left for America, haven of so many Jewish artists and intellectuals.

The war and the ghastly reports from the concentration camps continued to be reflected in the pictures of those years – crucifixions, cheerless wintry landscapes, gloomy and melancholy canvases recording a world in ruins. The pair of lovers appears again in *Between Darkness and Light*, but this time they are shadowy figures, he with a blue face, she disembodied, with chalk-white profile. In the foreground a woman, with the head of a bird, clutches a child, beyond stretches the snow-covered street, with a solitary lamp-lighter and a sinister sleigh, drawn by an undefined green creature.

Personal tragedy arrived when Bella, his beloved companion and artistic inspiration, died in September, 1945. He dedicated a touching painting to her, *Autour d'elle*, in the year of her death. Only in a group of colourful pictures inspired by a visit to Mexico was the gloom of the war years

Left: The Russian-born painter Marc Chagall, who left his native country after the Revolution to work in America and France.
Below: A typical Chagall painting, with many of his familiar motifs. This one dates from 1925 and is entitled *Russian Village (by kind permission of the Albright-Knox Art Gallery, Buffalo, New York).*
Bottom: General Moshe Dayan examines a pottery jar of the Biblical period. Dayan takes a keen interest in archaeology and has a valuable private collection.

Right: The 'Secret Annexe" in the house overlooking the canal in Amsterdam, where Anne Frank, her family and friends were concealed from the Gestapo for two years.
Below: This portrait of Anne Frank was unveiled at the opening of the Anne Frank Haven in Amsterdam – the house where she hid from the Germans, now used as a youth centre.

alleviated; and his links with Russia and the theatre were reforged in the vivid stage designs and costumes devised for the New York Ballet Theatre's production of Stravinsky's *Fire Bird*.

In the spring of 1947 Chagall returned for the third time to France. He lived in Paris for a time, then moved south to St Jean Cap-Ferrat, and later to his permanent home in Vence. Here, where so many other artists had found inspiration, he captured the beauties and joys of the countryside. His paintings glowed again with rich, turbulent colours – trees in leaf, blossom and flowers, birds, fishes, fruit, sunlight and song. In a series of twenty-nine paintings entitled *Thanks to Paris*, he evoked memories of the city he loved second only to Vitebsk. He married again in 1952. His wife, the charming and intelligent Valentine (Vava) Brodsky, brought him serenity of spirit once more. He returned to familiar subjects, the floating, entwined lovers and the circus acrobats, trapeze artists, clowns, equestriennes and animals. And he began to experiment in new media – sculpture and ceramics. To the latter he brought all his flair for intricate design, constructing bowls, dishes, vases, plates and wall-plaques, full of gaiety and light.

Yet there were still greater things to come. He turned to the difficult medium of stained glass. Two large windows were commissioned for Metz Cathedral, depicting scenes from the Old Testament. This was a prelude to an even finer achievement – one hesitates to say 'crowning' achievement, for this amazing man is still at work, though over eighty –, the group of stained-glass windows for the synagogue of the Hadassah Medical Centre in Jerusalem. These presented a new challenge, twelve windows, each over ten foot in height, representing the twelve tribes. But Jewish tradition prohibits the religious depiction of face and form. Chagall surmounted this problem brilliantly, treating his sacred subjects in swirling patterns and radiant colours, reaching back to the motifs of his childhood – the sacred objects, the trees, fruits, plants and animals – employing all the symbols of his unique world of dream and fantasy in a supreme expression of wonder and worship. During the Six-Day War of 1967 the windows were removed for safety, though one was damaged. Chagall wrote: 'I am not worried about them, only about Israel's safety. Let Israel be safe and I will make you lovelier windows.'

Many critics have tried to 'explain' Chagall and have failed. Once begin to analyse him and you threaten to destroy his very essence. No words can convey his spontaneity, his fertile imagination, the ease and power of his brush-work, the magic 'chemistry' of his colours. He himself has said repeatedly that all he cares about is painting and once told a questioner: 'I don't understand them at all. They are not literature. They are merely a pictorial arrangement of images that obsess me.' This is the sort of statement with which we have to be content. It cannot tell us anything about the warmth and variety of his work. For that we have to go to the paintings themselves, and happily they are there for all to examine and enjoy. And to enjoy them is to share modestly in Chagall's own unique experience.

Moshe Dayan
1915–

Out of the shambles of the Anglo-French Suez offensive of 1956, its muddle and mismanagement, the accusations and barefaced denials of collusion, the contradictory statements of objectives and the self-righteous storms of indignation, the lightning Israeli campaign in Sinai emerged as an undeniably brilliant operation. Whether one approved or condemned the motives, it was a case-book example of military strategy, meticulously planned and resoundingly executed. The mastermind behind this amazing desert campaign was Israel's Chief of Staff, General Moshe Dayan, whose familiar features, boyish grin, black eye-patch and all, gazed out from newspaper and magazine features and from cinema and television screens all over the world at an admiring public.

Just over ten years later, in the extraordinary Six-Day War of June, 1967, the process was almost exactly repeated, except that on this occasion the defeat of the Arab armies was more complete – on three fronts this time – and more speedily effected. As the crisis reached boiling-point, with the

291

Egyptian army massed in the Sinai desert and the Arab capitals ringing with paeans of hate and threats of exterminaation, Israeli popular opinion demanded the appointment of Moshe Dayan to the key post of Ministry of Defence. A divided government gave way and Dayan, having held no military post for six years, was recalled. Although the individual commands were in other hands, it was Dayan who made the vital military decisions during this most critical week in the nation's history. And once again his face, slightly more lined than before, dominated the newsreels and the centre pages of the newspapers, stared out from shop windows and cars; as before his name was in all the headlines. To those who sympathized with Israel, he was once more the hero of the hour.

How had it happened? How much of the credit was rightfully his? And how did it come about that twice within a troubled decade this outstandingly gifted soldier had led to victory an army, composed largely of civilian reservists, against forces vastly superior in numbers and incomparably better equipped and armed? Both campaigns were landmarks in the development of modern Israel, and both have occurred too recently to qualify as 'history'. Much still remains to be written and revealed, though the true facts about the earlier campaign are gradually coming to the surface. As for the other, it has given Israel a greater measure of security, a much needed breathing space, but it has brought in its wake tremendous political problems which can only be solved by patience, goodwill and understanding – virtues sadly lacking in today's turbulent world.

Lasting peace between Jews and Arabs is no closer today than it was ten or twenty years ago but it is towards this goal that Dayan and his colleagues, both in the army and in the government, must direct their energies in the years ahead. Dayan is one of the few men in Israeli public life who could be in line for the succession as the next Prime Minister. Though over fifty he is still regarded as one of the 'youngsters' – by his political opponents as an irresponsible one. Independent, outspoken, controversial, Dayan is undoubtedly going to play a colourful and influential role in Israel's future. Given what he has already done and the kind of man he is, it cannot be otherwise.

Moshe Dayan is a 'Sabra', born in what was then Turkish-occupied Palestine on 20 May, 1915, to Russian immigrant parents. They had helped to found the first *kibbutz*, or communal settlement, at Degania, near the Sea of Galilee, and it was there that he spent the first six years of his life. The most frequently quoted episode from those early years is when his father locked him in a chicken coop for being disobedient, a frightening experience from which he emerged unrepentant and as defiant as ever.

When he was six the family moved to a *moshav*, or co-operative farm, in Nahalal, in the Valley of Jezreel. Here too Moshe's father was a founder-member. Each family owned its hut and segment of farmland and, as on the *kibbutz*, the produce was marketed on co-operative lines. But here the family unit was separate whereas in the *kibbutz* life was communal. Dayan's son still runs the farm in Nahalal which his grandfather staked out fifty years ago.

Life in those pioneering days was tough, but for a boy of Moshe's mischievous and fearless temperament a perpetual challenge. He soon made his mark among older and stronger friends as a boy of unusual resourcefulness and courage, a natural leader. The only school in Nahalal was an Agricultural School for Girls and he was the first boy to be accepted in what soon became a co-educational establishment. The standard of teaching in both arts and science was high, and he was a good student, fond of reading and with an aptitude for the subject in which the school specialized – farming, both theoretical and practical.

He also learned how to use a gun. Marauders were common in the isolated settlements during the twenties, and the importance of self-defence impressed itself on him at an early age. Dayan was still in his teens when he joined *Haganah*, the Jewish underground movement founded in 1920 to protect the settlements against Arab attack, and regarded by the British as illegal.

In 1935 Dayan married a fellow agricultural student, Ruth Schwarz, daughter of a Jerusalem lawyer, and after a long honeymoon in England the couple settled modestly in Nahalal. These were increasingly troubled times and the Arab riots of 1936 ushered in a brief period of co-operation between Britain and the Jews of Palestine. Dayan was made a platoon commander in *Haganah*; another was a young man named Yigal Allon, also a future general and political rival. In the spring of 1938 they took part in a typical 'Tower and Stockade' operation on the northern border with Lebanon. A new *kibbutz*, Hanita, sprang up literally overnight. When dusk fell there was a patch of empty land. By dawn a group of young men and women had erected some flimsy buildings, a watch tower and an encircling fence. *Haganah* provided defence cover and Dayan and Allon fought off a succession of violent attacks before Hanita's security was assured.

Haganah was gradually transformed from a purely defensive organization into a deadly striking force. Ironically, it was a British soldier who showed how it should be done. Captain Orde Wingate, a brilliant and unconventional strategist with a mystical sense of Biblical mission, organized the famous *Haganah* Night Squads to step up the fight against Arab infiltrators and saboteurs. Under Wingate Dayan acquired the practical experience and expert tactical instruction which he was to put to such good use after the establishment of the State. Wingate based his methods on speed, mobility and surprise, and although the British removed him from the scene when his partisanship became too embarrassing, he left an indelible impression on Dayan and his colleagues.

After Wingate's departure the British decided to break up *Haganah*, at the very time when it would have been in the Allied interest to encourage and strengthen it. Dayan, with forty-two colleagues, was arrested and imprisoned for belonging to an illegal military organization. Facing a five-year sentence they were held in the old Crusader fort at Acre. Though the inactivity was frustrating, the time was far from wasted. Dayan polished up his English and Arabic, read and wrote poetry and planned for the future, for the realization of a Jewish State. Whatever the outcome of the war Dayan now knew that the Jews would have to fight for it, and that *Haganah* would have to be ready when the call came.

Developments in the Middle East made it expedient for the British to release their prisoners in 1941, after sixteen months in gaol, and to enlist their aid. A select Jewish commando force was formed to help the allies to clear the Vichy French out of Lebanon and Syria. Dayan, with his knowledge of Arabic and familiarity with the border terrain, was chosen to lead a pathfinding unit of some thirty men into Lebanon with the Australian 7th Division. The invasion took place on a calm summer night. At dawn Dayan's men attacked and captured a heavily fortified police station, but then they came under concentrated fire from snipers. Dayan blazed away from the station's roof with a machine-gun, a sitting target. As he paused to survey his surroundings a bullet smashed into his binoculars, destroying his left eye. It was the end of the campaign for him. After a long and agonizing journey back to Haifa he was committed to hospital. When he was discharged, fully recovered, he was wearing the buccaneer-type black patch which later became his hallmark.

He returned to Nahalal where he bought his own farm, and although he did not sever his links with *Haganah*, this was his home and headquarters for the next few years. The Dayans now had three children, Yael, born shortly before his arrest in 1939, and two sons, Ehud, born in 1941, and Assaf, born in 1945. This was victory year for the allies in Europe and the Far East. For the Jews of Palestine it brought an intensified struggle to save the remnants of European Jewry and pave the way for an independent State. *Haganah*, together with the crack commando force, *Palmach*, went over to the offensive, smashing Arab terrorist bases, raiding British arms dumps, escorting illegal immigrants in daring night-time landings, defending settlements, pipelines and vital communications, gaining in confidence and efficiency as every month passed. Dayan, on the permanent staff of *Haganah*, took little active part in its operations. His time came when five Arab armies advanced to crush the tiny State created by the United Nations in November, 1947.

Dayan's experience and personal courage now found their outlet in action, first on the Syrian front, then in the newly formed armoured brigade commanded by Yitzhak Sadeh, his old chief from the pre-war *Haganah* days. He was given charge of a specially picked commando battalion operating in the Arab-occupied bulge to the south-east of Tel-Aviv. It lay dangerously near the coast and threatened the road and rail communications between Tel-Aviv and Jerusalem. With typical panache Dayan led his men in frontal assaults on the Arab towns of Ramle and Lydda, capturing both, with the loss of nine dead and sixteen wounded. Without being allowed a breathing space they were then thrown into the battle on the southern front, capturing the Egyptian-held village of Caratia after bitter fighting.

Already, though on a comparatively small scale, Dayan was displaying the qualities for which he was to become notorious and which were frequently to cause embarrassment to his superiors – personal bravery, sometimes carried to the brink of rashness, the ability to inspire unquestioning loyalty among his troops (by example rather than exhortation), and determination to press home an attack regardless of cost.

Ben-Gurion had already marked him for promotion, and a few days later he was appointed commander in the Jerusalem area, with the rank of Lieutenant-Colonel. The Old City had been captured by King Abdullah's Arab Legion, and the Jewish section was under siege by land and air, cut off from the rest of the country. Dayan knew he was fighting against time. Two cease-fires had already come and gone. The construction of the relief route known as the 'Burma Road' saved Jewish Jerusalem, but an attempt to capture Hebron and to widen the corridor across the country proved unsuccessful. A divided Jerusalem remained an uneasy, unpalatable fact for twenty years and the link between the capital and the rest of Israel perilously insecure.

Ben-Gurion's choice of Dayan for Jerusalem was a wise one. Dayan believed then – and still believes today – in the need for a mutually beneficial agreement with the neighbouring Arab countries. At that time a far-reaching settlement with Jordan seemed feasible. Abdullah, grandfather of the present King Hussein, was a shrewd politician, a man of independent mind and great tenacity. Dayan, with his understanding of Arabic temperament and history, negotiated the armistice with Jordan and met Abdullah on several occasions at his palace at Shuna, near the Dead Sea. The two men liked and respected each other and a peace treaty was seriously discussed. Unhappily, British influence in Amman prevented anything more than a temporary cease-fire, and the tragic assassination of Abdullah in the Old City in July, 1951, put paid to any prospect of a Jordan–Israel agreement. From then on, relations between the two countries deteriorated steadily.

Dayan was launched on his military career. After the armistice in 1949 he was promoted to Brigadier-General and took over from his old friend Allon as chief of Southern Command. The great sandy expanse of the Negev down to the vital Red Sea port of Eilat was his responsibility, and it was now that he came to know the desert at first-hand. He would drive down the bumpy roads in a jeep, camp out under the desert stars, study the flora and fauna, relive three thousand years of history. Here, where the Children of Israel had wandered after the Exodus from Egypt, where Canaanite cities were buried beneath the shifting sands, Dayan's deep love of the Bible and lively interest in archaeology helped to compensate for the frequent stretches of inactivity. There were isolated cases of cattle rustling and sheep stealing by Arab guerillas, but few major incidents. Dayan's mobile patrols effectively policed the area and much valuable tactical information was stored away for the future.

After a couple of years he was switched to Northern Command, back to the familiar frontiers of Lebanon, Syria and Jordan, and then – over the heads of many seniors – appointed Chief of Military Operations on the General Staff. Here there was trouble in plenty, saboteurs crossing from Jordan during the night, destroying property, killing watchmen and stealing livestock. So continuous was the threat to the border settlements that the Israelis decided that the only answer was retaliation in force. One such raid on Kibya in October, 1953, caused a furore in the Security Council, but Dayan was not alone in concluding that the United Nations was powerless to keep the peace between Jew and Arab.

The last appointment which Ben-Gurion made before he resigned at the end of that year was that of his protégé as Chief of Staff of the Armed Forces, a remarkable gesture of confidence in a man then only thirty-eight. Shimon Peres, with whom Dayan was to work amicably in the years to come, was made Director General of the Defence Ministry, and the Defence Minister was the ill-fated Pinchas Lavon, centre of the controversy which split the Ben-Gurion government in 1961. Sweeping army reforms following the new appointments were not all to the liking of the top brass or the government. Both Dayan and Peres were individualists with a flair for swift, direct action – true disciples of the 'Old Man'. Both believed, particularly after Nasser's *coup* in 1954, that Egypt represented a real threat to Israel's interests. Let Israel seek what powerful friends she could, but let her ultimately rely on her own resources and capacities to defend herself.

Thus it was, in the face of increasing terrorist activity from the Gaza Strip and the newly formed *Fedayin* suicide squads, that Dayan set about streamlining army organization, strengthening the Air Force and the crack Parachute Corps – he himself going on a training course and gaining his Parachutist Badge – accompanying Peres on overseas missions to inspect military installations and buy military equipment. In the months leading up to the Sinai campaign they fell foul of the Israeli Foreign Ministry, especially in their dealings with the French High Command, for by-passing normal diplomatic channels. But by this time Ben-Gurion was back in the saddle. Lavon had been forced to resign after a mysterious spy operation in Cairo for which he was held responsible had failed. The new team was in no mood for softness.

Developments in Egypt in 1955 and the early months of 1956 had convinced Dayan that a showdown was imminent. Raids from the Gaza Strip were increasing in number and intensity, reaching a climax with the murder of five children and a teacher in a synagogue only eight miles from Tel-Aviv, and the killing of Roy Rothberg, secretary of a new *kibbutz* on the edge of the Gaza Strip. Additionally there were raids and reprisals on the Syrian and Jordanian fronts, with fishermen on the Sea of Galilee and farm workers in fields and orange groves at the mercy of Syrian guns on the heights overlooking the border.

Close links were forged with the French who saw in Israel a useful ally against Nasser, then actively assisting the rebels in Algeria. Britain had withdrawn from the Canal Zone, and international tension rose as Nasser promptly nationalized the Canal. By closing the Straits of Tiran he imposed a virtual blockade on the port of Eilat, Israel's maritime link with Africa and the Far East.

Israel was realistic enough not to attempt to 'go it alone', and they were assured of British and French moral support. Peres made sure of a plentiful supply of modern French weapons, including *Mystère* fighters. During that fateful summer Operation Musketeer was planned, a joint Anglo-French attack on the Suez Canal, accompanied by an Israeli strike into Sinai. All parties involved vehemently denied collusion at the time, but enough information has since emerged – including Dayan's own *Diary of the Sinai Campaign* – to show that there was close co-ordination, though, from the British and French angles, insufficient planning.

The ethical issues, so fiercely debated at the time, are by now academic. Nobody's hands were clean, including the Americans and the Russians (busy in Hungary) who made the most vociferous protests in the Security Council. But Israel saw it in terms of sheer survival. Rather than wait for the day when Egypt was strong enough to mount an overwhelming offensive in Sinai, better to strike now in the south – risking intervention by Egypt's allies which, in the event, never came. Put an end once and for all to the *Fedayin* and prove to Nasser that Israel, despite inferiority in numbers and arms, could and would use her teeth in self-defence.

The Israeli attack which began on 29 October caught the Egyptians and the world by surprise, and was an almost unqualified success. It took seven days for the hard-thrusting

Israeli infantry to sweep down into Sinai, capturing the frontier posts and main road junctions, opening the Tiran Straits with a parachute drop on Sharm el-Sheikh, overrunning the Gaza Strip, and driving to within ten miles of the Suez Canal. By the time the British and French had lumbered into action, the Israelis had no hesitation in accepting the Security Council's call for a cease-fire.

The speed and imagination of Dayan's campaign impressed the world's military experts, but he himself considered that it fell some way short of perfection. In the *Diary*, which he published nine years later, he severely criticized organizational and tactical failures among his own officers and men. They were not repeated eleven years later when Israel's vastly increased strength in armour and air-power made her an even more formidable opponent. Yet the Egyptian failings which Dayan correctly analysed – low morale, poor leadership, inadequate intelligence and lack of flexibility – were all reproduced, on a vastly larger scale and immeasurably greater cost, in the disastrous Six-Day War of 1967.

Dayan, in typical fashion, scandalized the politicians and worried his military colleagues by insisting on staying in the front lines and endangering his own life. At El Arish, on the way to the Canal, a signalman was shot dead at Dayan's side by a burst of machine-gun fire from a sniper.

'My absences are not viewed kindly by the General Staff,' he remarked laconically. 'I spent the first two days of the campaign mostly in the field. . . . True, I returned to GHQ command post each night, but of course my non-appearance during the day makes things difficult. . . . In the field there is a radio transmitter with me all the time and I am in constant contact with GHQ, but my staff officers complain that this is not enough. They may be right; but I am unable, or unwilling, to behave otherwise.'

Even in the heat of battle Dayan found the opportunity to indulge in his favourite hobby. Standing on a ridge outside Gaza he came across a Canaanite grave at the bottom of an Egyptian trench. Digging down, he uncovered a jug and a plate dating back some three thousand years, which he duly added to his private collection.

The repercussions of the Sinai campaign were decidedly not to Dayan's liking. Israel, under intense political pressure, was forced to withdraw from all captured territory, although Gaza and Sharm el-Sheikh were from now on policed by the United Nations Emergency Force. Ben-Gurion's decision was right, but Dayan felt strongly that to toss away the military advantage was to invite a repetition of trouble at a later date. Public opinion was largely on his side. In any event, a few months after the withdrawal was completed, he tendered his resignation as Chief of Staff and subsequently left the army altogether to study law, economics and political science.

The Old Guard under Ben-Gurion were still in control, their prestige high after Sinai. Dayan, though never a party man in the narrow sense, was still highly regarded by Ben-Gurion and broadly supported his chief's policies, particularly the reparations agreement with West Germany. But he was independent enough to launch occasional attacks on the government's economic policy and against the leaders of the *Histadrut*. As a public speaker he proved a spell-binder especially with the younger generation. He helped to draw enthusiastic crowds for Ben-Gurion's *Mapai* party at the 1959 elections. The victorious Prime Minister rewarded him with the post of Minister of Agriculture.

His political enemies – many of them within his own party – saw the writing on the wall. To the problems at the Ministry he brought the same sense of assurance and high confidence that he showed in military matters, and often the same lack of tact and delicacy. Clearly, as a politician he was a man to be reckoned with. The Old Guard closed ranks, losing no opportunity to discredit him and mounting vicious attacks both on public platforms and through the Press on his private life. Yet he was still popular enough to survive Ben-Gurion's final resignation in 1963 and to retain his post – though not to earn promotion – in Levi Eshkol's new government.

But with Ben-Gurion gone he was more vulnerable to attack. The rift widened between Dayan and Eshkol's cautious, conservative government, still dominated by the pre-war pioneers from Eastern Europe, whose hold on the mind and imagination of a new generation of *Sabras* was becoming precarious. Ben-Gurion, obsessed by the Lavon affair and pressing for a new inquiry, regardless of the fact that Lavon had been exonerated, lost much popular support. Nevertheless, Dayan stayed loyal to him. When, in February, 1965, Ben-Gurion left his old *Mapai* party to form a splinter group known as *Rafi*, Dayan and Peres joined him, the former resigning his post at the Ministry of Agriculture. Yet at the ensuing election *Rafi* won only ten seats out of one hundred and twenty. The country's economy was evidently booming, the security situation seemed no worse than usual, and the electorate rallied behind the old-timers.

After the election the harsh realities of the economic situation became clear and the pressure on the government to take drastic austerity measures was voiced by many besides Moshe Dayan. But equally he urged forceful action to deal with the increasing threat of the *El-Fatah* terrorists, Syrian irregulars, backed by their government but operating from bases in Jordan. Occasional reprisal raids were costly, controversial and only partially effective. Moreover, the entire Arab–Israel political problem was now part of the huge global struggle between the two major powers, America and Russia. Sentiment and morality played no part in shaping the policies of the two nations who were busy carving out their spheres of influence. Oil, commerce, capital investment, military bases, political prestige – these were the deciding factors.

Israel still had to seek allies where she could, bearing in mind that pledges of aid and friendship were temporary, perhaps lasting no longer than the next election or the next emergent nation revolt. Russia was now wholeheartedly behind Nasser, and the Communist bloc was pouring in supplies of the latest weapons – tanks, bombers, fighters, missiles – together with skilled technicians and instructors. Syria, Jordan and Iraq were receiving arms from both camps. France, her Algerian problem now settled, proclaimed herself strictly neutral. Israel could not even count on American backing.

The Middle East arms race was clearly going to culminate in an explosion, possibly with world-wide repercussions.

Although Arab unity was more impressive on paper than in reality, Dayan and those of his colleagues who called for a firm stand against Arab threats saw increased danger with every passing month. Dayan had recently visited Vietnam, sending back vivid reports for an Israeli evening paper. He realized that a clearcut American victory was impossible to achieve, but he was impressed by American power and convinced that Israel must continue to woo the Pentagon and the White House. But there would be no repetition of 1956. This time Israel, in all probability, would have to 'go it alone'. Dayan was confident that, provided the fighting was limited in time and scope, Israel could win.

The crisis gained momentum slowly during the early part of 1967. Syria kept up a continual stream of anti-Israel invective as her governments tottered; Nasser, on the verge of bankruptcy, struggling to bolster his prestige in the Arab world, found the situation slipping from his control; the terrorists – *El-Fatah* and Ahmed Shukairy's Palestine Liberation Organization – became ever more reckless, provoking strong Israeli reprisals. As the calls for revenge and united Arab action became daily more hysterical Nasser was forced into a sequence of ill-considered and ultimately self-destructive actions. Meanwhile, Israel, in the throes of economic crisis and political turmoil, watched uneasily, though without alarm.

Whether Nasser acted deliberately with the intention of provoking war or whether he suddenly found himself beyond the point of no return is now an academic question, of interest only to the historians. Even when his tanks and troops poured into Sinai there was no general feeling in Israel that war was inevitable. That feeling changed only when Nasser called on the United Nations Emergency Force to pull out of Gaza and Sharm el-Sheikh, and when U Thant, to the world's amazement, obliged. The closing of the Tiran Straits followed, and Israel once again was faced with the stark alternative – fight or be destroyed.

Yet the Israeli government still vacillated, the 'doves' and 'hawks' angrily debating into the early hours. The public mood was explosive. It demanded the return of the one man who could inspire confidence at such a time – Moshe Dayan. On 1 June, Eshkol reluctantly appointed him Minister of Defence. Full mobilization followed and on Monday, 5 June, the Six-Day War began with a devastating series of attacks by the small but highly efficient Israeli Air Force, which demolished Arab air power in a couple of hours.

The rest is familiar history. Israel's armed forces, outnumbered but vastly superior in training, fighting spirit and manœuvrability, captured the Sinai peninsula in a great pincers movement. When King Hussein ill-advisedly took the offensive, Israel, exploiting a completely unforeseen situation, took the Old City of Jerusalem and the entire West Bank of the Jordan, including Bethlehem, Jericho, Hebron and Nablus. Finally the Israelis turned on the Syrians, storming the Golan Heights and immobilizing the Russian-supplied guns that had lobbed shells down on to the *kibbutzim* of Upper Galilee with monotonous regularity but little accuracy.

To every Israeli the greatest prize was undoubtedly Jerusalem, united after two thousand years. General Dayan was among the first to enter the Old City and join his exhausted, emotion-filled troops at the Wailing Wall. To a reporter who asked how he felt he answered simply, 'We deserve this city.' Then, approaching the Wall, he placed a folded slip of paper between the stones, on which he had jotted down a short prayer – 'Let there be peace upon the House of Israel'.

The victory was swift and complete, but the aftermath of the war left many problems – old and new – to be solved. To the perennial, tragic plight of the refugees was now added the unfamiliar one of administering occupied territories, for which Dayan was immediately responsible. He brought to this enormous task his organizational genius and a deep sense of duty. Though at times his public pronouncements may have sounded uncompromising, the occupation has been constructive and humanitarian. Dayan has always liked the Arabs and most of them admire and respect him. Despite isolated and highly-publicized hostile incidents, it has been proved that co-operation between Arabs and Jews is possible. Although a permanent peace settlement still seems remote, such co-operation is the only solution for the Middle East.

Moshe Dayan

In March, 1968, Dayan was seriously hurt while digging on a site not far from Tel-Aviv. Completely buried by a miniature landslide, he was rescued in the nick of time, semi-conscious. It happened on the eve of a large-scale raid on a terrorist base in Jordan and the nation was plunged into gloom and concern. His convalescence was slow, but once more his courage and stamina pulled him through. This is the measure of the man's appeal, particularly to the younger generation. They rely on him and trust him.

Dayan will always remain a somewhat solitary man, often touchy and unsociable, impulsive and unafraid to speak his mind. Though charming and immensely likeable, he will never court popularity at the expense of deeply held principles. He is still one of Israel's 'youngsters' and has much to give her. One fervently hopes he will not have to lead her in yet another round of fighting, but were it to come he would be ready. In the political arena he also has much to contribute. Though many are wary of him, he has proved he has flair and imagination. What about diplomacy and judgement, difficult to acquire but essential for real statesmanship? Time will tell. Whatever transpires, Israel and the world may expect to hear much of Moshe Dayan.

Anne Frank
1929–1945

It is quite likely that the name of Anne Frank, a teen-aged Dutch girl, is more widely known than many of the eminent writers, scientists, statesmen and philosophers whose lives have been described in this book. Her story is included not so much because she herself was unusually gifted or outstanding, but because she spoke for the millions of voiceless victims of Nazi persecution throughout Europe, her diary a testament to the tenacity of those who suffered and the courage of those who gave a helping hand.

Over six million Jews are estimated to have died in Hitler's concentration camps, most of them silently and anonymously. While the battles raged on other fronts the evil machinery of the Final Solution steadily gathered momentum, unaffected by the ebb and flow of military events. The civilized world, despite confirmed reports, refused to believe that such things were happening. It was not until it was too late that the shocked victors saw the brutal evidence with their own eyes.

Some of Hitler's victims were able to record or portray the truth. A few fortunate ones survived and wrote about their experiences. Fragments of journals, poems, and drawings were smuggled out of the death camps. Photographs taken when the camps were liberated sent shock-waves of horror and indignation round the world. But Anne Frank's diary, first published in 1947, was no account of violence and terror. It was simply a day-to-day record, kept by a remarkably intelligent, sensitive Dutch girl, of how she, her family and a few friends hid from the Gestapo in the disused part of an office building overlooking an Amsterdam canal, for no less than two years. It tells of how they were assisted by a handful of brave men and women, describes the routine, mundane events from which there was no escape, the fear of discovery, the domestic tensions, the blossoming of young love, the hopes for the future. It is a beautiful, astonishingly mature and poignant record of courage and endurance. It is full of humour and completely devoid of self-pity. In normal circumstances it would have been a fine, sensitive account of growing-up. In its special context it is unbearably moving, a glowing tribute to the human spirit.

Summer, 1942, was the time when the fortunes of war swung at last in favour of the Allies. The spearhead of the Axis attack was blunted on all fronts. In Russia the long retreat of the Red Army halted at Stalingrad. In North Africa the Allies struck back at Alamein. In the Atlantic the battle against the U-boats was slowly being won, and in the air war the Allies were now able to mount massive thousand-bomber raids, striking deep into Germany itself. In occupied Europe resistance fighters girded themselves for the expected invasion from the west. Civilians, listening secretly to the news from London, watching the huge bombers flying eastward, waited and prayed.

For the Jews of Europe, however, it was already too late. The mass deportations continued, the sinister cattle trucks rattled across the continent towards the camps, and the methods of extermination grew ever more refined and efficient. In some countries civilians assisted the Germans in hunting down Jews, in others they risked their lives to save them. The stories of these thousands of courageous people will never be told, but there were many and in Holland the record was especially proud. The Dutch never gave their full co-operation to the Germans. The history of Anne Frank was remarkable; but it was surely not unique.

The Frank family, father, mother and two daughters, came originally from Frankfurt in Germany, settling in Holland during the early thirties. Mr Frank was a well-to-do business-man, and the girls attended the local Jewish Secondary School. Margot, three years the elder, was beautiful, clever and compliant, evidently her mother's favourite. Anne, not academically outstanding, had a wide range of interests, a lively inquiring mind, a gay, ebullient personality. Her diary which she began in June, 1942, on her thirteenth birthday, is the source of all the information which follows.

Holland, of course, was under Nazi occupation, and life for the Jews was harsh. They were forced to wear the traditional yellow six-pointed star, were subjected to a strict curfew, were forbidden to travel by public transport, visit cinemas and theatres or attend sports events. They were allowed to shop only during certain hours and then only in Jewish shops. They were not permitted to visit non-Jewish friends. They drew smaller rations than their Christian neighbours and were subject to every kind of social and professional discrimination. Behind the scenes they were slowly being rounded up and deported. The Franks' friends were vanishing overnight and it was clear that their turn would soon come.

On the day Anne received her examination results – 'My report is not at all bad,' she remarked – plans were made for the entire family to go into hiding, and three days later they made their way, with all the belongings which they could conveniently transport, to the building on the Prinsengracht Canal which was to be their home. 'I had on two vests,' wrote Anne, 'three pairs of pants, a dress, on top of that a shirt, jacket, summer coat, two pairs of stockings, lace-up shoes, woolly cap, scarf, and still more; I was nearly stifled.'

They were to live in the abandoned part of Mr Frank's office building and Anne described the layout in detail. There were a warehouse and offices on the ground floor, in use during the day, with storerooms on the first floor and an attic on the second. But on the first floor there was also a plain grey door, backed by a bookcase and box files, which swung open. Behind that door was the so-called 'Secret Annexe'. A narrow passage led into a large room which became the Franks' bed-sitting room; off that was a small, windowless room with wash-basin and W.C.; and beyond that the small bedroom occupied by Margot and Anne. Upstairs, linked by a flight of stairs, was another large, bright room which was to belong to the van Daans (who moved in three days later) and a smaller room for their son, Peter.

Mr and Mrs van Daan brought with them a strange collection of personal possessions including, to Anne's amusement, a large chamber-pot in a hat-box. Peter, aged sixteen, brought his cat Mouschi. Anne scathingly described him as 'a rather soft, shy, gawky youth; can't expect much from his company'. Mr van Daan was carrying a folding tea-table.

There, within the sound of the Westertorn clock, the two families settled in, gathering together at meal-times, dependent for their safety and livelihood on the assistance of five people, Mr Kraler and Mr Koophuis, business colleagues of Otto Frank's, Miep and Henk, a young married couple, and Elli Vossen, a typist. It was they who bought food, carried messages, kept watch and brought in news from the outside world. Without them the Franks and the van Daans could not have survived a month.

Anne brightened up her room by decorating the walls with pin-ups of film-stars and coloured postcards, and for a while it was like 'being on vacation in a very peculiar boarding-house'. When the date for the beginning of the school term came round she obediently tackled her French and her mathematics, the latter a subject she loathed. She spent most of her time reading, especially her favourite subjects, history, mythology, music and art. And she jotted down in her diary everything that went on, no matter how trivial – the daily routine, the news on the radio, the meal-time discussions, the frequent family rows, the sudden and startling raps on the door and footsteps on the stair – as well as her own feelings towards her own family, the quarrelsome van Daans and the shy Peter.

It was soon evident that the family tensions which had

existed outside were fifty times worse now that they were all crowded into a couple of rooms, unable to venture out, forced to keep their voices low for fear of being overheard, and increasingly aware of one another's failures and shortcomings. The van Daans spent much of their time arguing, Peter buried himself away in his room, and Anne, incessantly chattering, continually got on her mother's nerves. There were frequent clashes, and Anne recorded them vividly. What is astonishing is her lack of resentment, her mature analysis of her own failings and her gentle rebuking of the adults for their childlike behaviour. Take this passage:

'I'm not jealous of Margot, never have been. I don't envy her good looks or her beauty. It is only that I long for Daddy's real love: not only as his child, but for me – Anne, myself.

'I cling to Daddy because it is only through him that I am able to retain the remnant of family feeling. Daddy doesn't understand that I need to give vent to my feelings over Mummy sometimes. He doesn't want to talk about it; he simply avoids anything which might lead to remarks about Mummy's failings. Just the same, Mummy and her failings are something I find harder to bear than anything else. I don't know how to keep it all to myself. I can't always be drawing attention to her untidiness, her sarcasm, and her lack of sweetness, neither can I believe that I'm always in the wrong.'

In November they were joined by another refugee, a dentist named Dussell, with whom Anne was forced to share a room. She found him a 'stodgy, old-fashioned disciplinarian'. Typically, she made allowances for him, but the following entry is crushing: 'A person of fifty-four who is still so pedantic and small-minded must be so by nature, and will never improve.'

On *Chanuka*, the Jewish festival of lights, which coincided with St Nicholas' Day, they exchanged presents and a little later, at Christmas, they made the most of their extra ration of butter by baking cakes and biscuits. It was such occasions that livened the monotony of the short winter days, the boredom which so affected their tempers and spirits. Sometimes Anne gave way to depression; 'I would like to shout to Margot, van Daan, Dussel – and Daddy too – "leave me in peace, let me sleep one night at least without my pillow being wet with tears, my eyes burning and my head throbbing. Let me get away from it all, preferably away from the world!"'

Now and then she brooded on the news from outside, the deportations, the sufferings of the Jews – and she rebuked herself for daring to complain while she still had a warm bed and food to eat.

So the months passed. Spring and summer, 1943, brought more encouraging news from all fronts, Rommel in full retreat in North Africa, Italy invaded. Each such item of news brought them fresh hope as they watched the light fade yet again over the housetops and crouched together at night as the Allied bombers ran the gauntlet of German anti-aircraft guns. There were occasional alarms, one when the house was sold and the owner brought an architect round to inspect the premises, another after a burglary when the police snooped outside their secret cupboard, but failed to discover them. At such times they were drawn together instinctively and the trivial daily disagreements were forgotten.

Winter came again and there was no celebrating on St Nicholas' Day. But on Christmas Day there was a cake baked by Miep, a round of biscuits from Elli, a bottle of yoghourt for the children, and beer for the grown-ups. Then the long round of dark days, frayed nerves, lost tempers – and suddenly, for Anne, something new. From day-dreaming about old boy friends her thoughts veered, gradually and inevitably, towards the boy upstairs. Aware of her own mental and physical development, spring suddenly burst forth with new hope, new radiance. 'The sun is shining, the sky is a deep blue, there is a lovely breeze and I'm longing – so longing – for everything.'

No longer was Peter a shy, gawky youth. 'Kitty,' wrote Anne (Kitty was the name she gave her diary), 'I'm just like someone in love, who can only talk about her darling. And Peter really is a darling. When shall I be able to tell him so? Naturally, only if he thinks I'm a darling too.' Weeks of agony followed, but gradually Peter thawed. They spent long hours together, somewhat to their parents' disapproval, talking, reading and . . . 16 April, 1944: 'Darlingest Kitty, Remember yesterday's date, for it is a very important day in my life. Surely it is a great day for every girl when she receives her first kiss?' Nothing else mattered now. Three days later she wrote: 'Is there anything more beautiful in the world than to sit before an open window and enjoy nature, to listen to the birds singing, feel the sun on your cheeks and have a darling boy in your arms?'

Their idyll was, alas, short-lived. As spring lengthened into summer, the good news from every front brought renewed optimism. On 6 June they heard the announcement of the long-awaited invasion. On her fifteenth birthday Anne was deluged with presents – Sprenger's *History of Art*, a set of underwear, a book on botany from her parents, a bracelet from her sister, a bunch of peonies from Peter. By mid-July the allies had broken out of their bridgeheads and were heading east. Anne and Peter made plans for the future. The entry for Tuesday, 1 August again analysed herself – 'the little bundle of contradictions', and then – silence.

On 4 August the Gestapo broke in and took away all the occupants of the 'Secret Annexe'. With them went Kraler and Koophuis, who survived the concentration camp. Otto Frank, Anne's father, also survived. The rest perished, Anne herself dying in Bergen-Belsen in March, 1945.

Among a pile of old books, newspapers and magazines left on the floor of the 'Secret Annexe', Miep and Elli came across Anne's diary. It was published in Holland in 1947 and was later translated into more than a dozen languages. It was then adapted for the stage and shown throughout the world, including Germany.

Had she lived Anne Frank would most probably have been a writer. 'I know that I can write, a couple of my stories are good, my descriptions of the "Secret Annexe" are humorous, there's a lot in my diary that speaks, but – whether I have real talent remains to be seen,' she confided to her diary in April, 1944; and further on comes the short entry which sadly was to serve as her epitaph: 'I want to go on living even after my death! And therefore I am grateful to God for giving me this gift, this possibility of developing myself and of writing, of expressing all that is in me.'

Bibliography

C. Roth (ed.) *The Standard Jewish Encyclopedia* (Massadah, 1962)
A. H. Hyamson & A. M. Silbermann *Vallentine's Jewish Encyclopedia* (Shapiro, Vallentine, 1938)
A. L. Sachar *A History of the Jews* (Knopf, 1965)
C. Roth *A History of the Jews in England* (O.U.P., 1941)
C. Roth *The Jewish Contribution to Civilisation* (East & West Lib., 1956)
M. Wurmbrand & C. Roth *The Jewish People – 4000 Years of Survival* (Thames & Hudson, 1966)
T. H. Robinson *A History of Israel* (O.U.P., 1932)
D. Ben-Gurion (ed.) *The Jews in Their Land* (Aldus, 1966)
F. Kobler (ed.) *Letters of Jews Through the Ages* (East & West Lib., 1952)
J. Picciotto *Sketches of Anglo-Jewish History* (Soncino, 1956)

H. M. Orlinsky. Essay in *Great Jewish Personalities in Ancient and Medieval Times* (Farrar, Straus, 1959)
L. Ginzberg *Legends of the Bible* (Jewish Publication Sty., 1966)

S. Baron. Essay in *Great Jewish Personalities in Ancient and Medieval Times* (Farrar, Straus, 1959)
J. S. Minkin *The World of Moses Maimonides* (Yoseloff, 1957)
C. Roth *The Guide for the Perplexed* (Hutchinson, 1948)
D. Yellin & I. Abrahams *Maimonides* (Macmillan, 1903)
S. Zeitlin *Maimonides* (Bloch, 1935)

C. Roth *The House of Nasi* (2 vols. Jewish Publication Sty., 1947, 1948)

J. Slotki *Manasseh ben Israel*

J. Kastein *The Messiah of Izmir* (Bodley Head, 1931)
H. C. Schnur *Mystic Rebels* (Beechhurst, 1949)
L. Magnus *The Jews in the Christian Era* (Benn, 1929)

P. Maguet (ed.) *The Memoirs of Daniel Mendoza* (Batsford, 1951)

F. Morton *The Rothschilds* (Secker, 1963)
I. Balla *The Romance of the Rothschilds* (Eveleigh Nash, 1913)
J. Reeves *The Rothschilds* (Sampson Low, 1887)

A. Maurois *Disraeli* (Bodley Head, 1927)
G. E. Buckle & W. F. Monypenny *Life of Benjamin Disraeli* (6 vols. John Murray, 1910–20)
R. Blake *Disraeli* (Eyre & Spottiswoode, 1967)
H. Pearson *Dizzy* (Methuen, 1952)
H. Bolitho *Twelve Jews* (Rich & Cowan, 1934)
G. R. Stirling Taylor *Seven Nineteenth Century Statesman* (Cape, 1932)

S. Hensel *The Mendelssohn Family* (Sampson Low, 1881)
H. E. Jacob *Felix Mendelssohn and his Times* (Barrie, 1963)
P. Radcliffe *Mendelssohn* (Dent, 1954)
G. Selden-Goth (ed.) *Letters of Felix Mendelssohn* (Elek, 1946)

J. Richardson *Rachel* (Reinhardt, 1956)
F. Gribble *Rachel* (Chapman & Hall, 1911)

313

J. Agate *Rachel* (Howe, 1928)
Madame de B——— *Memoirs of Rachel* (Hurst & Blackett, 1858)

E. Jones *Sigmund Freud: Life and Work* (Hogarth, 1953, 1955, 1957)
S. Freud *An Autobiographical Study* (Hogarth, 1936)
E. L. Freud (ed.) *Letters of Sigmund Freud* (Hogarth, 1961)
M. Freud *Glory Reflected* (Angus & Robertson, 1957)

S. Alexander *Space, Time and Deity* (Macmillan, 1920)
S. Alexander *Philosophical and Literary Pieces* (Macmillan, 1939)

M. Lowenthal (ed.) *The Diaries of Theodor Herzl* (Gollancz, 1958)
T. Herzl (trans. S. d'Avigdor) *Der Judenstaat* (1904)

G. R. Isaacs *Rufus Isaacs, First Marquess of Reading* (Hutchinson, 1942)
S. Jackson *Rufus Isaacs* (Cassell, 1936)
M. Hyde *Lord Reading* (Heinemann, 1967)
A. L. Goodhart *Five Jewish Lawyers of the Common Law* (Jewish Historical
    Sty., 1949)
Lord Birkett *Six Great Advocates* (Penguin, 1961)

J. Monash *The Australian Victories in France in 1918* (Hutchinson, 1920)
F. M. Cutlack (ed.) *War Letters of General Monash* (Angus & Robertson,
    1935)
V. R. Northwood *Monash* (State Electricity Commission of Victoria, 1950)
J. Hetherington *John Monash* (O.U.P., Melbourne, 1962)

B. Baruch *My Own Story* (Odhams, 1958)
B. Baruch *The Public Years* (Odhams, 1961)
M. L. Coit *Baruch* (Gollancz, 1958)

C. Weizmann *Trial and Error* (Hamish Hamilton, 1949)
M. Weisgal & J. Carmichael (ed.) *Chaim Weizmann – A Biography by
    Several Hands* (Weidenfeld, 1962)

M. Samuel *Blood Accusation* (Jewish Publication Sty., 1966)
M. Beilis *The Story of My Sufferings* (1926)

P. Michelmore *Einstein: Profile of the Man* (Muller, 1963)
A. Vallentin *Einstein* (Weidenfeld, 1954)
P. Frank *Einstein: His Life and Times* (Cape, 1948)
C. Seelig *Albert Einstein* (Staples, 1956)

J. Epstein *An Autobiography* (Vista, 1963)

B. Litvinoff *Ben-Gurion of Israel* (Weidenfeld, 1954)
R. St. John *Ben-Gurion* (Jarrolds, 1959)
M. Edelman *Ben-Gurion* (Hodder, 1964)

J. Cassou *Chagall* (Thames & Hudson, 1967)
W. Erben *Marc Chagall* (Thames & Hudson, 1957)
M. Chagall *My Life* (Orion, 1960)

M. Dayan *Diary of the Sinai Campaign* (Weidenfeld, 1965)
N. Lau-Lavie *Moshe Dayan* (Vallentine Mitchell, 1968)
D. Kimche & D. Bawly *The Sandstorm* (Secker, 1968)

A. Frank *The Diary of a Young Girl* (Doubleday, 1952)

Index

Index

Index

Index

Index

Index